New Perspectives in History

In Search of a Meaningful Past

Edited by

ARTHUR N. GILBERT
University of Denver

Houghton Mifflin Company • **Boston**

New York • *Atlanta* • *Geneva, Illinois* • *Dallas* • *Palo Alto*

Printed in the U.S.A.

Library of Congress Catalog Card Number: 77-169903

ISBN: 0-395-12567-7

To my parents

Introduction

The cry for relevant education has not spared the historian. In recent years historians in increasing numbers have felt called upon to defend their profession from attacks by those who see no purpose in studying ancient Greek inscriptions or the landholding records of Tudor England. The pace of change in the twentieth century and the dramatically different future projected by those who peer into the twenty-first make the historian's craft seem particularly irrelevant to large numbers of college students. In the minds of many young people the generation gap involves more than the rejection of one's *biological* parents; it involves as well the rejection of one's *historical* parents—the countless generations of the past whose life styles created and reflected the development of civilization.

Every generation, of course, feels itself unique, and there have been other times in history when people believed that the past held no solutions to their problems. Today's questioning of the meaningfulness of the past seems different, however, because it is based upon changes and projected changes in our environment which far exceed anything known to historic man. We are told that we are sitting on a biological time bomb which may explode at any moment, casting its fragments into every sphere of human life. Biologists are talking seriously about the artificial creation of life, and with increasing frequency we read about some startling new discovery that brings us closer to that goal. It is probable that genes will be intentionally modified within our lifetime or at least within that of our children. The future holds the possibility not only of creating life but of delaying the aging process and even death itself. Increasingly men talk about immortality for some or many in the next century.

Meanwhile, every year the communication revolution, with its computers, satellites, and new modes of influencing and shaping men, marks new generations all over the world in ways which we only dimly understand. Why look backward when the future is about to turn the past into a relic? Why look backward when we may be moving into an age which is truly post-historic?

Many writers, not all of them dreamers and visionaries, have contributed, perhaps unwittingly, to anti-historical thinking. History is the story of collectivities and these writers feel that radical changes in man's allegiance to collectivities may occur in the future.

The noted psychiatrist, Philip Reiff, informs us that the traditional tension between the Freudian poles of culture and civilization on the one hand and instinctual gratification on the other is disappearing in middle-class Europe and America.[1] In the future it may no longer be necessary for men and women to sublimate or suppress instinctual desires in order to preserve cultural and civilizational norms. Economic surplus in the future may enable individuals to follow their inclinations without worrying about the needs and the survival of the group to which they belong.

Norman O. Brown, whose writings have been very popular in recent years, calls for a new man who literally leaps out of history and becomes the polymorphously perverse being that Freud associated with childhood purity.[2] Again instinct will triumph and man will achieve happiness because he no longer must sacrifice his desires to the demands of collectivities. He frees himself from the tyranny of the state, the nation, the class, and the dead weight of tradition: the dead weight of history. He no longer, in Ortega y Gasset's phrase, "stands on the shoulders of past generations like acrobats in a circus."[3] He leaps from their shoulders and swings to the top of the circus tent alone and free.

Robert Lifton writes of a new "Protean man" who, because of the impact of communications, can change his life style and his beliefs as easily as he can don a new shirt.[4] Our children will try on new personalities and shed the old without a backward glance or a pang of regret. The new man is Proteus who can be and do what he wants. He has no entangling past, no historical corpse to drag around throughout his life.

History is also being called before the bar by those who are trying to free themselves from a past that they see characterized by war, poverty, racism, and other assorted evils. To them the past seems to reveal only how bad things have been. They are interested in how much *better* things *can* be and feel that attention paid to the follies of history will hamper the process of making a new world.

In addition to recognizing the possibility that history may be irrelevant, historians have increasingly become aware that their own

---

[1]Philip Reiff, *The Triumph of the Therapeutic: The Uses of Faith After Freud* (New York: Harper & Row, 1966).

[2]Norman O. Brown, *Life Against Death* (New York: Vintage Books, 1959).

[3]Ortega y Gasset, *Man and Crisis* (New York: Norton, 1962), p. 53.

[4]Robert J. Lifton, "Protean Man," *The Partisan Review,* XXXV (Winter 1968), pp. 13-27.

profession may have had a corrosive impact on the mythic pasts that once made life meaningful for men. The ideas of progress and of national destiny have been the victims not only of the catastrophic events of the twentieth century but also of new professional standards. Before the rise of modern historical writing historians wrote history to justify a new religion, glorify a monarch, or celebrate the virtues of a particular nation-state. We had Christian history in which Christian heroes fought pagan villains. We had Tudor heroes overcoming with the help of God the evil Yorkist and later Papist threats. We had history that celebrated the rise of the Prussian state or the political virtues of those superhuman founders of the American Republic. And we had history which proclaimed the steady march of the English-speaking people from their rude Celtic beginnings to democracy and world-wide imperialism.

It is this "use" of history which writers like John Marcus and J. H. Plumb see disintegrating in our time. Of course, we cannot be sure of the extent to which people have lost faith in traditional mythical interpretations of the past. Lingering in the public mind is a quasi-mythic past which the professional historian touches only marginally. Parson Weems' biography of George Washington may be out of print but the images of honest George and his cherry tree remain embedded in popular imagination. The quasi-mythic past has a life of its own that seems to be impervious to the latest findings of scholars. Historians, for example, know a great deal about the origins of Christianity, its relationship to Judaism, and its role in the Roman Empire. Yet a mythic history of Christianity survives in the minds of Christians whose acquaintance with the birth of their religion is limited to Sunday morning sermons, inspirational verse, and movies about the greatest story ever told.

Added to the persistent quasi-mythic past are newly generated counter-pasts which may commit sins of omission as serious as those of earlier historical world views. In the United States we have recently seen the emergence of an image of the American past characterized by violence, imperialism, and poverty: a past that runs counter to the one most of us recall from high school American history courses. It is too early to make judgments on this new view of the past, but it may be as distorted and "mythic" as the paeans to America written by earlier generations of historians.

Yet although the creation of arbitrary pasts for use by the present may not be dead, it has been seriously wounded by the general acceptance of professional standards in writing history. We may still believe in any one of a number of pasts which suit our fancy but we believe in them with less assurance. We do not proclaim our version of history to all within earshot for fear that someone in the audience may have read a recent authoritative text which proves conclusively that our version of history is inadequate, that America has (or has not) been a racist, imperialist state, that the early church fathers may have destroyed documents in the name of orthodoxy, or that progress exists in the eye of the beholder of the historical record and not in history itself. Those who seek solace in the past are troubled not by a lack of interpretations, but by an inability to have complete faith in any one version of history.

This uncertainty about the uses and value of the past has given rise to a large and growing literature on the purpose and meaning of history. Some writers like J. H. Plumb and E. H. Carr have called for a new idea of progress to give meaning to the jumble of past events and to provide a vision of a better future for all mankind. Their new idea of progress is more sophisticated and restrained than that of some nineteenth-century historians. It has been tested in World Wars I and II and tempered by the chilling thought that nuclear annihilation may make a mockery of its vision. The new idea of progress recognizes that human history has had disastrous setbacks as well as halting steps forward and that man's achievements in science and technology certainly outstrip any advances made in the social and political spheres. For some historians the idea of progress is little more than a hope, a wager that the future can be better than the past and that it is more noble and humane to attach one's faith to that star than to any other. As Voltaire says in Peter Gay's dialogues, "In the end, after all experimentation and investigation are over, philosophy rests on a wager. Pascal advised the doubter to wager on God's existence. I advise man to wager on the possibility of improvement."[5]

To many of today's action-oriented historians, a generalized faith in progress is not enough. History is a weapon in the arsenal of those who feel that their job is to make a better future as well as to comment on the past. History, they believe, should be used to beat swords into plowshares and to destroy the vestiges of racism and imperialism in human affairs. Howard Zinn calls for historians to direct their research to the great problems of our time. While paying heed to professional standards, Zinn wants a committed radical

[5]Peter Gay, *The Bridge of Criticism* (New York: Harper & Row, 1970), p. 149.

history that does violence to some historians' concepts of objectivity. Although Zinn proposes only that historians ask questions relevant to our time, there is always the danger that the questions will be asked in such a way that the answers will not be in doubt. There is a difference between questions like "Why does war occur?" and "Why is war declared by a handful of men at the top who manipulate public opinion . . . just before and after the decision, to build support for it?"[6] The second question prejudges the case. It simplifies the reasons for war. The question itself controls the answer and there is little chance for the historian to discover that the reasons for war in human affairs go beyond the cabalistic approach that some radical historians seem to favor.

Zinn does, however, bring into focus a major problem, namely: What is the point of studying history? Although most of the historians who have written on this subject in recent years are not looking for salvation or ultimate meaning in the historical process, they are nonetheless trying to find some utility, however marginal, to justify the enormous effort required to interpret and reinterpret past events and pass the findings on to others. If history cannot give meaning to life, if its lessons are too complex to be applied to present problems, what is its value? Can analogies drawn from the past enlighten us about the present and the future? Should we forget the past which, after all, tyrannizes as often as it enlightens? Look at the terrible errors diplomats, generals, and entire countries have made in our time because past experiences taught them lessons that were at best only partially relevant to new situations. Perhaps we should have courses in historical forgetting.

The selections in this volume were chosen in order to give the reader an idea of how some historians have dealt with questions of relevance and purpose. They range from attempts to revive the idea of progress to exhortations on the dangers of forgetting one's past and living a one-dimensional existence outside of the historical process. There are essays calling for history which is socially and politically relevant and essays that challenge the idea that the historian must or should see the past in terms of present utility. To some of these writers the best historian is involved in the process of trying to make a better world; to others he is, in Siegfried Kracauer's words, "an exile" who has the ability to detach himself from the problems of his age. To some, then, detachment, not involvement, is

---

[6]Howard Zinn, *The Politics of History* (Boston: Beacon Press, 1970), p. 305.

the ideal. Some of these historians advocate drawing analogies and making generalizations whereas others see great dangers in this use of history.

There are also historians who value their discipline more for what it can do for the individual than for what it can do for society as a whole. History puts us in touch with times and with men uniquely different from those we know. History opens up a panorama of possibilities for the human condition that we cannot see by concentrating on our own times. Rilke's poem, "The Archaic Torso of Apollo," sums up this function of the past quite succinctly. A man is looking at the remains of an ancient Greek statue. To him, the statue represents a different way of life and of doing things, and the shock of confronting the past *as something new* shakes the observer loose from a self-satisfied present. Paradoxically the past feeds his discontent. He must change his life because he has confronted an historic moment and has found his life style (and perhaps the life style of his generation) wanting.

We find similarities as well as differences in past ages, however. In spite of the enormous differences between our age and the Elizabethan age, we share enough for sympathetic understanding to be possible. This is why the plays of Shakespeare have relevance and meaning for us even though civilization has changed in countless ways since the sixteenth century. We can still find kinship with a past in which men lived, died, fought wars, knew suffering and joy, and faced problems somewhat like our own. Both the similarities and the differences embedded in the past can be instructive, but only in the broadest sense. This is what Peter Geyl meant when he wrote:

> History is not to be searched for practical lessons, the applicability of which will always be doubtful in view of the inexhaustible novelty of circumstances and combinations of causes, but just this, that the mind will acquire a sensitiveness, an imaginative range.[7]

These essays will not provide easy answers to the difficult questions of meaning and purpose in history. They are, however, eloquent testimony to the fact that historians have begun to approach their discipline in new and searching ways. I hope that the reader will discover in these pages why some men look backward to an uncertain past as well as forward to the problems of an uncertain future.

[7]Peter Geyl, *Use and Abuse of History* (New Haven: Yale University Press, 1955), p. 84.

Contents

I The Death of the Past

In the selections below, John Marcus and Page Smith reveal their deep concern about the fate of the past in our time. Marcus' writings have a strong "theological" bent in that he is disturbed by the fact that history no longer provides mankind with meaning and a sense of destiny. In a sense, he is responding to the criticisms of men like Karl Löwith and Reinhold Niebuhr who, writing under the impact of World War II, chided mankind for putting its faith in the essentially unpredictable and fickle muse of history. Along with others, these men argued that salvation must be sought and found outside of the historical process, in some sort of transhistorical faith, such as Christianity. Although Marcus is not attempting to proselytize, he does share with some theologians a sense of despair and foreboding about the consequences of a loss of faith in the meaning of the historical process. In the epilogue to his book, he sums up these fears when he writes:

> ... When in the western view of time and of historical destiny the individual lost his sense of a final goal, or even of a direction of movement, he was left in a moral void. Western man found himself facing a relentless process of historical change heading into an endless emptiness. The grinding force of historical tragedy intensified the individual's feelings of impotence, converting it into the terror of oblivion within the infinite abyss of time. Detranscendentalization left man without any escape from annihilation, either beyond worldly reality or within it.[1]

Page Smith shares some of Marcus' concern about the fate of the past in the twentieth century but he is less concerned with questions

---

[1]John Marcus, *Heaven, Hell, & History.* New York: Macmillan, 1967, p. 75.

of ultimate meaning and salvation. Smith is worried about the effects of presentism on men who have no understanding of the importance of studying history. History is useful to us not because it provides us with final answers about the fate of man, but because it offers us an inexhaustible storehouse of life styles, civilizational modes, and ways of acting that we can draw on as we face the future. History gives us balance, patience, and a deeper understanding of what it means to live and die. History cannot save us in any ultimate sense, but it can deepen our understanding of humanity's potentialities and limitations.

JOHN T. MARCUS
The Historical Crisis

THE HISTORICAL CRISIS OF OUR TIME

Is history the latest and last of the human gods that have failed? Is the despair of finding any meaning in man's experience the most starkly revealing discovery of the mind, and the sense of futility the end result of our civilization? These pessimistic questions, which are explicitly raised or half-consciously implied in many key elements of modern thought, reflect the anxiety and sense of purposelessness underlying much of contemporary life. Disillusion in its most general form manifests itself through a pervasive nihilism, destructive of all human values and hopes. In its more limited and specific form, it expresses itself as a profound alienation from the traditions, values and, in particular, the historical aspirations of Western culture. Fear of the abyss arises above all from disenchantment with our glorified historical expectations. History appears as the tragic story of human failure, devoid of the redemptive role of classic tragedy, from Orestes or Job to Faust.

Since the appearance of Spengler's *Decline of the West,* a concern with the pathology of our civilization has become a morbidly fascinating theme for historical philosophers and the literate public. Cultural introspection has been refined, and sometimes overrefined. Under the stress of the historical crises and the chaos of recent years, social comment has gone from pessimism about Western civilization to pessimism about man.

New political movements, wars and revolutions have confirmed many of the social prophets' hypotheses of irrationalism and violence. These forces seem to have taken on in our time a new universality and relentlessness. The assumption that violence and irrationalism are the ultimate reality of man is the basic premise of some modern ideologies and is implicit in others. Such ideological currents have led to growing apprehension that the problems confronting our civilization cannot be resolved through hope, work and time, but are not capable of solution at all—that the human condition, in sum, is uncontrollable. Confronted today with the possibility of omnicide on one hand and the growing rejection of all suprahuman values on the other, we have watched the age-old philosophical theme of the possible futility of existence take on new psychological immanence in Western life and thought. Doubt has become the common solvent of many contemporary attitudes, both among intellectual elites and among the mass. Totalitarian movements have sought escape from the frustration of our aborted hopes of social redemption through identification with the charismatic will of the leader and the forced certitude of imposed beliefs. Meanwhile, the deep-seated uncertainty of an influential part of the intelligentsia has turned into a pervasive sense of moral chaos, or a nihilistic philosophy of absurdity. The survival of Western civilization is held in jeopardy. It is significant that cultural historians have taken a renewed interest in the study of late Rome, and that some social philosophers find disturbing comparisons between the temper of our own time and that of the decaying Roman Empire.

At the heart of this crisis of values lies a crucial problem of ideology and psychology: the repudiation of all sense of order and meaning in human experience. The course of civilization is seen as an incoherent sequence of events, or as a relentless movement of superhuman forces against which the individual and humanity itself are helpless. In its intellectualized expression, this anxiety has manifested itself in repeated proclamations of the ultimate purposelessness of man's existential condition *in history,* i.e., that there exists no redemption from man's meaningless role as an historical being. The denial of a meaningful continuum in history has fostered a sense of void. Individual life appears futile in the larger context of man's lack of destiny. This loss of the sense of an historical objective seems to deprive human experience of its moral *raison d'être.* Indeed, when history as a whole seems futile, the notion of coherent purpose in the individual is shattered, and each event seems an isolated, purposeless phenomenon in the abyss of time. In this view there is no escape from death, no lingering effect from the light of one's own brief candle. This fear cuts to the very heart of the ideological drive in man, namely his yearning to transcend his present state and to "break free." In short, the present crisis of values has its root in an intimation of the untranscendability of the human condition in an historical world devoid of rhyme or reason.

The sense of incoherence and untranscendability is mirrored in a host of intellectual movements. It is clearly evidenced in the shock techniques and aggressive irrationality characteristic of much of modern art. Twentieth-century aesthetic forms have been rife with expressions of the chaotic unconscious within us, and of the mindless chaos around us. Each successive art movement has manifested to some degree man's fear of alienation in modern industrial society and of the imprisonment of each individual psyche in a permanently unfulfilled state.

Science, for all its intellectual and technological successes, has also contributed substantially to the climate of anxiety. Conclusions drawn in a vulgarized form from the revolution in the physical sciences—conclusions often misapplied or misinterpreted—have proved to be influential intellectual forces. Based on imprecisely understood scientific concepts of time and space, certain social philosophies proclaim that, in a universe where all positions are relative, subjective and indeterminate, man can find little hope of escape from his own mortal frame of reference into an absolute and eternal Being.

Of all the sciences, however, it is psychology which has most reenforced the fear of the inherent untranscendability of the human condition. The rationalism of early psychoanalytic clinical theory was overshadowed by the emphasis on man's unconscious drives as the decisive elements in his life and culture. This notion was readily distorted in popularized form into a new determinism that reduces human actions to the play of irrational forces within the psyche. In this view, civilized man is still chained to his baser self and its aggressive impulses. According to Freud, he is irretrievably trapped in the contradiction between his basic urges and his guilt feelings.

This pessimism is also reflected in contemporary philosophic movements. From Plato through the mid-nineteenth century, the predominant mode of philosophical enquiry was the quest for some absolute truth and for an ultimate good. Through philosophical knowledge, man hoped to find justification for his life. Socrates' remark that the purpose of philosophy is to teach men how to die suggests the implicit psychological motivation towards metaphysics, epistemology and ontology, not to mention ethics, social philosophy and theology. The goal of philosophy was to reach towards immortality by somehow apprehending the eternal, for the notion of seeking an absolute has an inherently redemptive aspect, insofar as it appears to offer access to a transcendent truth beyond the individual's subjective experience and a purpose beyond his mortal life. But most twentieth-century philosophers reject the idea of a transcending absolute. Indeed, this repudiation provides one of the few common elements between such generally unrelated philosophical movements as the positivist and existentialist schools.

That this disorientation among intellectuals has also affected larger groups of society is clear from the history of two world wars and the repeated social and political crises of contemporary industrial civilization. The rise of various totalitarian movements provides especially devastating testimony of man's apprehension about his "imprisonment" in history and his fear of being trapped in an aimless existence. Industrial mass society, economic dislocation and total war have created mass values susceptible to totalitarian ideologies as a counterattack on the despair born of historical futility and purposelessness. The irony is that this reaction adopts the very weapons of irrationalism and violence which it purports to counteract.

The nihilism suggested in much of contemporary literature appears related to the major events of modern history. Despite its frequently pretentious forebodings and artificial mood of self-pity, the literary vogue of despair touches a real chord in modern experience. It is particularly noteworthy that Western man's sense of anxiety arose as a direct consequence of the collapse of our sense of historical purpose: it emerged from the inherent self-contradiction in seeking human redemption within history. The full dilemma is revealed in the individual's vain attempt to escape mortality within the frame of historical time and in terms of specific historical expectations. The problem of meaning in historical consciousness becomes crucial in a civilization which has come to place upon the individual's conception of historical destiny the full burden of his vicarious transcendence of death. It is largely the fear of history and the loss of hope in historical redemption that has brought the crisis of our time.

THE PROBLEM OF SELF-TRANSCENDENCE
AND HISTORICAL CONSCIOUSNESS

Why should the sense of history play such a key role in our scale of values? What has made it serve in Western society as the fulcrum of our ideals? Why did history provide, for a while, a sense of order in human experience and purpose in individual life? To answer these questions, we must consider the nature of man's yearning for transcendence. We must see how the desire for eternity is related to man's impulse to seek unity and coherence in his world, and how sometimes it manifests itself in the awareness of time. Then we can discuss the role of redemptive aspirations of history in the life-forms of Western culture.

Like all biological organisms, man seeks direct gratification of his basic drives. As he develops towards civilization, he formulates a consciousness of time. He develops a collective memory and a sense of individual self-projection into the future. He no longer lives solely in the present moment and in the immediate satisfaction of wants. With the development of a sense of temporality, the wish to gratify present impulses is transformed psychologically into a wish to ensure their future satisfaction. Death, which will put an end to the fulfillment of desire, becomes relevant to his present life—a prospect he strives desperately to veil from his consciousness even if, as Freud argues, another force within his psyche drives him towards it. Fear of an absolute end to his being alters the life principle itself from a present-centered survival impulse into an overpowering yearning for immortality, or for "presence" through the eternity of time.

To gratify this urge for perpetuity, the individual seeks to transcend himself and his finite, temporal span. The notion of an afterlife appears. There emerges the idea of a distinct "spirit" that will survive the mortal body. Since the encounter with death and the desire to transcend it are common to all civilizations, this "spirit" finds universal expression, from the Egyptian *ka* to the Christian soul. The universality of funeral rites, apparent even in prehistoric cultures, attests man's concern with some form of posthumous identity. Many of man's great endeavors and cultural triumphs rise from the psychological impulse to immortality through preservation of the individual's spirit or in eternalizing his memory, whether in the form of the pyramids or of the Taj Mahal. Were there no sense of transcending death, there would be no occasion for burial ceremonies, monuments and elegies. Even in secular perspectives, entombment in a shrine is intended to perpetuate the memory of the dead hero. It symbolizes a human transcendence within an historical frame. A similar function is performed for some individuals by ideals and goals. Such hopes of transcendence often arouse a true altruism and self-sacrifice. They may awaken a person's love of country, of humanity, or of God. For some people, these sentiments are unselfish in that they love their nation solely for the sake of its destiny, humanity purely for the sake of man, and God for His perfection. For most others, however, the sentiments represent more self-centered values, being essentially an idealized egocentricity in disguised form—a hope of salvation through self-denial and sacrifice. But in any case, all such values stem, psychologically, from a person's desire to achieve somehow the immortalization of his own identity and the identification with eternal Being.

Self-transcendence, then, means primarily man's going beyond himself and his moment in time—his reaching for identification with something beyond his own finite and mortal ego. It entails the development of an idealized alter ego that signifies his eternal identity, either directly as a spiritual being or indirectly in some human legacy. Transcendence, we will see, depends upon the power of empathy and fellow-feeling; it involves an imaginative displacement of the psyche, for example, in the capacity to envisage a perfect or heavenly state. It appears in countless forms of religious beliefs, and myths of immortality. It appears also in immortalizing objectives, such as the raising of sons who will duly worship their ancestors, or the passing on of a moral legacy to men who will admire their legendary and historical heroes. We may conclude that the urge to self-transcendence is basic to civilization, for it is one of the most fundamental impulses of the psyche, namely to secure its own being from extinction.

Man's desire for vicarious immortality manifests itself in his conception of the ideal. Identification of oneself with an ideal object, such as the spirit of an ancestor, or with an ideal value, such as the good society, constitutes an indirect method of eternalization. For the quest of ideality expresses the universal desire for a self-transcending objective. Thus, while prevalent contemporary thought holds that moral values can exist only in relation to particular cultures and contexts, and that their forms are necessarily transitory, it does not deny that the quality of idealness—or some conception of good and right—is a basic element in human consciousness and a notable force in history. Indeed, no society is without both its ethical consciousness and its ritual forms representing some kind of enduring value transcending individual life.

The desire to find some coherence in life, or to evoke a semblance of order out of chaos, constitutes a general aspiration of mankind. It is reflected in the myths, archetypes and sacred rituals of all primitive cultures. This universality arises from the function that the ideal of unity performs in enabling the individual to formulate a sense of his own place and purpose, and to conceive of some meaning to his experience extending beyond his mortal existence. By providing the person with an intimation of his role, the particular conception of order, in effect, defines his social and cultural identity. Thus the distinctive unifying ideals in a civilization indirectly frame its transcendent goals and establish the concrete forms of the individual's aspiration to eternity.

In each culture, specific values and rituals give shape to man's underlying urge for unity and order, and to his desire for harmony with the transcendent forces of life. *In our own secularized civilization, thus urge has found its basic expression in historical consciousness.* Indeed, one of the ways of seeking unity and meaning in things is through *the coherent organization of experience in historical time.* The unifying principle then becomes the temporal structure; the organizing theme of thought and action becomes man's conception of an evolutionary development that can be directed towards achieving a moral order in history. For example, much of the impetus behind our traditional social and political ideals has been the expectation of attaining morally rewarding historical goals, such as manifest destiny, social justice or universal peace.

These historical objectives seemed to confer upon the disconnected or erratic elements of life some consistency and redemptive meaning. They served an eternalizing function because men tended to presume that their historical goals, for example, the British Empire, the Thousand-Year Reich or the Classless Society, would extend indefinitely into the future. Each of these historical ideals thus appeared to confer a symbolic immortality upon those who associated themselves with its historical triumph. In short, the basic yearning for eternity comes to manifest itself in redeeming objectives, whether these take mythical, religious or historical form. Particular historical ideals merely serve as the means through which the individual seeks a self-transcending identification with the encompassing unity that gives purpose to human existence and a form of vicarious release from death.

In historical consciousness, the individual's desire to identify himself with an immortal object expresses itself in his contributing to a transcended state—a state occurring within the historical process. That is, the redemptive value must have here a temporal quality. In sacred archetypes, the transcendent objective is eventual removal of the self *from* the process of time. In the secular-historical model (epitomized by Faust), the transcendent objective is the unending record of one's presence *in* time. Historical redemption offers not an other-worldly existence of the spirit but a moral goal embodied in the anticipated society of the future. It envisions an ideal world of human creation, if not as an attainable reality, at least as a desirable goal. In contrast to those forms of self-transcendence that seek an atemporal communion with nature or the spirit world, or which proclaim the undifferentiatedness of being, historical redemption calls for a personal impact upon the contemporary course of events. It requires a distinctive legacy to posterity, such as memorable acts and creations that carry the name of their author into the unending future, or the unsung contributions of countless anonymous individuals to the destiny of a nation or of mankind. But in any case, it is marked by the uniqueness of each person's role in the linear unfolding of events and in the cumulative process of culture. By projecting his idealized alter ego upon the vision of a redeeming future state, the individual seeks to overcome the sense of alienation induced by the prospect of his own mortality. He achieves through historical consciousness a feeling of personal liberation and of eternal worth.

When the sense of history, which we shall hereafter call historicity, serves in this self-transcending capacity, its concern is not the past for its own sake. Its focus is rather the relation between the past and the future, whether as an inevitable process of destiny or as an opportunity for man's fulfillment and ideal aspirations. Here the past presents not a model for emulation in some cyclical regeneration of time, but the source out of which the future state arises. The process of history is seen as drawn towards certain teleological goals, in reference to which the "meaning" of present events is to be evaluated. In some historical perspectives, the teleology appears predetermined and inevitable, arising out of a divine plan or a law of historical necessity. In others, it appears simply as the unpredestined consequence of conflicting human wants and desires. Thus under given material and social conditions, such as industrialization, nationalism or the demand for social justice, these wants channel men's actions in a particular direction. According to this view, there is no single movement of history immutably imposed upon man by Providence or by the inherent order of things; but there is still a teleological quality to the historical process, in the sense that men are possessed of intentions and that, within the limiting frame of cultural and economic circumstances, they pursue goal-directed activities. The various ideal objectives to which individuals and groups direct their efforts provide the distinctive "futuricity" of our historical consciousness, which enables it to serve in a redemptive capacity.

Redemptive historicity implies the presence of inherent tendencies and immanent forces within the historical process, even if they do not predetermine the course of events. For example, an acorn has the inherent potential to become an oak, but fulfillment of this potential depends upon external conditions, or contingencies, which cause the acorn to germinate into a new tree, or to rot on the ground. Similarly, based upon past developments, the historical process may be seen as exhibiting certain tendencies which limit the future range of choices. These tendencies become manifest in occasional momentous events, such as the French and Russian Revolutions, which reveal to the believer the "immanent forces in the historical process." They provide the faithful with a sense of security in their conception of historical destiny. But these tendencies depend upon individual acts in order to be realized or completed. In the cumulative legacy of the historical past, there are always implicit certain unfinished tasks of the moment. Our responses to them, which depend upon circumstances and culturally formed values and individual desires, may lead towards certain historical objectives, such as democracy and freedom. In the transcendent conception of history, the process of developing these inherent capacities into actual realities (such as the *risorgimento*) gives a sense of redemptive purpose to individual existence. Thus historical consciousness comes to serve as a unifying principle in human experience. It answers man's basic need for a meaningful ordering of things. In the end, it seems to transcend even its secular origins, as in the case of the patriot who finds a religious quality in his national ideal.

It is evident that, given such a perspective of history, the collapse of the sense of historical destiny would provoke an acute moral disorientation. It would engender a fear of the philosophical void and a crisis of identity. If there is no historical meaning or continuity in the succession of experiences, then little seems left, psychologically, on which to anchor a person's sense of place and role. The individual is still conditioned by our culture to search for the nature of his identity within a coherent historical world. But he is deprived of traditional historical goals—hence the severe aggravation of the sense of alienation in our society. Indeed, we may propose that the crisis of values of our time is basically a consequence of our loss of a redemptive historical hope.

PAGE SMITH
History and the Search for Identity

THE CLASSIC SEARCH of our time is the search for identity. But we cannot ask "Who am I?" and expect to find an answer without asking Kant's question "What is Man?"[1] We might well recall Heidegger's famous diagnosis: "No age has known so much, and so many different things, about man as ours. . . . And no age has known less than ours of what man is."[2]

In earlier chapters[3] we touched on the modern impulse to escape from history. Here we propose to carry the matter somewhat further and suggest a number of ways in which the attenuation of the historical sense is impoverishing modern society and thwarting the "self" in its search for identity.

One of the most conspicuous characteristics of our society is oversensitivity. This oversensitivity deprives modern man of the deeper emotions—love, hatred, compassion, loyalty.[4] The relation between sensitivity and sentiment corresponds on the one hand to the moment and on the other to the historic. Sentiment has its roots in the past, in memories and associations, loves and loyalties that command our allegiance. Sensitivity presses upon the immediate and has little or no power to sustain itself in the absence of the present objects which evoke it. Sensitivity, without the counter-

[1]"What we once were, how we developed and became what we are, we learn from the way in which we acted, the plans which we once adopted, the way in which we made ourselves felt in our vocation, from old letters from judgments on us which were spoken long ago. . . We understand ourselves and others only when we transfer our own lived experience into every kind of expression of our own and other people's life." [Wilhelm Dilthey, from "The Peculiar Nature of the Human Studies," in *Wilhelm Dilthey: An Introduction,* translated and edited by H. A. Hodges (London: Routledge & Kegan Paul; 1949), p. 142.]

[2]From *Kant and the Problem of Metaphysics,* quoted by Martin Buber in *Between Man and Man* (New York: Macmillan; 1948), p. 181.

[3]See, e.g., the discussion of free will vs. determinism in Chapter 13, Page Smith, *The Historian and History,* pp. 200-217.

[4]J. D. Salinger is the perfect literary expression of this characteristic. He has explored the psyche of his characters with such an exquisite sensitivity that he has finally destroyed them, for we no longer believe in their power to act in a real world and thus no longer care to read about them. He has refined them out of existence, most typically in the strange case history of Seymour Glass.

balance of sentiment, progressively destroys the capacity of the individual to be deeply engaged. Moreover, oversensitivity produces sentimentality, which is misplaced sentiment, as in one of the classic literary vulgarities of our day, when Salinger's Zooey Glass assures his sister that "Christ is the fat lady." This is gross sentimentality and, as such, has a strong appeal to the deracinated intellectual; it avoids the problems and burdens of historic religion and offers instead a mild and inoffensive religiosity—the liberal doctrine of empathy.[5] In the absence of a sense of the historic, the oversensitive cannot handle sentiment without having it degenerate into sentimentality.[6]

Contemporary man is often both extraordinarily sensitive and extraordinarily impotent. It is hard not to feel, for instance, that the matter of sensitivity is related to the rapid increase in homosexuality; homosexual relations provide an opportunity for great sensitivity between partners to the relationship, without the risks and complex *historical* demands of heterosexual relations. When a man loves a woman, he faces the possibility of having a child by her—already an extreme and drastic involvement in history—and perhaps even of marrying her—then, together with his wife, he forms a unity that becomes part of history. If he and his wife have a child, the child immediately asserts its place in the continuity of generations by demanding grandparents and great-grandparents and threatening, in turn, to have children of its own one day.[7]

An excess of sensibility erodes all meaning and falls at last into mannered posings. *Last Year at Marienbad* is a cinematic example of such an excess which abandons meaning and coherence for effect. The film is conspicuous for its outspoken rejection of any recognizable historical framework. Whether the unhappy lovers met last year or the year before or, indeed, ever is not clear to them or to

[5]Such sentimentality is equally evident in the work of Tennessee Williams, around whose derelicts, psychopaths, and homosexuals a kind of dim religious light plays—the hero of *The Night of the Iguana* is a defrocked Episcopal priest of enormous sensitivity. *The Milk Train Doesn't Stop Here Anymore* features a Christ-like figure as hero. Edward Albee's *The Zoo Story* indulges in the same sentimental vulgarity: "It's just that if you can't deal with people, you have to make a start somewhere. WITH ANIMALS. . . . WITH GOD WHO IS A COLORED QUEEN WHO WEARS A KIMONO AND PLUCKS HIS EYEBROWS."

[6]It is probably no accident that one of the most robust and prolific writers of our time, William Faulkner, was obsessed by history.

[7]Today one often hears childless couples declare self-righteously that they "would not think of bringing a child into such a frightful world."

the audience; the film offers a calculated ambiguity which serves to annihilate time.

One of the principal causes of the oversensitivity which results in alienation and withdrawal (seen most dramatically, though not necessarily most typically, in the beatnik living a life of rebellious inactivity in some desolate pad) is the modern city. It is in the city that history most often seems nullified. The feverish activity of the metropolis hangs upon the moment. What yesterday loomed solidly in brick and concrete is today replaced with steel and glass. Landmarks disappear almost overnight; children are conspicuously absent and old people are invisible, segregated in crumbling slums or in senior-citizens developments. There is little sign of death or birth, and the sequence of generations which is the backbone of history is hardly to be observed. The city lives in a kind of prolonged today whose symbol is the metropolitan newspaper, which tells every morning of various horrors—deaths, mutilations, terrible accidents—but seldom makes any subsequent mention of these tragedies (except where it focuses with morbid sentimentality on the lingering death of a child or a celebrity from some incurable illness).

The city prides itself above everything else on being up-to-date and works in a hundred direct and indirect ways to erode the sense of a historical dimension in our lives. It is, for example, the citadel of the senses; most of its inhabitants learn to live on sensations of the most transient kind, a constant and ingenious titillation of superficial emotions. Daniel Bell, writing primarily about art, has suggested that our technical civilization, of which the city is the most characteristic accomplishment, has "eclipsed distance"—that psychic interval which has traditionally existed between the observer and the object observed. Bell attributes this eclipse to certain elements of our "style" as a society, which he comprehends in the terms *"novelty, sensation, simultaneity, immediacy, and impact."*[8] As Bell puts it, "the loss of psychic distance means the suspension of time." It is in just this timeless, a-historical void that modern man wanders, often hopelessly lost, searching for his authentic self. Time and space are the walls and roof of the home in which the soul of Western man has grown to its present estate. The eclipse of these dimensions threatens that soul in its innermost being.

Ironically, we are especially susceptible to despair as a consequence of having been able to imagine a better world than the one we live in. We are, in fact, overcome by the discrepancies between

[8]"The Eclipse of Distance," *Encounter*, XX, No. 5 (May, 1963), pp. 54-6.

the ought-to-be and the is or, more accurately, by the apparent absence of any readily accessible path from the is to the ought-to-be. As the eighteenth century was sustained by faith in reason, the nineteenth was supported by a belief in some form of evolutionary process. The twentieth century, however, is painfully aware that process is no longer to be relied upon. Our century has faced too many horrors to believe that progress is part of the structure of the universe. We are thus left with the grim fact that the progress of the race depends on the good will and intelligence (and, one is tempted to add, luck) with which we solve the crises that seem to press on us from every side. The authority vested in abstract thought induced us to believe that society could be reconstructed according to some planner's blueprint, whereas history, if we would listen, speaks with a somewhat different voice and reminds us of "the risks we have to run, the partial obscurity in which we have to take decisions . . . the state of dispossession, insecurity and hardihood which is the climate of all great action."[9]

It is not accidental that the optimism of the Enlightenment with regard to the power of man over himself and the cosmos has been replaced, in our own day, with the contradictory sense of man's powerlessness over his own psyche and over the social and political arrangements that obtain in the contemporary world. As man's power over nature has grown, his power over himself seems to have diminished. But the extremes of optimism and pessimism are, to a considerable degree, the consequences of inadequate or faulty history. The Enlightenment was convinced that what seemed evident about man in the past—his superstition, cruelty, and vice—must vanish in the light of reason and thus could not condition the future. This delusion enabled the French to accept the horrors of their Revolution; when you are convinced that you are about to cure the patient (man) from the disease of history, you will stop at no cruelty to effect the cure. In our century Russia was driven by the same terrible lust of idealism that propelled the French Revolution in its course.

Yet, Western man, as we have seen, has dared to hope and the balance of mankind has been infected with this fever of aspiration. Gabriel Marcel has expressed man's universal aspiration: to be in the future "as before but differently and better than before."[10]

While it is doubtlessly true that the self today has taken much

[9]Emmanuel Mounier. *Personalism* (New York: Grove Press; 1952), p. 93.

[10]*Homo Viator: Introduction to a Metaphysic of Hope* (Chicago: Henry Regnery; 1951), p. 67.

more upon itself than in earlier times—a truly staggering load—it condemns itself to ineptitude if it does not constantly carry the awareness of the darker areas of life back to the active world. In other generations people have known just as vividly the sordidness, degeneracy, and falsity of much of life, but they have also known delights and pleasures that were not purchased at the cost of insensitivity to the desperate needs and frustrations of the world.

At the other end of the spectrum from that excess of sensitivity, which is so sensitive that it rejects the world as misshapen and intolerable and refuses to enter into its dilemmas and crises, are the "overadapted," whose spokesmen tirelessly congratulate us on our technological achievements and exhort everyone to avail himself gratefully of the rich bounty that this technology has produced. The overadapted gives himself up to bondage to "things"; the bondage itself degrades his "productive or social function to automatism." He is the victim of the transient fads that our society presses on him without end, claiming that some new revelation of the good life is to be found in each one: swimming pool, deep freeze, patio, electric rotisserie, powerboat, color TV, electric toothbrush, motion-picture projector, an endless cornucopia of *things,* an enchanted forest of materiality. Small wonder the oversensitive, who, although he may not know how to save his soul, at least realizes it is in desperate peril, turns away in revulsion.[11] The oversensitive knows in his heart that "man's exploitation of nature was not destined to erect upon the web of natural determinism another network of conditioned reflexes."[12]

The oversensitive suffer from an excess of self-consciousness and indeed from that very narcissism which such neo-Freudians as Marcuse and Brown celebrate; the overadapted are afflicted by a spiritual nullity that is the consequence of being devoured by an omnivorous present. They, who have given themselves so willingly to the fancied delights of an abundant technology, go as restlessly and as aimlessly as butterflies from one gleaming, machine-made flower to another, sucking up a nectar which eventually poisons them. The only thing that can save them from the tyranny of the middle-class standard of living is the knowledge that other people have lived differently and lived better by subordinating "things" to

[11]"The supreme despair," Kierkegaard wrote, "is not to feel desperate."

[12]Mounier: *Personalism,* p. 12; see also p. 85. Speaking of those whom I have called the oversensitive, Mounier writes that their "almost visceral repugnance to commit themselves, and an inability to bring anything to realization, betray the dried-up sources of feeling that underlie their sometimes highly-colored eloquence."

human values. Surely they will not improve by visiting a psychoanalyst, for he will tell them that the solution to their problem lies in freeing themselves of any lingering sense of guilt over their self-indulgence.[13] The basic malady of the oversensitive and the over-adapted is indeed the same: they are destroying themselves for want of history.

Another contemporary manifestation of oversensitivity is subjectivism. The subjective spirit believes that it can heal the schism between subject and object by absorbing the objective, but finds that, instead, the objective triumphs. The unexpected accomplishment of the subjectivists has been to turn the world, human and material, into objects, objects which seem to have no relation to one another and whose symbol is "the now pure lordship of the eye," the detached, coolly observing gaze which, like that of Robbe-Grillet and his school, ranges impersonally over the world. In the film *Last Year at Marienbad,* the facades, gardens, and interior details of the hotel are more substantial and seem to promise more meaning than the wan people who act out deliberately impenetrable anti-dramas before them.

It is well to recall Paul Weiss's concept of the historic as that which objectively happened in the past *rather than simply that which happens in the mind of the historian.* The working historian is hardly apt to be led astray on this point, but the theoretical ground may be washed out from under him by philosophers (Croce, Ortega y Gasset, and Collingwood are cases in point) or attitudes which, in effect, destroy the power of the historic. The dimension of the historic alone prevents us from being crushed by the weight of the present; it is equally important to hold fast to the objective nature of the historic as a bulwark against the encroachment of the subjective.

Thus, to repeat, it is essential that the objective nature of the historic be insisted upon in all discussions of history, because it is the objective nature of our historic life which offers the means for drawing modern man out of his increasingly sterile subjectivism and back into an inhabitable, if grossly imperfect, world.

[13]It is the fate of the overadapted to "have no secret, no contents, no background" and, "having no experience of any depth," to have "no respect for privacy, their own or anyone else's." Mounier: Ibid., p. 35. Marcel writes of them: "The more we allow ourselves to be the servants of Having, the more we shall let ourselves fall a prey to the knowing anxiety which Having involves, the more we shall tend to lose not only the aptitude for hope, but even I should say the very belief, indistinct as it might be, of its possibility." *Homo Viator,* p. 61. It is this spirit which apparently motivates many members of the "radical right" in the United States.

In the world of art, abstract expressionism might be called "art without history," an art which undertook to free the painter from the constraints and inhibitions of traditionalism and thus allow him to express his inner, that is, his "true" self.[14] This movement has resulted, ironically, in works that lack individuality—suggesting that all "inners" are curiously alike. This might serve to convince us that the "true," inner man is indistinguishable from his fellows; he is only individualized as he appears in the world—that is, as he acquires a history. Moreover, he does not make that history, nor, more precisely, does he make himself. As Mounier has expressed it: "If every man *is* nothing but what he *makes himself,* there can be no humanity, no history, and no community."[15] The individual acquires an identity by being involved in a common enterprise. If between all individuals there existed that "absolute discontinuity" which is so prominent in much existential thought, mankind could have no history and no real future.

Another area of contemporary life where the impulse to annihilate the past is inescapably evident is in modern architecture. In the brutal and impersonal buildings that sprout like mushrooms all over the urban landscapes there is "no trace of the forms which lived in the centuries before us, none of their arrogance, their privilege, their aspiration, their canniness . . . their vulgarities."[16] They are coldly antihuman monoliths whose promise is death. Indeed, there is a spirit abroad, armed with such cant words as *progressive, modern, functional, dynamic,* which would gladly pull down all buildings with any dignity, with any power to evoke a past, and erect in their places structures as cruel as knives and as graceless as blocks. These banal and monotonous erections are like congealed pieces of the present, and it is for their very contemporaneity that they are prized. Devoid of any suggestion of the richness and variety of the past, they are the perfect monuments of an anti-historical age.

It might be said that the peculiar curse of America has been its preoccupation with individualism, rugged or otherwise. A good many Americans have had the notion, whether they acted upon it or

---

[14]In the words of Willard Gaylin, there is "a prevalent tendency to think of the 'inner' man as the 'real' man and the 'outer' man as illusion or pretender. But the unconscious of a man represents *another* view, not a 'truer' one. Though a man may not always be what he appears to be, what he appears to be is always a significant part of what he is." "Psychoanaliterature: The Hazards of a Hybrid," *Columbia University Forum,* VI, No. 2 (Spring, 1963), pp. 11-16.

[15]*Personalism,* p. 30.

[16]Norman Mailer: "The Big Bite," *Esquire,* LX (August, 1963), p. 21.

not, that they as individuals could, without study or prayer, re-capitulate the experience of the race; they have not hesitated to attempt to found new religions or novel sects. That the self has insatiable appetites was known to Christian theology long before it was discovered by Freud. Moreover, the ingenuity with which the self masks its appetites and the skill with which it uses reason or religion as the servant of its interest is equally well known and is not, in any sense, a modern discovery.[17] These facts make even more dangerous and futile the effort of modern man to escape from history. "Self-expression" and "self-realization" are two of the cant phrases of our time. What is thought to be the ultimate reality—the self—becomes in fact the ultimate unreality, and the tormented individuals who continue to probe the depths of their psyche become increasingly unreal.

Self-expression and self-realization are, much as their advocates would be repelled by the idea, the lineal descendants of nineteenth-century rugged individualism. Individualism, with its rapacious and exploitative attitude toward the world, is the antithesis of that individuality which is the authentic self realized within a genuine community. One of the principal fallacies of those who pursue individualism in one form or another is the notion that it is achieved by the rejection of all authority, within which history is included. Certainly, history is authoritative. We are capable of saying with reasonable accuracy what happened.[18] The historic appears as form and order, which, while it discloses areas of choice, i.e., freedom (which often, from later perspectives, also appears to be inevitable), also imposes limitations on our actions. But the framework of necessity within which history binds us cannot be escaped by ignoring history. Indeed, it could be said that to ignore it is, ultimately, to turn its authority into tyranny.

The fact is that the individual, per se, is without history; the

---

[17]Reinhold Niebuhr has pointed out that the self's desire "for security or for prestige is, like all human desires, indeterminate. There is no point at which the self . . . can feel satisfied and free to consider others than itself." *The Self and the Drama of History* (New York: Charles Scribner's, 1955), p. 139.

[18]"The historian never arrives at certainty; he rarely ends with more than a not altogether sifted totality of plausible, hypothetical, guessed-at and imagined formulations of what had been. One will more likely achieve more truth by turning away from the study of history than by engaging in it. . . . The historian does not find this fact as regrettable as others do, for he is primarily concerned not with achieving pure and well-tested truth but with providing a comprehensive, illuminating account of what had been." Paul Weiss: *History Written and Lived* (Carbondale: Southern Illinois University Press, 1962), p. 45.

community is historic. The individual is powerless; the community has the power to re-form its members and the world as well. In the words of Robert Oppenheimer, with the disintegration of the community (the public), "we have had neither the time nor the skill nor the dedication to tell one another what we have learned, nor to listen, nor to welcome its enrichment of the common culture and the common understanding. Thus the public sector of our lives, what we have and hold in common, has suffered. . . . Our specialized traditions flourish; our private beauties thrive; but in those high undertakings where man derives strength and insight from the public excellence, we have been impoverished. We hunger for nobility; the rare words and acts that harmonize simplicity and truth." Our public life is pre-eminently our historic life, and it is this life that is shrunken and attenuated.[19]

Another serious flaw in the modern psyche is a lack of "patience." We cannot wait for anything; we must snatch with rude violence everything that time might properly withhold in order that it should come to fruition. If the teen-ager must have adult pleasures at once, he can never become an adult. It is a sad fact that "too soon" means "never."

The curse of impatience can be seen in almost every aspect of our lives. Young people cannot wait to get married and once married cannot wait for that deepening of understanding and sympathy which would enhance their sexual relations. Few people are willing to sacrifice today for a prospective joy. The talented young writer sits down at once to write the great American novel and ends up making a hundred thousand dollars a year in Hollywood. The novice actor wishes to be a star long before he has learned his craft. All fail to recognize that without patience it is impossible to achieve anything more than brief sensations. One of the principal sources of patience is to be found in the contemplation of the historic, which teaches us that the most significant transformations of society are the work of decades and generations. To enter consciously into the great enterprise of carrying history forward is to learn, almost inevitably, the meaning of patience. We might well recall the Pauline in-

---

[19]Man's common nature and his historic being are perhaps best seen in the liturgies for the dead that are found in every great religion. In such solemn moments secular efforts to summon up some "personal" or "individual" traits to commemorate the deceased inevitably seem trivial and banal beside the profound religious utterances which bind all mankind in the common bond of death: To try to speak "individually" at this instant is presumptuous and futile.

junction to glory in tribulation, "knowing that tribulation worketh patience; and patience, experience and experience, hope."[20] History, in this sense, is collective experience. And whoever has known historic man in the hours of his profoundest defeats and triumphs will not easily lose faith in the possibilities of our common future. It is the impatient who most readily abandon hope when their often puerile expectations are frustrated.

Another aspect of the search for identity which is related to history is the tendency of our time to rob life of its dramatic content. Life without drama becomes flat and tasteless; yet today the demolition of the dramatic is pursued with a spirit of almost demonic intensity. We see it, for instance, in the destruction of the various arts by their practitioners. In the realm of ethics, good and bad are dissolved into neutral grays; the devil is banished and God with him; conflict is at all odds to be avoided; adjustment is the national ideal; the case study replaces the imaginative narrative.

One of man's most basic needs is for the dramatic representation of life. It is hard to escape the feeling that much of the senseless violence of juvenile delinquents stems from a desperate effort to endow marginal lives with some dramatic meaning, however perverse. Certainly the names they give their gangs—the Dukes, Royals, Kings, Jets, Earls, Sharks, etc.—suggest this most strongly.

History, as the story of the race, is a tale of unparalleled drama, but today it too is stripped of its dramatic quality and reduced to a series of dreary dates and bland formulas. The supreme importance in written history of the imaginative rather than the analytical powers can hardly be overemphasized. The imaginative reconstruction of the past, if done faithfully and scrupulously through narrative history, involves an extention of the affective life; it trains us to extend our sympathies so as to include the alien and the unfamiliar and thus reproduces in the historical arena that most painful and exemplary of exercises—the enlargement of our capacity for participation in the needs, hopes, anxieties, and expectations of others. The restoration of a sense of the dramatic in history will do much to fortify the individual in his effort to discover his identity, for an essential part of that identity is to be found in the story of his past—his collective "autobiography," as Rosenstock-Huessy has called it.

The point where the historic and the individual most frequently intersect is in the high-school or college classroom. I have spoken at

[20]*Romans:* 5:3-4.

length of the stultifying character of most instruction in history.* It does the devil's work by convincing most of the young people exposed to it that it is, at least for them, quite irrelevant. We must admit, I think, the validity of Mounier's criticism of the university as the distributor of a "formal knowledge which predisposes men to ideological dogmatism, or, by reaction, to sterile irony."[21] Martin Buber most effectively contrasts the modern pedagogue with his predecessor: "The 'old' educator represented particularly the historical world, the past. He was the ambassador of history to this intruder, the 'child'; he carried to him, as the Pope in the legend did to the prince of the Huns, the magic of the spiritual forces of history; he instilled values into the child or he drew the child into values."[22] The modern teacher who reduces the encounter between the historic and "its eternally new chaos" to "facts" or "interpretations" destroys the power of history to become a part of the student and wrench him out of his self-centeredness. What the old teacher knew that his present-day counterpart seems to have forgotten is that "education worthy of the name is essentially education of character."[23]

The individual finds the courage to be, in Paul Tillich's formulation, in a resolute confrontation of nothingness or non-being; and he derives the courage to act from the examples of others who have acted in history.[24]

We turn to history, then, as an inexhaustible reservoir of "life styles," of models and examples, as a means of identification and completion. The man who participates in history even "incidentally and somewhat vicariously" overcomes his "impotence, guilt and worthlessness."[25] Paul Weiss echoes the words of Boris Pasternak when he writes: "Only by directly involving himself with other Actualities can a man really manage to survive. . . . When he enters history he is, by means of an effective life, able to continue in being long past the end of his natural span. He does this in the course of an effort, through the use of nature, to contribute to the work of

---

*Editor's Note: See *The Historian and History*, pp. 161-164.

[21] *Personalism*, p. 94.

[22] *Between Man and Man*, p. 93.

[23] Ibid., p. 104.

[24] "The reenactments [of history] make us more vividly aware of the full nature of our being. . . . History, by bringing before us the memorable past, gives us material for desirable enactments today." Weiss: *History*, pp. 41-3.

[25] Paul Weiss: *History*, p. 136.

mankind in time."[26] Selfhood, or identity, or authenticity is only achieved when larger dimensions are opened to the individual—the community, the nation, mankind, the transcendent, history. Solovyev tells the story of the huntsman lost in a dense forest. As he sits, filled with despair at his plight and eaten with feelings of futility, a bent and repulsive old woman touches him on the shoulder. She assures him that beyond the stream he faces lies her homeland, a paradise. If he will carry her over, she will lead him to this golden land. The young huntsman, skeptical though he is about her story, good-naturedly undertakes to carry the poor old woman. But when she mounts his back she is heavy as lead and he can hardly move. With a heroic effort he pushes out into the stream and with each step his burden grows lighter. When he reaches the other side, the ancient granny has turned into an enchanting maiden, who, true to her promise, guides him to her homeland.

The old crone, Solovyev tells us, "is the sacred antiquity of tradition"; the stream is history. Man, instead of being repulsed by the past, instead of "idly looking for phantom-like fairies beyond the clouds," should undertake the task of carrying this unappetizing burden "across the real stream of history." He dare not let the old woman perish in the forest because if she does he can never find his way out of the wilderness. "Those," Solovyev adds, "who do not believe in the future of the old and sacred, must at any rate remember its past," and in respect and gratitude for it, take it up. *"He who saves shall be saved,"* he tells us. "That is the secret of progress—there is not and there can be no other!"[27]

History is, of course, no panacea. I would not wish to leave the impression that I am attempting here to re-establish history as the source of all meaning, in some neo-Hegelian exercise, or as somehow a substitute for the Divine. (Such a view seems to me to require the belief that the salvation of man, however imagined, lies in the process, or dialectic, of history.)[28] Man lives in the light of some

[26]Ibid., p. 136.

[27]Vladimir Solovyev: *An Anthology,* edited by S. L. Frank, translated by Natalie Duddington (London: SCM Press; 1950), pp. 224-6.

[28]Karl Löwith makes this point very effectively in *Meaning in History: The Theological Implications of the Philosophy of History* (Chicago: University of Chicago Press, 1949). History in this sense has no meaning *within* it. Paul Weiss, in *History: Written and Lived,* has pointed out also that ultimately it is the transhistorical which gives meaning and direction to history. See also Nathan Rotenstreich: *Between Past and Present: An Essay on History* (New Haven: Yale University Press; 1958).

faith, even if it is only faith in himself, in his ability to live without a faith. Many men, the Marxists prominent among them, have lived by a faith in the redemptive power of history, which in most such systems will ultimately annihilate history. My point is much less pretentious: to wit, that many of the ills which maim and distort the modern psyche have their source, in large part, in a faulty sense of history or of the historic.[29]

To the philosophical historians, the Utopians, and the idealists (who wish to appropriate history), we might add those who simply wish to escape from history through a form of modern stoicism that submits to it as a blind and brutal process. To live simply in the present, as so many have undertaken to do in this age, destroying systematically the links which bind them to preceding generations, is to leave oneself at the mercy of all those neuroses for which our society has proved so fertile a breeding ground. The modern odyssey—the search for identity—is doomed to shipwreck if it does not take unto itself the historic dimension of man's experience.

Historiography defined as the process of thinking and writing about the past in some orderly and systematic way has had a very short life; we might date its birth from the middle years of the eighteenth century. A sense of history as the unfolding of time pregnant with Divine, if only dimly perceived, potentiality has had a rather longer life. This concept has been associated, if we except the Greeks, with the notion of linear time moving to an anticipated end, however variously interpreted, in an inherently orderly universe. It is this older and profounder sense of history (which today we seem intent on destroying) that has provided the assumptions within whose scaffolding our world has taken shape. We may deplore the form; we may hate the world and ourselves, but it is a world made by countless generations of ancestors and if we lose faith in its potentialities we foreclose the future of mankind on this vastly shrunken planet.

---

[29]"Nothing less than the whole panorama of history will tell us what man is as fully expressed in time. At every moment he reveals himself in a new way. By taking account of the totality of his manifestations, we can have a knowledge of him more detailed and better structured than we otherwise could get by speculation or introspection." Paul Weiss: *History: Written and Lived,* p. 55.

II Progress Revisited

Two aspects of the idea of progress merit our attention. On the one hand, a belief in progress has utilitarian value. One can argue that whether or not it exists, we must maintain some modicum of faith in it in order to make life meaningful and to give us the courage to face the future. This argument, of course, is similar to the claim of some theologians that belief in God has utilitarian value in that it protects us against a variety of social and personal ills like totalitarianism, crime in the streets, anomie, and suicide. On the other hand, we can approach progress with the thought of scientifically measuring whether or not mankind is advancing in certain desirable directions. This is extremely difficult to do, since the question, Is mankind making progress? invites the rejoinder, What is progress? Is not everyone's concept of progress somewhat different? Progress for what? Progress for whom? If we tie the concept of progress to certain specific technological, social, and political goals, however, we can perhaps begin to arrive at some tentative conclusions. We can speak of progress in the abolition of slavery, or the improvement of the lot of the working man, or the increase of academic freedom, or the making of history scientific. Ultimately, of course, talking about progress in specific areas has its limitations. To the man who likes slavery, its abolition is regression, and to the man who believes academic freedom is a great evil, we are marching backward, not forward. Still, most liberal and humane individuals can reach agreement today on the desirability of certain goals, and progress in these areas can be measured by historians. George Iggers has noted, "Progress as yet is only a hypothesis and a very questionable one."[1] But it may be possible, and the writing of books

[1] George Iggers, "The Idea of Progress: A Critical Reassessment," *American Historical Review*, LXXI (October 1965), p. 17.

that treat some aspects of history with greater attention to the idea of progress would be an important undertaking in this age of cynicism and despair. This is what John Roche does in his history of civil liberties in the United States.[2] It could be done in other areas as well.

The selections in this section reaffirm progress because it is a useful concept for our age and because progress is demonstrable in certain areas by most humane standards. Both Plumb and Carr are deeply concerned about the corrosive effects of professional history on the man in the street. Having been stripped of faith in history as philosophers stripped him of faith in God, he is left morally footloose but not very fancy free. Perhaps this process began during the Enlightenment when God was read out of the historical process. Although man-centered history was a great step forward in many ways, it has created difficulties for those attempting to find meaning in the historical process and especially for those living through times of great stress. It is very difficult to hold to even a limited faith that things are getting better when they seem visibly worse. History can never provide us with the same assurance that faith in a trans-cendental, salvation-granting God gives the believer. But perhaps the striving for human betterment and the deep commitment to humane values that make Plumb and Carr the heirs to Peter Gay's Voltaire are all we can and should expect from the mysterious progression of life and death.

[2]John Roche, *The Quest for a Dream: The Development of Civil Rights and Human Relations in Modern America* (New York: Macmillan, 1963).

J. H. PLUMB
The Role of History

THE GREAT CHRISTIAN PAST, with its nineteenth-century variations—for they were no more than variations—on that old majestic
theme of man's fall and salvation, has collapsed. Rubble, broken
arches, monuments crumbling to dust, roofs open to the sky litter
this world of thought and loom forebodingly against the horizon. A
strange collection of men walk amidst the debris, some full of
lamentation, calling for urgent repairs, for an immediate restoration
of the old house of the intellect; others climb on to a prominent
broken pillar and in self-confident voices explain it all away; others
are blind and stumble over the ruins not knowing what has happened. From none of this does humanity derive much comfort. Can
this litter of a dead past be cleared away? Can its subtle distortions,
or its complex interrelations with all we think and feel, be eliminated
from our intellectual heritage. Is to do so desirable, even if possible?
And if possible, can man face the future with hope and with
resolution without a sense of the past? And if not, can a new past,
truer than the old, be manufactured to give him a like confidence?
These problems, I venture to suggest, lie at the very heart of our
society. And they are problems which no historian can ignore. For
many centuries now history has burrowed like a death-watch beetle
in this great fabric of the past, honeycombing the timbers and
making the structure ruinous. Now that it has fallen, can the
historian reconstruct a more viable past for mankind? Or is that like
demanding of a surgeon that he gives up his skill and turns to the
problem of creating life?

So far I have dealt with the past. I have used the word "history"
as sparingly as I could, but I would have been happier not to have
used it at all—at least, until this moment. Although historians spend
assiduous lives in its practice and perhaps write more than they
should about its nature and methods, few in the West are agreed
about its purpose or its validity.[1] In Communist countries, from

---

[1]The literature on the nature, let alone the philosophy, of history is vast, and
growing. For a quick glance at some of the more notable pronouncements over the
last hundred years, see *The Varieties of History,* ed. Fritz Stern (New York, 1956),
and Hans Meyerhoff, *The Philosophy of History in our Time* (New York, 1959).

From *The Death of the Past* by J. H. Plumb (Boston: Houghton Mifflin Company,
1970), pp. 102-145. Reprinted by permission of the publisher.

Poland to China, the situation is, of course, simpler, for there history and the past are but a two-headed Siamese twin. History is the exegesis of a dogmatic past. It may refine but it cannot change. But even this situation in Communist Europe and Asia is more apparent than real, more desired than practised, for the historical methods of the West, developed over so many centuries, possess an inherent destructive force for all dogmatic assertion. Furthermore, the remodelling of the old Bolshevik past by Stalin, the de-Stalinization of the past by Krushchev, both requiring the immediate past to be rewritten, have undermined dogma and bred scepticism as well as criticism. Serious cracks have appeared in the ideological furniture into which the historian can burrow. Had the Russians been as isolated as Imperial China, such reconstructions of the past might have been possible and become effective for generations; but Russia cannot detach itself from the West. The dogma of history, as now practised in Russia, is unlikely to remain in its present form for many more decades. Soon Russia and her satellites will be facing the problem of a past corroded by the practice of history.

It would, however, be profitless to enter into a philosophic discussion of the nature of history or of its capacity to establish objective truth. The practising historian is like the practising scientist. Just as the latter has no great interest in or use for the philosophy of science, so the active historian is not much concerned with the philosophy of history. He knows history exists and he has been trained in the methods necessary for its investigation. And he knows, too, that increasingly historical studies have been in conflict with the accepted past.

But so that there can be no mistake, it might be as well to define my own position. The aim of history I believe, is to understand men both as individuals and in their social relationships in time. Social embraces all of man's activities—economic, religious, political, artistic, legal, military, scientific—everything, indeed, that affects the life of mankind. And this, of course, is not a static study but a study of movement and change. It is not only necessary to discover, as accurately as the most sophisticated use of evidence will allow, things as they actually were, but also why they were so, and why they changed; for no human societies, not one, have ever stood still. Although we carry within ourselves and within our societies innumerable relics of the past, we have discarded, outgrown, neglected and lost far more. But we have been moulded by Time, all of us, from the naked Negrito in the Malayan forest to the Nobel prizewinners of the Rockefeller Institute. This is a truism, but how this happened poses a problem of exceptional intellectual complexity. The materials for its solution are the debris of Time itself—the records, the artifacts, the monuments, even the landscapes we live in and the languages we speak—materials that are infinite in their number and combination, yet capable of order and interpretation. The historical methods and techniques for the investigation of this process are comparatively young; most of them, such as archaeology, palaeography, topography, sociology, linguistics, demography and the like, have been used by historians for little more than a hundred years. The purpose of historical investigation is to produce answers, in the form of concepts and generalizations, to the fundamental problems of historical change in the social activities of men. These generalizations about societies will, of course, not be immutable but always tentative. They must, however, be as accurate, as scientific, as detailed research and a profound sense of human reality can make them. The historian's purpose, therefore, is to deepen understanding about men and society, not merely for its own sake, but in the hope that a profounder knowledge, a profounder awareness will help to mould human attitudes and human actions. Knowledge and understanding should not end in negation, but in action.[2]

This view of history, which is essentially that of the greatest historian of modern times—Marc Bloch—would, I think, command a considerable measure of assent from working historians. Bloch combined two qualities. He possessed the power to abstract himself from any preconceived notions about the past and to investigate an historical problem with detachment. And yet, detached as he was, his imagination, his creative invention, his sense of humanity infused all that he did. And although it may seem odd, his historical work gained from his wonderful, omnivorous appetite for life that was secure in the delight he derived from living. He loved life—in himself, in others—and because he did his craft of history had to be active. It could not for Bloch be a mere scholarly and imaginative investigation leading nowhere. It had to lead to positive statements

---

[2]There is a common fallacy amongst historians that the pursuit of objectivity must end in negation, e.g. Professor Robert Lynd: "History, thus voyaging forth with no pole star except the objective recovery of the past, becomes a vast, wandering enterprise." Quoted by Howard Zinn, "History as Private Enterprise," in *The Critical Spirit: Essays in Honor of Herbert Marcuse* (Boston, 1967), ed. Kurt H. Wolff and Barrington Moore, Jr., 174.

about human life, to the acceptance of principles about social living and, I would stress this strongly, create hope. Very many historians who would embrace Bloch's methods with delight would reject the purpose he required historical studies to contain. Indeed, Bloch here was in a very small minority. For an increasing number of historians of the twentieth century, the critical method and the professional debates to which it has given rise are sufficient in themselves. Let us turn, however to the practice of history itself, and glance at Bloch's own work, particularly his remarkable investigation and reconstruction of the life of medieval Europe; in so doing we turn to an extraordinary phenomenon. No other society, no other civilization, has ever given rise to investigations such as these. By the early twentieth century Western civilization had developed a completely new form of history, and Bloch well knew that the science that he practised was very young:

> For history is not only a science in movement. Like all those which have the human spirit for their object, this newcomer in the field of rational knowledge is also a science in its infancy. Or to explain more fully, having grown old in embryo as mere narrative, for long encumbered with legend, and for still longer preoccupied with only the most obvious events, it is still very young as a rational attempt at analysis.[3]

Professional history of the twentieth century is as remote from the history produced by our ancestors as modern physics is from Archimedes. Also, as with science, so with history in another aspect. There are more historians alive and practising in the world today than ever before; indeed, there are almost certainly more historians now than the total of all who have ever lived. Hence as a social force their potentiality must be very great, especially so as the vast majority are involved directly in the education of the young. Hence we are presented with a paradox—a past that is in ruins and a proliferating world of historical studies. These are not separate phenomena; they are thoroughly entangled with each other.

To understand the present position, to comprehend the intellectual strength of history and its social weakness, one must turn to the history of history itself, and grapple with the complex problem of why Western European society and its American counterpart began to be so concerned to discover historical truth, no matter where the

---

[3]Marc Bloch, *The Historian's Craft,* trans. Peter Putnam (Manchester, 1954), 13.

results might lead. Why did history become a pursuit in itself? Even in those years in embryo, to use Bloch's phrase, history was struggling not only towards accuracy, but to analysis, to the description of growth and, in an elementary sense, to the reconstruction of past societies in their own terms.

The contrast between the role of history in China and in the West is illuminating. China, as dynasty followed dynasty, acquired a large historical archive, as diverse and as mountainous as the historical material of Western Europe, and stretching over a longer period of time. Yet Chinese methods of using this material and generalizing about it did not fundamentally change from dynasty to dynasty, and Chinese scholars were using historical materials for the same pragmatic purposes in the early twentieth century as in the T'ang or Han dynasties. Within the tenets of their traditional generalizations they could be subtle and on occasion glimpse the problem of the growth of institutions outside the dynastic context, but Chinese history never developed the process of self-criticism and discovery, the relentless testing of generalization, the purposeful search for documentation to prove hypotheses which marks Western history. In consequence, when traditional Chinese historiography began to collapse in the late nineteenth century, the result was chaos and confusion. Chinese historians, aided and abetted by Western students of their country, snatched at Western generalizations, particularly Marxist ones, and applied them to Chinese data. But this was rather as if the detailed concepts of advanced chemistry were used on a large quantity of freshly discovered biological facts. The generalizations of Western history were the refined end-product of years of patient argument in which generalization and fresh facts had created an ever more sophisticated dialogue. To apply these in any meaningful way to China on the data available was well-nigh impracticable. Once the traditional generalizations were removed, Chinese history collapsed into fragments. The narrative of dynasties remained, of course, but explanation vanished. They possessed neither a usable past nor a core of historical analysis and explanation.[4]

[4]See the most important and suggestive article by Arthur F. Wright, "On the Uses of Generalization in the Study of Chinese History," in *Generalization in the Writing of History* (Chicago, 1963), ed. Louis Gottschalk, 36-58; also J. Gray, "Historical Writing in Twentieth Century China: Notes on its Background and Development," in *Historical Writing on the Peoples of Asia: Historians of China and Japan*, ed. W. G. Beasley and E. G. Pulleyblank (Oxford, 1961), 186-212. This volume also contains a

Why did history develop in Europe, whereas in China it never extracted itself from the iron grip of the past in the service of the present? The usual answer is to stress the isolation and self-sufficiency of China.[5] But the problem goes deeper than this. China was not without interest in or contact with other civilizations, particularly Japan, Vietnam, Cambodia, Indonesia and India, whose beliefs and social structure differed from her own. And Chinese sages, confident and arrogant as they were about Chinese culture, were not devoid of curiosity.[6] *What closed their minds to the historical problem was its absence.* For the Chinese scholar the past stretched out from his own time like the sea—ruffled here and there by storm and tempest, but limitless. There was no dramatic collapse of a civilization which had lasted for centuries; there was no great revolution in belief that had half obliterated the culture of former times. The area of necessary explanation confronting a Chinese and Western historian was quite different.[7] The European intellectual, even in the fourth and fifth centuries of our era, had two pasts to contend with. By the time of the Enlightenment he had three. Always in subterranean contact, or overt conflict, there were two others, deeply involved in his own, yet different in interpretation and different, too, in usage of materials—the past of the Jews and the past of Islam. Hence the European's past never possessed the coherence or the unity, the all-embracing certainty of the Chinese. And here lies the key to why Europe could, indeed was bound to, develop critical history. There was in Europe's past no unity; the

---

fascinating essay (pp. 135-66), "Chinese Historical Criticism: Liu Chih-chi and Ssu-ma Kuang," by E. G. Pulleyblank, which demonstrates the great sophistication of Chinese historiography within its own rigid framework of generalization. Of course, the generalization was no more and no less rigid than that of the Christian West, and the arrangement of sources and the detail contained in them was infinitely greater. But I would maintain that the Chinese were concerned solely with creating an educative past—subtle, complex, highly detailed, accurate in commission, but not history.

[5]Wright, loc. cit. 39.

[6]See two brilliant books by Edward H. Schafer, *The Golden Peaches of Samarkand* (University of California Press, 1963), and *The Vermilion Bird: A Study of T'ang Images of the South* (University of California Press, 1967), which discuss the interest of the Chinese of the T'ang dynasty in Central Asia and the tropical South and the exotics which they produced.

[7]No Chinese historian suffered even the surprise of Herodotus at Thebes when, confronted by three hundred generations of high priests, he was made to realize the youthfulness of Greek society.

pagan past could not be obliterated, and the catastrophe of Rome's decline fascinated the curious and created an intellectual problem that insisted, generation after generation, on explanation.

Now problems of conflicting pasts do not necessarily lead to historical methods as we know them, but they do present quite formidable problems which require explanation. The huge output of quasi-historical theology and Church history both in the fourth and sixteenth centuries is an indication of the need to explain the revolution in attitude to the past which took place at these times. And both these critical periods of European ideology deeply influenced the growth of historiography; or, at least, embryos were implanted in the womb of the past which could develop into true history.

The changeover from the pagan to Christian ideology was particularly seminal. The delay of the Second Coming, the development of an organized, hierarchical Church, the growth of the concept of heresy, and the final marriage between Church and State created a need, in the fourth century, to explain the past in a way which differed profoundly from that employed by pagan historians. The hand of God in the Christian's destiny had to be traced to remote times, back indeed to the Creation; the power of the Church, the supremacy of bishops (and later the authority of the Pope) required proof, historical and documentary proof. Again, the definition of heresy relied on decisions of historical synods and councils; the relations between Church and State, which ranged widely over property and privileges, again needed the authenticity of document. And the result had to be so much more exclusive than pagan history. Christianity was exclusive, yet all-embracing, so the past required explanation or rejection; it could not be simply neglected. And it was this necessity which, as Momigliano has shown us, created a new form—ecclesiastical history—whose first great practitioner was Eusebius. The features of ecclesiastical history which are important in the present context are its documentation and its controversial nature. One did not merely record the annals of the past, or use the past as an illustration of ethics or philosophy; one needed, also, to prove its validity by argument. In the new Christian past, enshrined in ecclesiastical history, which came to dominate European ideology for the next thousand years, there were two vital aspects for the further development of history as we know it; one was the belief in documentary proof, the other was the sense that there was another interpretation, the pagan one, that had to be refuted.[8] Two pasts existed in conflict no matter how victorious the Christian past was with the majority of men.

Even in the Dark Ages, the past of Rome and Greece beckoned. Its salvation lay partly in the preservation and extension of Latin as the language of belief, administration and culture, and partly in the sense of loss created by the visible monuments of former greatness, above all in Rome, but also throughout Italy, Greece, southern France and parts of Spain. This old past might be pagan, but it was undoubtedly impressive. And although the monuments crumbled and decayed, suffering the slow obliteration of Time, the literature remained, copied by monks and preserved in monastic libraries, and,

[8]"Perhaps we have all underestimated the impact of ecclesiastical history on the development of historical method. A new chapter of historiography begins with Eusebius, not only because he invented ecclesiastical history, but because he wrote it with a documentation which is utterly different from that of the pagan historians": A. Momigliano, "Pagan and Christian Historiography in the Fourth Century A.D." in *The Conflict between Paganism and Christianity in the Fourth Century,* ed. A. Momigliano (Oxford, 1963), 92. The whole essay is profoundly important and I am deeply indebted to it. Professor Momigliano stresses the rejection by Christian historians of the pagan past. He points out that the Christians of the fourth century made no serious attempt to provide a Christian version of Livy or Thucydides. "A reinterpretation of ordinary, military, political or diplomatic history in Christian terms was neither achieved nor even attempted": ibid. 88. And, of course, the whole Pantheon of pagan heroes was rejected. Biography ceased and was replaced by hagiography. No such total rejection of a sophisticated ideology of the past is comparable to this until modern times. The Islamic revolution in Arabia certainly had a profound influence on the Arabs' view of their past, but there was far more continuity. See Julian Obermann, "Early Islam," in Robert C. Dentan, *The Idea of History in the Ancient Near East* (New Haven, 1955); also Franz Rosenthal, "The Influence of the Biblical Tradition on Muslim Historiography," in Bernard Lewis and P. M. Holt, *Historians of the Middle East* (Oxford, 1962). And, in any case, the pre-Muslim past of the Arabs was very unsophisticated. Elaborate and coherent pasts which become the prerogative of a band of trained professional scholars can only be found in complex and highly sophisticated societies. For the philosophical naïveté of the historian of medieval India, see P. Hardy, *Historians of Medieval India* (1960), 18-19, 125-31. The same is true of Indonesian history, which is largely a complex of myths in which some historical facts are buried. This was quite adequate for the primitive and courtly societies of Indonesia until the present time when the need for a unifying, socially usable past became keenly felt. See C. C. Berg, "The Javanese Picture of the Past," in *An Introduction to Indonesian Historiography,* ed. Soedjatmoko, Mohammad Ali, G. J. Resink and G. McT. Kahin (Ithaca, 1965), 87-117. Soedjatmoko's essay on "The Indonesian Historian and his Time" is a fascinating discussion of the problems facing a Western-trained historian confronted by a society with a very primitive sense of the past. However, no society, primitive or advanced, has suffered such ideological fractures as Europe.

when copied, often revered for its own intrinsic worth.[9] The old past was never entirely lost; it survived in sufficient depth to make recovery both possible and likely. In the darkest times it retained amongst scholars and writers a tenuous life, even in its most secular aspects. It always promoted curiosity and respect, and time and time again enriched philosophy, science, mathematics and geography. Nevertheless, it posed a question—the vast and daunting problem of why this splendid, sophisticated, cultured world had vanished. God's will was one easy and, perhaps, satisfactory answer for the majority of monkish scholars. The more elaborate explanations of St. Augustine satisfied the sophisticated, but with the growth of a more secular culture from 1200 onwards, the question could not be so easily answered. Two great periods, two great epochs, began to loom large as cultivated and scholarly men looked back at their past; and with gathering momentum men began to regard the time which stretched between themselves and the ancients as a time of darkness, of barbarism, of obscurity,[10] a process which was not stopped by the Reformation but intensified by it, for the religion itself acquired two pasts—the pure past of the primitive Church and the corrupt past of Rome. Of course, this duality of the past did not immediately lead to the historical method as we know it, but it did posit problems of great complexity to any historian. At first, the great historians of the Renaissance—Machiavelli and Guicciardini—wished to emulate the ancients, particularly Livy: to divorce history of their own time from the providential and the miraculous and to discover the truths of humanity in the actions of men.[11] Their purpose was basically moral and educative. Also they were primarily concerned with contemporary or near-contemporary

[9]See R. R. Bolgar, *The Classical Heritage and its Beneficiaries* (Cambridge, 1954), for a brilliant discussion of what the Middle Ages made of their classical inheritance.

[10]Joseph Anthony Mazzeo, *Renaissance and Revolution: The Remaking of European Thought* (New York, 1965), 61: "Petrarch and his humanist successors . . . were, in fact, able to view the classical past in an historical perspective, as something distant, yet accessible, different, yet intelligible and eminently usable. As the natural landscape that the Renaissance artist painted existed in a mathematically intelligible space, so the ancient world existed for the humanists in a well-defined structured historical space."

[11]This is, in a sense, only half true of Guicciardini. He describes the portents and miracles—the monstrous births, the sweating images, etc.—which preceded Charles VIII's invasion of Italy, and obviously he believed in God. But within the framework of destiny he attempted a complex and detailed explanation in terms of human

history. Good as they were, they were in intention nearer to Thucydides than to ourselves. And yet there was a powerful difference. From the time of Eusebius, records, the written evidence, had acquired immense prestige as validitators of the truth, and the critical use of records for the writing of history had made considerable progress. True, the canons of criticism were often primitive by our standards, but not always. Guicciardini achieved a level of documentation for his *Storia d'Italia* that was almost modern in its range and complexity.[12]

The concept of a dual past therefore, was clarified and greatly strengthened in the fifteenth century. For the first time there was a sense of anachronism, which can be discerned in painting and illumination as well as in literature. Livy is no longer illustrated by Romans in medieval costume, and Masaccio's apostles wear the toga; Alberti does not use Gothic ornament to decorate his classical villas; Donatello and Brunelleschi deliberately searched in the ruins of Rome for pure forms of the antique.[13] The same desire for purity, to re-achieve the ancient world without the accretions of time, was at work even more strongly in the fields of scholarship. Both philologists and lawyers realized that language and law had changed vastly since the days of Cicero or Justinian. The knowledge that words meant different things at different epochs, that law derived from an historical context, obviously enriched the sense of time in scholars who practised these disciplines. The divergences which they discovered created an acute sense of the duality of the past. This led to absurdities, to the silliness of those Ciceronians who

---

character and action. Both Machiavelli and Guicciardini are much closer in attitude to Herodotus, Thucydides, Livy and Tacitus than to their monkish predecessors of the Middle Ages, but some credulity, at least with Guicciardini, lingers powerfully on.

[12]Herbert Butterfield, *The Statecraft of Machiavelli* (New York, 1955); also R. Ridolfi, *The Life of Francesco Guicciardini* (New York 1967), 259: "In the *Storia d'Italia* Guicciardini used documents with a method more rigorous than any had done before him and few did after."

[13]On the other hand there is a deliberate Gothicism in Uccello's work. For this see Erwin Panofsky, *Renaissance and Renascences in Western Art* (Stockholm, 1960) and *Studies in the History of Iconography: Humanistic Themes in the Art of the Renaissance* (New York, 1939). Of course, there were bound to be many anachronistic features of religious art, when ignorance of the actual world of the ancients was so widespread. What is interesting is that the attempt was made, which implies the consciousness of a different past. See also J. H. Plumb, *The Renaissance* (New York, 1961), 95-96.

refused to use any Latin word not to be found in Cicero's works, but even foolishness can propagate seminal ideas. More important and more far-reaching in the effect on the development of history was the furious battle between those lawyers who followed the *mos italicus* and the innovators who preferred the *mos gallicus.* This approach—to attempt to see classical language and law as they were—before time had done its work, was in a most profound sense the beginning of historical criticism. The attempt to discover or verify universal truths, through historical knowledge, was almost as old as man, but the development of historical criticism—to see things as they were in their own time—we owe to the late Middle Ages and the Renaissance. It quickly proved, as it was to remain, dangerous and subversive. A method which could be applied to law and language could be used to test theology or to enquire into the institutions of the Church. After all, Lorenzo Valla was an exceptionally fine lawyer, and one who had attacked the traditional views of Bartolus of Sassoferrato at Pavia with such ferocity that he had been forced to quit the university.[14] Lawyers were amongst the intellectual leadership in criticism of the Church for a generation or so before Luther nailed his thesis to Wittenberg's church door, and a vast amount of Protestant propaganda was based on historical criticism of the Church of Rome's historical claims. Moreover, in a desire to revive the essence of the primitive Church, the same intellectual process is at work that agitated the lawyers of the *mos gallicus* or the Ciceronians. We can discover in grammar, in law, in theology a swelling tide of critical erudition that possessed, as its mainspring, this sense of a duality of the past. And, indeed, there was a further dimension which gradually began to assert itself in men's consciousness of themselves in Time. The ancient world was the world of greatness which they wished to recover. As their disdain for the immediate past deepened, and the sense of their own achievement strengthened, so they began to feel that they belonged to a new age; the great discoveries of America and the East, the revolution in religion, the development in technology, led a few if not many scholars and philosophers to a tentative confidence that they might surpass all that had gone before, that recovery of the past would lead to advance in the future. They felt that this might be best

[14]See Myron P. Gilmore, *Humanists and Jurists: Six Studies in the Renaissance* (Cambridge, Mass., 1963), 31-32.

achieved by applying the critical spirit to Nature to see things as they truly were.[15]

This is no place to discuss the deepening preoccupation with scientific enquiry which stimulated so many European scholars of the sixteenth and seventeenth centuries, but it became a factor in the intellectual climate of the age and strengthened the new attitude to the past that was rapidly developing; indeed, these centuries witnessed an historical revolution in every way as profound as the scientific or the geographical ones. All were linked. The origin of this revolution in historical studies can be found in the spirit of historical criticism in law and philology in the fifteenth century. It was given great impetus by the invention of printing and the growth of the study of antiquities. For some time the number of scholars involved in critical studies remained very small; tiny bands worked in the universities of Padua or Pavia, or lone scholars, such as Alciato, who took the message to the universities of France.[16] As the decades passed, the material for criticism grew vast—ancient classics, chronologies, editions of all the Fathers of the Church were published in a never-ending stream. Knowledge was disseminated and scrutinized; private libraries, far larger than any the largest monasteries had known, became by the end of the sixteenth century commonplace. Gentlemen whose ancestors possessed one or two illustrated books of devotion now owned hundreds of volumes ranging over history, philosophy, literature, rhetoric, grammar— above all well-edited editions of the classics, usually Latin, in which Cicero and Plutarch figured most prominently. This, of course, was a haphazard process; often scholarship and the cult of antiquities was a pastime for gentlemanly dilletantes. There was no concerted drive for historical studies in the universities, but preoccupation with the ancient past—its arts, its literature, its coins and artifacts—spread far and wide over Europe in the sixteenth century. This secularization of historical studies is very important. The Church had dominated history throughout the Middle Ages and had been responsible for its interpretation. After 1400, history could be the pursuit of anyone with time and inclination. And here is a notable contrast with developments in the East. China, very much earlier, had developed

---

[15]J. B. Bury, *The Idea of Progress* (Dover, ed., 1955), 39-41. Also Geoffroy Atkinson, *Les Nouveaux Horizons de la Renaissance Française* (Paris, 1935), for the effect of geographical knowledge.

[16]See Gilmore, op. cit., 30-33, 61-86.

bureaucratic control of historical materials and interpretation. The new universities of Europe never attempted to bureaucratize history; hence historical criticism had a far freer soil in which to develop, with the result that concentration quickly arose on difficult questions of scholarly interpretation, not only on the validity of chronologies but also on the relation of customs described in the Old Testament with pagan rites and sacrifices. A whole world of critical erudition began to develop. Sometimes it settled erratically on curious problems. In the seventeenth century a furious and learned debate broke out concerning the longevity of the patriarchs, where the new scientific attitude seemed to be at sharp variance with holy record.[17] Graver problems were caused by the Flood. As men read more and knew more, the historical improbabilities of a Judaeo-Christian past became more difficult to maintain. Nevertheless historical criticism was more like a woodworm working in the heart of a beam—always active, but rarely seen on the surface. Now and again it punctured a hole, but the vast complex edifice of the Christian past remained intact for the large majority of literate and illiterate Europeans. The scholars themselves had no thought of destroying it; the idea would have filled them with pious horror. They wished to accumulate knowledge, to render it accurate and, some of them, to solve the conundrums their accuracy produced.

Yet the fascination of antiquity, particularly its visible relics, grew steadily; inscriptions, coins, medals were all collected with fervour, catalogued and printed. From the fifteenth century onwards interest in antiquities became one of the dominant themes of scholarship and led to the acquisition by European scholars of a large amount of new historical material. Scholarship became, like European society itself, deeply acquisitive, but acquisition led to knowledge and method, and the same antique spirit found rich pastures not only in the classical world but also in the Middle Ages and in local and national history. In many ways, seventeenth-century scholarship was dominated by the antiquarians whom the philosophers of the Enlightenment dismissed as *les érudits*.[18]

[17]N. Egerton, "The Longevity of the Patriarchs," *Journal of the History of Ideas,* xxvii (1966), 575-84.

[18]A. Momigliano, "Ancient History and the Antiquarian," in *Studies in Historiography* (London 1966), 1-39, for a brilliant summary of the growth of antiquarianism after the Renaissance and its effect on the development of the techniques of historical scholarship.

Both historians and antiquarians increased considerably in number during these centuries. And many of them preferred to work in a limited and exact field of scholarship, with the result that available sources in good texts multiplied. Here the work of the Maurists and Bollandists, who set about clarifying the great records of the Church and of Catholic Christianity, was outstanding in range and method.[19] The spirit of scholarship permeated secular as well as clerical society. In England it is the age of Parker, Cotton, Bodley, Dugdale, Wanley, who preserved so much of the English past and provided some of the first serious historical criticism in our language.[20]

In the pursuit of erudition, new historical techniques were established—epigraphy, palaeography, diplomatics and numismatics—as well as edited texts, dictionaries, catalogues, improved chronologies and encyclopedias, without which the practice of history as we know it could never have developed. Yet this vast extension of historical literature and of historical knowledge did not lead, initially, to the type of historical understanding which we attempt. Its intention was largely to purify and establish the "how" of history, not the "why." The great works of Mabillon illustrate this point. Here was a scholar of powerful intellect and acute sense of criticism, who established fundamental rules in his *De Re Diplomatica* for sifting the true from the spurious in medieval charters. His editions of the works of St. Bernard were not surpassed for centuries. And yet he never asked himself a question of fundamental historical analysis—why medieval society needed, let alone believed, the grotesque legends of its saints or why saints were so plentiful or so necessary. Neither did the Bollandists working steadily through their calendar of saints. They tried to establish the most authentic life of a saint, to refine from the legend the accretions of time. But the whole process of historical change, of why legend? why forgery? why saints? was inconceivable to them. They were not concerned to rewrite history nor to reinterpret the past; they wished to purify and authenticate and make available what existed. Nevertheless they are the fathers of modern historical scholarship as we

[19]For the Maurists and Bollandists, see M. D. Knowles, *Trans. Royal Hist. Soc.,* 5th ser., viii (1958), 147-66, and ibid., ix (1959), 169-92.

[20]David C. Douglas, *English Scholars* (London, 1939); *English Historical Scholarship in the Sixteenth and Seventeenth Centuries,* ed. Levi Fox (Oxford, 1956); T. D. Kendrick, *British Antiquity* (1950), and F. Smith Fussner, *The Historical Revolution* (New York 1962); J. S. A. Pocock's fundamentally important *The Ancient Constitution and the Feudal Law* (Cambridge, 1957).

know it. They proved the value of two things: accumulation of material and critical method.

And they improved, not directly but indirectly, the level of historical discourse. King Lud, the fables of Gildas about the origins of the British people, began to fade from the ordinary historical narrative; similarly, in France kings were no longer descended from the heroes of the Trojan war. Narrative, inexact still by our standards, improved immeasurably. The writing of history itself recovered its critical standards—indeed improved on them. Sarpi was a far greater historian than Livy. And yet, good as the historical scholarship was, and as good as the writing became, history and the past still lived in a curious schizophrenic relationship. Even a scholar as profound as Vico was still locked in historically antique concepts, such as his three ages, which has stronger links with Hesiod than with the historical scholarship of his day. It was not really until the second half of the eighteenth century that historians, notably Gibbon, began to attack the traditional interpretation of the past at its foundations.

Gibbon was not only the heir of the antiquaries and of the great fathers of classical scholarship to whose works he had been constantly drawn since a boy, but also of *les philosophes,* particularly of Bayle, whom he venerated, and of Montesquieu and Voltaire. Their attitude to the past was novel. Bayle and Voltaire, at least, took a sceptical, often malicious, view of the Christian past and all of its works. Voltaire jeered frequently enough at the mole-like activities of *les érudits* and mocked their beliefs. Nevertheless the philosophers were deeply concerned to understand the past in all of its variety and seeming contradiction, searching for laws which would be both rational and convincing. Their interest in historical evidence was largely superficial; it was needed, of course, to underpin an argument or to illustrate a theme, but was not in itself a necessary pursuit in the search for historical truth. Nevertheless their role in the development of historical studies was profound and, for Western society, deeply original. They were attempting to reconstruct the past in non-Christian terms and they were trying, for the first time, to explain the destiny of man by his own nature.[21] At the same time, their purpose was educative, but in the broad, not the precise, sense. The main aim was the understanding, not a mere

[21]See P. Gay's most illuminating work, *The Enlightenment: The Rise of Modern Paganism* (New York, 1966).

realizing, of man and his past. Gibbon combined within himself both attitudes. He valued knowledge for its own sake, yet he was aware that erudition could not be an end in itself. History needed to be philosophic and purposeful. But the history of what?

Gibbon's indecision, recorded in his *Journal,* about the subject of his life's work is fascinating and illustrates the basic theme of this chapter to perfection. He considered for some time a variety of subjects, from a life of Sir Walter Raleigh, a history of the Third Crusade to the foundation of the Swiss Republic. They stirred his imagination, but wisely he dropped them. Raleigh was too parochial, the Swiss demanded a knowledge of German language and literature that he was not prepared to undertake.[22] But all these excuses were rationalizations. They posed great historical problems—the Swiss a major one—as did the history of the Medicis with its conflict of cultures, which he considered for a while. He was, however, drawn inevitably to the great problem of European history and the duality of its past. Indeed, his life had largely been a preparation for this work, long before he made his famous journey to Rome. Yet it was in Rome that Gibbon found the image that is a key not only to his own work, but also to the development of historical studies in Europe. He writes in his *Autobiography:*

> It was at Rome, on the 15th of October, 1764, as I sat musing amidst the ruins of the Capitol, while the barefooted friars were singing vespers in the Temple of Jupiter, that the idea of writing the decline and fall of the city first started to my mind.[23]

Here, in succinct symbolism—the bare-footed friars, the Temple of Jupiter—Gibbon placed in juxtaposition the two great cultures that Western Europe had experienced, the question that had haunted scholars of two centuries or more, the condition which had produced the inner dynamic of so many historical studies of which Gibbon was the heir. He never forgot his debt to the scholars, to the

---

[22]Gibbon remained attached to this idea and wrote an introductory piece about Switzerland. His preoccupation is not surprising, for the success of Switzerland in achieving and maintaining its independence presents a curiously difficult problem of historical understanding. Everything that makes for social and political stability would seem to be absent—geography, language, economic integration, religion, or even a common social structure. Yet Switzerland survived, prospered, avoided revolution. Why? The problem still awaits its historian. Gibbon had an unerring instinct for major problems, but luckily chose the largest.

[23]Edward Gibbon, *Autobiography* (Oxford, 1907), 169.

masters of historical criticism and method who made his work possible. What Gibbon did, however, was to absorb their work and make it a part of historical literature for all time. After Gibbon, history was fully fledged. The success of his book brought, as did the works of other historians of the Enlightenment, a new depth to the understanding of European history amongst the educated élite. As with Voltaire or Hume, Gibbon interpreted history in purely human terms. Of course, he made moral judgments and he stressed the effects of chance. But his moral judgments were those of men, not God, and his chance was purely human, not a great external force, not *Fortuna* playing grimly with the lives of men. History had to be understood in human terms, be motivated by human forces; follies and iniquities abounded, but they were neither the result of ignoring the gods nor of original sin. Gibbon raised the writing of history to a new level. He was aware, more acutely than any of his predecessors, both of its possibilities and its limitations. He sought a detached and truthful past, free from preconception or the idea of inherent purpose. Yet his detachment was infused with a warm and generous attitude to mankind in spite of its immeasurable follies and iniquities. Gibbon frequently spoke of the candour of history, because it could display, not truths about the universe, or immutable laws of social development, but merely the truth of ourselves as living human beings.[24] History contained causes and events, not laws or systems. And yet Gibbon did not believe he was writing merely to entertain. History possessed a purpose and this was to deepen experience, to make men wiser about themselves and, also, about the social processes in which they were necessarily involved. After all, he wanted to explain the greatest cataclysm of European history.

But Gibbon stood in lonely detachment; most of the philosophic historians of the Enlightenment wished to wring more than he did from their study of history, to find immutable laws of historical change and development. They discovered their overall design in Progress, about which they grew both rhapsodic and optimistic. Gibbon shared little of their enthusiasm. He did, however, give a highly qualified assent to their general proposition that the condition of mankind had improved. To this we will return later.

Gibbon had demonstrated that historians could rewrite the history of antiquity with a wealth of detail and knowledge that surpassed

---

[24]Per Fuglum, *Edmund Gibbon: His View of Life and Conception of History* (Oslo, 1953), 41.

classical historians. Herodotus, Thucydides, Livy, Tacitus and the rest were no longer the occupants of Olympian heights, unattainable by moderns. And scholars turned to the history of Greece and Rome with a new vigour. But the historical ferment went deeper. Through the discoveries of archaeology, Time itself was given a vast extension towards the close of the eighteenth century. The decipherment of the Rosetta Stone, the quickening pace of discovery in Assyria and Babylonia, the deepening knowledge of India and China brought a new sense of the diversity of man's past and enlarged the problems of history. Nor did erudition wane, indeed it waxed. New archives, particularly medieval archives, became available in the early nineteenth century. The spread of Maurist and Bollandist methods to the great national sources of history in Germany, in France and in England made history not only a widespread profession but also a highly technical craft.[25] Against this huge deluge of material, historians struggled manfully. Leopold von Ranke still hoped to write a Universal History; indeed, he settled down to write it at the age of eighty-six. He wrote in the 1860's that

> In my opinion, we must work in two directions: the investigation of the effective factors in historical events and the understanding of their universal relationship . . . .
> The investigation of a single detail already requires profound and very penetrating study. At the present time, however, we are all agreed that the critical method, objective research, and synthetic construction can and must go together. Historical research will not suffer from its connection with the universal: without this link, research would become enfeebled, and without exact research the conception of the universal would degenerate into a phantasm.[26]

Ranke's intention is still Gibbon's—to combine the most exact erudition with philosophic history.

The professional historian, as the nineteenth century progressed, was forced into narrower and narrower fields of study, and often his studies were still the servants of an overall concept of the past. Indeed, there is no outstanding historian of the nineteenth century who did not accept a large structural interpretation of the destiny of

[25]See David Knowles, *Great Historical Enterprises* (New York, 1963), 65-134; also Herbert Butterfield, *Man on His Past* (Cambridge, 1955), particularly pp. 75-85.
[26]Fritz Stern (ed.), *The Varieties of History,* 62.

man, and usually of his nation too. The task, however, grew ever more difficult. And the twentieth century brought a change. Time and time again large-scale and small-scale assumptions about the purpose or meaning of history were sharply attacked. Professional historians began increasingly to reduce their generalizations to the professional areas of their interest. Did the Norman Conquest introduce feudalism into England? Was slavery a cause of the American Civil War? Did the *philosophes* help to provoke the French Revolution? Specialization confined itself to professional and not philosophic concepts. As in the seventeenth century, erudition dominated historical studies; the pursuit of scholarship became more important than the interpretation of history. Periodically, the professional historian lifted his head and tried to make up his mind what could or could not be derived from historical study. His answers expressed doubt, uncertainty, perhaps even bewilderment, and many thought it better not to embark on generalizations as perilous and as disputatious as these. After all, the debris of the past, shovelled wholesale into thousands of libraries and national and local record offices, provided material for work for tens of thousands of professional historians who were content to reduce it into some kind of order in fields of ever increasing specialization. Ten years of the history of Seattle or Sienna could provide a lifetime's work and a lifetime's academic career. And, on occasion, rightly so; for such studies in the hands of a professional historian of ability can help to solve technical and scholarly problems of great importance. After all, Bloch's own work was deeply rooted in local history.

Hence, history tended to become in the twentieth century, for the majority of its practitioners, a study for professionals by professionals. The purpose of history was limited; it trained the mind in criticism and in judgment, satisfied curiosity and made the wise wiser. What they would not allow was the old philosophic attitude of the Enlightenment, that history should interpret the destiny of mankind. This attitude of limited objectives and intentions has been common to those historians who have attempted, during the last sixty years, to keep history as a part of general culture, as well as of highly professional scholars who are concerned with the rigours of historical method. And, indeed, even today this is as far as the majority of historical writers and historical scholars would go in giving meaning and purpose to history. The business of the historian is to make sense of the past.[27] That is his primary task, but it is far from simple, for the complexities of historical forces are very intricate and their elucidation never easy. Hence it is natural for the professional historian to limit his field and concentrate his powers. He is likely to achieve greater mastery and deeper understanding, even though his vision in the terms of the history of mankind may be very limited.

This is, of course, a highly defensible attitude. Limited it may be, but it is sound, sensible and cautious. It has commanded respect over the last two centuries. The professional purpose is to understand, neither more nor less. This attitude can be traced back to the Enlightenment, to Herder who, concerned as he was with moral judgment in history, nevertheless realized that empathy was essential to the historian's task. Empathy, imagination, the attempt to place oneself in an historic situation and into an historic character without pre-judgment, rose in public favour throughout the nineteenth century. Indeed, Marc Bloch in the twentieth called "understanding" the beacon light of our studies.[28] However, this restricted view still leaves unanswered the deeper question—the understanding of what? A human character, an event in time, the nature of an institution, of the reasons for belief? The progression rises. Dare it lift to the process of history itself? It would seem not. Bloch, unlike Ranke, could not contemplate a universal history. By his day, history itself had rendered this impossible. Or rather, not impossible, but intellectually useless. To the trained historian, erudition by its very bulk had obliterated the possibility of that universal synthesis so much desired by Ranke. The historian's business may be to make sense of the past, but only of his own patch and not the vast panorama that stretches back to the beginning of time.

And so we come to the heart of the paradox. History began because scholars perceived a problem which faced no other civilization—the problem of the duality of Europe's past, its conflicting ideologies and of their different interpretations of human destiny.

[27]Richard Pares, *The Historian's Business and Other Essays* (Oxford, 1961), 10: "The sense (of the past) that historians make is an increasingly complicated sense. It may perhaps be suggested that professional classes always create complications in order to make themselves indispensable. But I think that such an explanation would do the professional historians less than justice. It is a matter of scientific conscience. The historical process is very complicated: it has its laws and its uniformities, but it can only be explained in terms of itself."

[28]Bloch, *The Historian's Craft*, 143.

Once historical criticism developed, the Christian explanation of the past could not maintain its supremacy. It slowly collapsed under criticism, but just as slowly and just as surely did the interpretations which replaced it—the concept of progress, the manifest destinies of competitive nationalism, social Darwinism, or dialectical materialism. History, which is so deeply concerned with the past, has, in a sense, helped to destroy it as a social force, as a synthesizing and comprehensive statement of human destiny.

Because of this, most historians in this century have avoided any attempt to explain the history of man. This has been left to the journalists, the prophets or the philosophers, but some of those who have attempted it acquired great popular success. H. G. Wells, Oswald Spengler and Arnold Toynbee, who sought to mould history into a meaningful past, secured millions of readers but the almost universal condemnation of historians. Yet the reception of their books points to the need of ordinary people, as well as to the difficulty of fulfilling it.[29] Although the past manufactured by his ancestors will no longer do, it would seem that man in the West still seeks a meaningful past, one which will confer as much significance on his life as the Marxist past does for those who can believe in it. Can historians fulfil this need? And is it their rightful task?

The historian, I believe, has a twofold purpose. He must pursue and test the concepts with which he deals. And because of the amount of material and its complexity, these concepts are likely to be limited in time. Much of his life must be spent, therefore, working with, and writing for, fellow professionals. These, as yet, are very early days for exact, professional history. But this cannot be the historian's sole *raison d'être*. Some would argue that the training which experience, even a short experience, gives in the techniques of historical study is a sufficient argument for its existence. This is the old argument for classical studies in a new guise. It is, of course, true that historical study does exercise memory, capacity for argument and clarity of expression. And it is excellent that it should do so, but there are plenty of academic disciplines which can do this, perhaps better than history.[30] The study of history can, of course,

[29]Apart from the excellent and stimulating world history of William H. McNeill, *The Rise of the West* (Chicago, 1963), the most successful attempts have been made by archaeologists—Carleton S. Coon and Gordon Childe.

[30]On the argument for classical studies as a training for the intellect, see M. I. Finley, "Crisis in the Classics," in *Crisis in the Humanities,* ed. J. H. Plumb (Baltimore, 1964), 18-19.

and does extend human experience in a peculiarly vivid way, but so do literary studies, so should sociology or anthropology or the study of politics.[31] Again, this is in no way peculiar to history. The combination of all these virtues would justify a minor academic discipline and fulfil a minor social role in satisfying curiosity and gratifying nostalgia. History as entertainment, whether of the intellectual or of the romantic housewife, would persist. If this, however, were all that a study of history could do, no one would insist that it fulfils a vital and major social role. Yet if the past is allowed to die, or, having died, a new one fails to be conceived, that will be the fate of history. Its place as the interpreter of man's destiny will be taken by the social sciences.

In many ways the historian of today is in the position of the historian of the Enlightenment. He cannot accept the interpretation of the past of his immediate ancestors or even of the mass of society in which he lives. Crude ideological interpretations, Marxist or nationalist, conservative or liberal, religious or agnostic, providential or progressive, cyclical or linear, are a violation of his discipline and an offence to his knowledge. Many historians, therefore, have taken refuge in the meaninglessness of history, in the belief that history can only make a personal or neutral statement; it is a game for professional players who make the rules. Others, more conservative, have taken refuge in its providential nature. The Christian myth dies hard. We need again a compulsive sense of the value of man's past, not only for ourselves as historians, but also for the world at large.

The historians of the Enlightenment could discover with delirious joy the antique past that beckoned them in Greece and Rome; the multiplicity of historical worlds that rose above their intellectual horizon—Egypt, Persia, India, China—gave them new stimulus, fresh ideas, and a deep sense of recovery, of escape into a fresher, more viable historical understanding. Alas, such an experience cannot revitalize the historian of this century.[32] There are no new pasts to discover. They are all exposed and all peopled by professional experts, digging in their minute concessions in the hope of finding a new sherd. The very limitations of professional historical

[31]"Its true value is educational. It can educate the minds of men by causing them to reflect on the past": G. M. Trevelyan, *Clio: A Muse and Other Essays* (new impr., London, 1949), 147. See also G. R. Elton, *The Practice of History* (Sydney, 1967), 48-50.

[32]Gay, *The Enlightenment: The Rise of Modern Paganism*, 46-47.

study make it difficult for historians to deal with any messages that might be derived from the vista of man's past, even if he believed in them. He does not look for them. He does not wish to lift his eyes from what he can see with clarity to what may be baffling, obscure and misleading. Philosophical history is at a discount, and antiquarianism, transmuted into scholarship, triumphs. After two world wars, after Hitler and Hiroshima, after the brutalities of Stalin and the sad failures in Africa, in India, in Indonesia, historians cannot help but look at the immediate, as well as the distant, past with foreboding and with pessimism. But blind optimism has rarely been the fault of the perceptive historian; Voltaire and Gibbon, the greatest historians of the Enlightenment, were conscious enough of the follies, the iniquities, the stupidities of mankind. But they were sufficiently detached to qualify their pessimism and to use a balanced judgment. To them the gains made by mankind were obvious and remarkable. They still are. Any historian who is not blindly prejudiced cannot but admit that the ordinary man and woman, unless they should be caught up in a murderous field of war, are capable of securing a richer life then their ancestors. There is more food in the world, more opportunity of advancement, greater areas of liberty in ideas and in living than the world has ever known: art, music, literature can be enjoyed by tens of millions, not tens of thousands. This has been achieved not by clinging to conservative tradition or by relying on instinct or emotion, but by the application of human ingenuity, no matter what the underlying motive might be. The great extension of rationalism has been a cause and a consequence of this development. In field after field, rationalism has proved its worth. It still has vast areas left to conquer in politics and social organization which may prove beyond its capacity, owing to the aggressive instincts built so deeply into man's nature. Nevertheless, the historian must stress the success, as well as point out the failure. Here is a message of the past which is as clear, but far more true, than the message wrung from it by our ancestors. The past can be used to sanctify not authority nor morality but those qualities of the human mind which have raised us from the forest and swamp to the city, to build a qualified confidence in man's capacity to order his life and to stress the virtues of intellect, of rational behaviour. And this past is neither pagan nor Christian, it belongs to no nation and no class, it is universal; it is human in the widest sense of that term. But this past must not be too simple. Just as the Christian past stressed the complexity of the battle between good and evil, so should the historian's past dwell on the difficulties which have faced those who have fought for intellectual and moral enlightenment. Nor need we gloss their motives. The historian's duty is to reveal the complexities of human behaviour and the strangeness of events. The past which mankind needs is no longer a simple one. Experience as well as science has made the majority of literate men aware of the vast complexity of human existence, its subtle interrelations. What, however, is becoming less and less stressed is the nature of the past, not only its successes, but also the shadows it casts across our lives. History, the dimension of Time, is ignored too frequently by sociologists, economists, politicians and philosophers; even theologians wish to escape from its clutches.

Any past serviceable to society, therefore, must be complex even though its base may be simple. That simple base I have described above. It is to me the one truth of history—that the condition of mankind has improved, materially alas more than morally, but nevertheless both have improved. Progress has come by fits and starts; retrogressions are common. Man's success has derived from his application of reason, whether this has been to technical or to social questions.[33] And it is the duty of the historian to teach this, to proclaim it, to demonstrate it in order to give humanity some confidence in a task that will still be cruel and long—the resolution of the tensions and antipathies that exist within the human species. These are limited objectives. Historians can use history to fulfil many of the social purposes which the old mythical pasts did so well. It can no longer provide sanctions for authority, nor for aristocratic or oligarchical élites, nor for inherent destinies clothed in national guise, but it can still teach wisdom, and it can teach it in a far deeper sense than was possible when wisdom had to be taught through the example of heroes.

Because of the complexities of its dual past—pagan and Chris-

---

[33]I do not, of course, believe in a simple dichotomy between reason and unreason. Reason can bolster folly, lead to absurdity and employ itself in the most dangerous ways. It is reason, controlled on the one hand by facts, by experiment and by experience, and energized on the other by man's deepest biological instincts to increase and protect his kind, that has led to success. (Nothing would unify mankind with greater alacrity than an attack from outer space.) No historian can consider the triumphs of rationality to have been easily secured, nor free from the admixture of many other motives. On the other hand, man's rationality, his capacity to think about himself and his environment and to communicate his thoughts is obviously his most precious gift, and makes him unique in the animal world.

tian—because of the collapse of the Roman Empire, because the Christian past after the Reformation became multiple, because of the impact of great civilizations with a past of their own, because of the discovery in Europe of the huge time-span of man's existence in the world, Western society has been forced not only to study but to accept the fact of social change, of not only the complexity and variety of human existence, but also of its restless social movement in time. As soon as history began to free itself from the past, it was this aspect which drew the best minds to history. It is as true of Gibbon as of Marx, of Michelet as of Bloch. And here lies the greatest contribution that the historian can make. History can teach all who are literate about the nature of social change; even to tell the mere story of social change would be a valuable educational process in itself and help to fulfil a need in present society of which we are all aware. Of course, there will not be agreement; historians will speak with different voices. This no more matters than the lack of unity in wisdom literature [sic] did in the past. The importance lies in the nature, the cogency, the presentation of argument. We need to teach people to think historically about social change, to make them alert to the cunning of history which, as Lenin emphasized, always contains a quality of surprise. We must add the depth of time to studies which so singularly lack it. And it should be remembered that history is constantly growing in insight and probing ever deeper into questions which affect our daily lives. The knowledge of the mechanics of historical change is far more profound than it was two generations ago. But much of the professionalism of history remains professional; in spite of the huge output of paperback histories, the results of professional history are not conveyed with the emphasis and cogency that society needs. The historians have, very rightly, been active agents in the destruction of the past to which society has so frequently turned to acquire either confidence or justification or both. This critical, destructive role is still necessary; illusions about the past, even in professional circles, are abundant enough, but the historian, as with other members of society, is being freed from the trammels of the past by the changes in society itself. Paradoxically, what allows the sociologist to ignore the past, enables the historian to see it more clearly. Hence the historian's opportunity is similar, although far from identical, to that of the philosophers of the Enlightenment. They too were slipping off the shackles of the past, destroying its pretensions and its follies, but they also attempted to create out of the debris a more extended, a more rational, a more detached sense of human destiny. And so by his writings, by his thinking, even by his example, the historian today should be similarly engaged.

The old past is dying, its force weakening, and so it should. Indeed, the historian should speed it on its way, for it was compounded of bigotry, of national vanity, of class domination. It was as absurd as that narrow Christian interpretation which Gibbon rightly scorned. May history step into its shoes, help to sustain man's confidence in his destiny, and create for us a new past as true, as exact, as we can make it, that will help us achieve our identity, not as Americans or Russians, Chinese or Britons, black or white, rich or poor, but as men.

EDWARD HALLETT CARR
History as Progress

LET ME BEGIN by quoting a passage from Professor Powicke's inaugural lecture as Regius Professor in Modern History in Oxford thirty years ago:

> The craving for an interpretation of history is so deep-rooted that, unless we have a constructive outlook over the past, we are drawn either to mysticism or to cynicism.[1]

"Mysticism" will, I think, stand for the view that the meaning of history lies somewhere outside history, in the realms of theology or eschatology—the view of such writers as Berdyaev or Niebuhr or Toynbee.[2] "Cynicism" stands for the view, examples of which I have several times quoted, that history has no meaning, or a multiplicity of equally valid or invalid meanings, or the meaning which we arbitrarily choose to give to it. These are perhaps the two

---

[1]F. Powicke: *Modern Historians and the Study of History* (London: Odhams Press; 1955), p. 174.

[2]"History passes over into theology," as Toynbee triumphantly asserted *(Civilization on Trial,* London: Oxford University Press; 1948, preface).

---

most popular views of history today. But I shall unhesitatingly reject both of them. This leaves us with that odd, but suggestive, phrase "a constructive outlook over the past." Having no way of knowing what was in Professor Powicke's mind when he used the phrase, I shall attempt to read my own interpretation into it.

Like the ancient civilizations of Asia, the classical civilization of Greece and Rome was basically unhistorical. . . . Herodotus as the father of history had few children; and the writers of classical antiquity were on the whole as little concerned with the future as with the past. Thucydides believed that nothing significant had happened in time before the events which he described, and that nothing significant was likely to happen thereafter. Lucretius deduced man's indifference to the past:

> Consider how that past ages of eternal time before our birth were no concern of ours. This is a mirror which nature holds up to us of future time after our death.[3]

Poetic visions of a brighter future took the form of visions of a return to a golden age of the past—a cyclical view which assimilated the processes of history to the processes of nature. History was not going anywhere: because there was no sense of the past, there was equally no sense of the future. Only Virgil, who in his fourth eclogue had given the classical picture of a return to the golden age, was inspired in the *Aeneid* momentarily to break through the cyclical conception: *"Imperium sine fine dedi"* was a most unclassical thought, which later earned Virgil recognition as a quasi-Christian prophet.

It was the Jews, and after them the Christians, who introduced an entirely new element by postulating a goal towards which the historical process is moving—the teleological view of history. History thus acquired a meaning and purpose, but at the expense of losing its secular character. The attainment of the goal of history would automatically mean the end of history: history itself became a theodicy. This was the mediaeval view of history. The Renaissance restored the classical view of an anthropocentric world and of the primacy of reason, but for the pessimistic classical view of the future substituted an optimistic view derived from the Jewish-Christian tradition. Time, which had once been hostile and corroding, now became friendly and creative: contrast Horace's

[3]*De Rerum Natura,* iii, 992-5.

"Damnosa quid non imminuit dies?" with Bacon's *"Veritas temporis filia."* The rationalists of the Enlightenment, who were the founders of modern historiography, retained the Jewish-Christian teleological view, but secularized the goal; they were thus enabled to restore the rational character of the historical process itself. History became progress towards the goal of the perfection of man's estate on earth. Gibbon, the greatest of the Enlightenment historians, was not deterred by the nature of his subject from recording what he called "the pleasing conclusion that every age of the world has increased, and still increases, the real wealth, the happiness, the knowledge, and perhaps the virtue, of the human race."[4] The cult of progress reached its climax at the moment when British prosperity, power, and self-confidence were at their height; and British writers and British historians were among the most ardent votaries of the cult. The phenomenon is too familiar to need illustration, but I need only quote one or two passages to show how recently faith in progress remained a postulate of all our thinking. Acton, in the report of 1896 on the project of *The Cambridge Modern History . . .* referred to history as "a progressive science"; and in the introduction to the first volume of the history wrote that "we are bound to assume, as the scientific hypothesis on which History is to be written, a progress in human affairs." In the last volume of the history, published in 1910, Dampier, who was a tutor of my college when I was an undergraduate, felt no doubt that "future ages will see no limit to the growth of man's power over the resources of nature and of his intelligent use of them for the welfare of his race."[5] In view of what I am about to say, it is fair for me to admit that this was the atmosphere in which I was educated, and that I could subscribe without reservation to the words of my senior by half a generation, Bertrand Russell: "I grew up in the full flood of

---

[4]Gibbon: *The Decline and Fall of the Roman Empire,* Ch. xxxviii; the occasion of this digression was the downfall of the Western empire. A critic in *The Times Literary Supplement,* November 18, 1960, quoting this passage, asks whether Gibbon quite meant it. Of course he did; the point of view of a writer is more likely to reflect the period in which he lives than that about which he writes—a truth well illustrated by this critic, who seeks to transfer his own mid-twentieth century scepticism to a late eighteenth-century writer.

[5]J. Acton, *The Cambridge Modern History: Its Origin, Authorship and Production,* p. 13; *The Cambridge Modern History,* I, p. 4; XII (London: Macmillan, 1910), p. 791.

Victorian optimism, and . . . something remains with me of the hopefulness that then was easy."[6]

In 1920, when Bury wrote his book *The Idea of Progress,* a bleaker climate already prevailed, the blame for which he laid, in obedience to the current fashion, on "the doctrinaires who have established the present reign of terror in Russia," though he still described progress as "the animating and controlling idea of Western civilization."[7] Thereafter this note was silent. Nicholas I of Russia is said to have issued an order banning the word "progress": nowadays the philosophers and historians of Western Europe, and even the United States, have come belatedly to agree with him. The hypothesis of progress has been refuted. The decline of the West has become so familiar a phrase that quotation marks are no longer required. But what, apart from all the shouting, has really happened? By whom has this new current of opinion been formed? The other day I was shocked to come across, I think, the only remark of Bertrand Russell I have ever seen which seemed to me to betray an acute sense of class: "There is, on the whole, much less liberty in the world now than there was a hundred years ago."[8] I have no measuring-rod for liberty, and do not know how to balance the lesser liberty of few against the greater liberty of many. But on any standard of measurement I can only regard the statement as fantastically untrue. I am more attracted by one of those fascinating glimpses which Mr. A.J.P. Taylor sometimes gives us into Oxford academic life. All this talk about the decline of civilization, he writes, "means only that university professors used to have domestic servants and now do their own washing-up."[9] Of course, for former domestic servants, washing-up by professors may be a symbol of progress. The loss of white supremacy in Africa, which worries Empire loyalists, Africaner republicans, and investors in gold and copper shares, may look like progress to others. I see no reason why, on this question of progress, I should *ipso facto* prefer the verdict of the 1950's to that of the 1890's, the verdict of the English-speaking world to that of Russia, Asia, and Africa, or the verdict of the middle-class intellectual to that of the man in the street who, according to Mr. Macmillan, has never had it so good.

[6]Russell: *Portraits From Memory,* (New York: Simon and Schuster, 1956) p. 17.
[7]Bury, *The Idea of Progress,* (New York: Macmillan, 1932) pp. vii-viii.
[8]Russell: *Portraits From Memory,* p. 124.
[9]*The Observer* (June 21, 1959).

Let us for the moment suspend judgment on the question whether we are living in a period of progress or of decline, and examine a little more closely what is implied in the concept of progress, what assumptions lie behind it, and how far these have become untenable.

I should like, first of all, to clear up the muddle about progress and evolution. The thinkers of the Enlightenment adopted two apparently incompatible views. They sought to vindicate man's place in the world of nature: the laws of history were equated with the laws of nature. On the other hand, they believed in progress. But what ground was there for treating nature as progressive, as constantly advancing towards a goal? Hegel met the difficulty by sharply distinguishing history, which was progressive, from nature, which was not. The Darwinian revolution appeared to remove all embarrassments by equating evolution and progress: nature, like history, turned out after all to be progressive. But this opened the way to a much graver misunderstanding by confusing biological inheritance, which is the source of evolution, with social acquisition, which is the source of progress in history. The distinction is familiar and obvious. Put a European infant in a Chinese family, and the child will grow up with a white skin, but speaking Chinese. Pigmentation is a biological inheritance, language a social acquisition transmitted by the agency of the human brain. Evolution by inheritance has to be measured in millennia or in millions of years; no measurable biological change is known to have occurred in man since the beginning of written history. Progress by acquisition can be measured in generations. The essence of man as a rational being is that he develops his potential capacities by accumulating the experience of past generations. Modern man is said to have no larger a brain, and no greater innate capacity of thought, than his ancestor 5,000 years ago. But the effectiveness of his thinking has been multiplied many times by learning and incorporating in his experience the experience of the intervening generations. The transmission of acquired characteristics, which is rejected by biologists, is the very foundation of social progress. History is progress through the transmission of acquired skills from one generation to another.

Secondly, we need not and should not conceive progress as having a finite beginning or end. The belief, popular less than fifty years ago, that civilization was invented in the Nile valley in the fourth millenium B.C. is no more credible today than the chronology which placed the creation of the world in 4004 B.C. Civilization, the birth of which we may perhaps take as a starting-point for our hypothesis of progress, was surely not an invention but an infinitely slow process of development, in which spectacular leaps probably occurred from time to time. We need not trouble ourselves with the question when progress—or civilization—began. The hypothesis of a finite end of progress has led to more serious misapprehension. Hegel has been rightly condemned for seeing the end of progress in the Prussian monarchy—apparently the result of an overstrained interpretation of his view of the impossibility of prediction. But Hegel's aberration was capped by that eminent Victorian, Arnold of Rugby, who in his inaugural lecture as Regius Professor of Modern History in Oxford in 1841 thought that modern history would be the last stage in the history of mankind: "It appears to bear marks of the fullness of time, as if there would be no future history beyond it."[10] Marx's prediction that the proletarian revolution would realize the ultimate aim of a classless society was logically and morally less vulnerable; but the presumption of an end of history has an eschatological ring more appropriate to the theologian than to the historian, and reverts to the fallacy of a goal outside history. No doubt a finite end has attractions for the human mind; and Acton's vision of the march of history as an unending progress towards liberty seems chilly and vague. But if the historian is to save his hypothesis of progress, I think he must be prepared to treat it as a process into which the demands and conditions of successive periods will put their own specific content. And this is what is meant by Acton's thesis that history is not only a record of progress, but a "progressive science," or, if you like, that history in both senses of the word—as the course of events and as the record of those events—is progressive. Let us recall Acton's description of the advance of liberty in history:

> It is by the combined efforts of the weak, made under compulsion, to resist the reign of force and constant wrong, that, in the rapid change but slow progress of four hundred years, liberty has been preserved, and secured, and extended, and finally understood.[11]

History as the course of events was conceived by Acton as progress towards liberty, history as the record of those events was progress towards the understanding of liberty: the two processes advanced

---

[10]T. Arnold: *An Inaugural Lecture on the Study of Modern History* (London: Longmans, Green, 1841), p. 38.

[11]J. Acton: *Lectures on Modern History*, (New York: Macmillan, 1906) p. 51.

side by side.[12] The philosopher Bradley, writing in an age when analogies from evolution were fashionable, remarked that "for religious faith the end of evolution is presented as that which . . . is already evolved."[13] For the historian the end of progress is not already evolved. It is something still infinitely remote; and pointers towards it come in sight only as we advance. This does not diminish its importance. A compass is a valuable and indeed indispensable guide. But it is not a chart of the route. The content of history can be realized only as we experience it.

My third point is that no sane person ever believed in a kind of progress which advanced in an unbroken straight line without reverses and deviations and breaks in continuity so that even the sharpest reverse is not necessarily fatal to the belief. Clearly there are periods of regression as well as periods of progress. Moreover, it would be rash to assume that, after a retreat, the advance will be resumed from the same point or along the same line. Hegel's or Marx's four or three civilizations, Toynbee's twenty-one civilizations, the theory of a life-cycle of civilizations passing through rise, decline, and fall—such schemes make no sense in themselves. But they are symptomatic of the observed fact that the effort which is needed to drive civilization forward dies away in one place and is later resumed at another, so that whatever progress we can observe in history is certainly not continuous either in time or in place. Indeed, if I were addicted to formulating laws of history, one such law would be to the effect that the group—call it a class, a nation, a continent, a civilization, what you will—which plays the leading role in the advance of civilization in one period is unlikely to play a similar role in the next period, and this for the good reason that it will be too deeply imbued with the traditions, interests, and ideologies of the earlier period to be able to adapt itself to the demands and conditions of the next period.[14] Thus it may very well happen that what seems for one group a period of decline may seem to another

[12]Mannheim: *Ideology and Utopia* (New York: Harcourt, Brace), p. 236, also associates man's "will to shape history" with his "ability to understand it."

[13]F. H. Bradley: *Ethical Studies* (1876), p. 293.

[14]For a diagnosis of such a situation, see R. S. Lynd: *Knowledge for What?* (Princeton: Princeton University Press; 1939), p. 88: "Elderly people in our culture are frequently oriented towards the past, the time of their vigour and power, and resist the future as a threat. It is probable that a whole culture in an advanced stage of loss of relative power and disintegration may thus have a dominant orientation towards a lost golden age, while life is lived sluggishly along in the present."

the birth of a new advance. Progress does not and cannot mean equal and simultaneous progress for all. It is significant that almost all our latter-day prophets of decline, our sceptics who see no meaning in history and assume that progress is dead, belong to that sector of the world and to that class of society which have triumphantly played a leading and predominant part in the advance of civilization for several generations. It is no consolation to them to be told that the role which their group has played in the past will now pass to others. Clearly a history which has played so scurvy a trick on them cannot be a meaningful or rational process. But, if we are to retain the hypothesis of progress, we must, I think, accept the condition of the broken line.

Lastly, I come to the question of what is the essential content of progress in terms of historical action. The people who struggle, say, to extend civil rights to all, or to reform penal practice, or to remove inequalities of race or wealth are consciously seeking to do just those things: they are not consciously seeking to "progress," to realize some historical "law" or "hypothesis" of progress. It is the historian who applies to their actions his hypothesis of progress, and interprets their actions as progress. But this does not invalidate the concept of progress. I am glad on this point to find myself in agreement with Sir Isaiah Berlin that "progress and reaction, however much the words may have been abused, are not empty concepts."[15] It is presupposition of history that man is capable of profiting (not that he necessarily profits) by the experience of his predecessors, and that progress in history, unlike evolution in nature, rests on the transmission of acquired assets. These assets include both material possessions and the capacity to master, transform, and utilize one's environment. Indeed, the two factors are closely interconnected, and react on one another. Marx treats human labour as the foundation of the whole edifice; and this formula seems acceptable if a sufficiently broad sense is attached to "labour." But the mere accumulation of resources will not avail unless it brings with it not only increased technical and social knowledge and experience, but increased mastery of man's environment in the broader sense. At the present time, few people would, I think, question the fact of progress in the accumulation both of material resources and of scientific knowledge, of mastery over the environment in the technological sense. What is questioned is

---

[15] *Foreign Affairs,* xxviii, No. 3 (June 1950), p. 382.

whether there has been in the twentieth century any progress in our ordering of society, in our mastery of the social environment, national or international, whether indeed there has not been a marked regression. Has not the evolution of man as a social being lagged fatally behind the progress of technology?

The symptoms which inspire this question are obvious. But I suspect none the less that it is wrongly put. History has known many turning-points, where the leadership and initiative have passed from one group, from one sector of the world, to another: the period of the rise of the modern state and the shift in the centre of power from the Mediterranean to Western Europe, and the period of the French revolution have been conspicuous modern examples. Such periods are always times of violent upheavals and struggles for power. The old authorities weaken, the old landmarks disappear; out of a bitter clash of ambitions and resentments the new order emerges. What I would suggest is that we are now passing through such a period. It appears to me simply untrue to say that our understanding of the problems of social organization or our good will to organize society in the light of that understanding have regressed: indeed, I should venture to say that they have greatly increased. It is not that our capacities have diminished, or our moral qualities declined. But the period of conflict and upheaval, due to the shifting balance of power between continents, nations, and classes, through which we are living has enormously increased the strain on these capacities and qualities, and limited and frustrated their effectiveness for positive achievement. While I do not wish to underestimate the force of the challenge of the past fifty years to the belief in progress in the Western world, I am still not convinced that progress in history has come to an end. But, if you press me further on the content of progress, I think I can only reply something like this. The notion of a finite and clearly definable goal of progress in history, so often postulated by nineteenth-century thinkers, has proved inapplicable and barren. Belief in progress means belief not in any automatic or inevitable process, but in the progressive development of human potentialities. Progress is an abstract term; and the concrete ends pursued by mankind arise from time to time out of the course of history, not from some source outside it. I profess no belief in the perfectibility of man, or in a future paradise on earth. To this extent I would agree with the theologians and the mystics who assert that perfection is not realizable in history. But I shall be content with the possibility of unlimited progress—or progress subject to no limits that we can need or envisage—towards goals which can be defined only as we advance towards them, and the validity of which can be verified only in a process of attaining them. Nor do I know how, without some such conception of progress, society can survive. Every civilized society imposes sacrifices on the living generation for the sake of generations yet unborn. To justify these sacrifices in the name of a better world in the future is the secular counterpart of justifying them in the name of some divine purpose. In Bury's words, "the principle of duty to posterity is a direct corollary of the idea of progress."[16] Perhaps this duty does not require justification. If it does, I know of no other way to justify it.

This brings me to the famous crux of objectivity in history. The word itself is misleading and question-begging. In an earlier lecture I have already argued that the social sciences—and history among them—cannot accommodate themselves to a theory of knowledge which puts subject and object asunder, and enforces a rigid separation between the observer and the thing observed.* We need a new model which does justice to the complex process of interrelation and interaction between them. The facts of history cannot be purely objective, since they become facts of history only in virtue of the significance attached to them by the historian. Objectivity in history—if we are still to use the conventional term—cannot be an objectivity of fact, but only of relation, of the relation between fact and interpretation, between past, present, and future. I need not revert to the reasons which led me to reject as unhistorical the attempt to judge historical events by erecting an absolute standard of value outside history and independent of it. But the concept of absolute truth is also not appropriate to the world of history—or, I suspect, to the world of science. It is only the simplest kind of historical statement that can be adjudged absolutely true or absolutely false. At a more sophisticated level, the historian who contests, say, the verdict of one of his predecessors will normally condemn it, not as absolutely false, but as inadequate or one-sided or misleading, or the product of a point of view which has been rendered obsolete or irrelevant by later evidence. To say that the Russian revolution was due to the stupidity of Nicholas II or to the

16Bury: *The Idea of Progress*, p. ix.
*Editor's Note: See *What is History?*, pp. 3-35.

genius of Lenin is altogether inadequate—so inadequate as to be altogether misleading. But it cannot be called absolutely false. The historian does not deal in absolutes of this kind.

Let us go back to the sad case of Robinson's death.* The objectivity of our enquiry into that event depended not on getting our facts right—these were not in dispute—but on distinguishing between the real or significant facts, in which we were interested, and the accidental facts, which we could afford to ignore. We found it easy to draw this distinction because our standard or test of significance, the basis of our objectivity, was clear, and consisted of relevance to the goal in view, *i.e.* reduction of deaths on the roads. But the historian is a less fortunate person than the investigator who has before him the simple and finite purpose of reducing traffic casualties. The historian, too, in his task of interpretation, needs his standard of significance, which is also his standard of objectivity, in order to distinguish between the significant and the accidental; and he, too, can find it only in relevance to the end in view. But this is necessarily an evolving end, since the evolving interpretation of the past is a necessary function of history. The traditional assumption that change has always to be explained in terms of something fixed and unchangeable is contrary to the experience of the historian. "For the historian," says Professor Butterfield, perhaps implicitly reserving for himself a sphere into which historians need not follow him, "the only absolute is change.[17] The absolute in history is not something in the past from which we start; it is not something in the present, since all present thinking is necessarily relative. It is something still incomplete and in process of becoming—something in the future towards which we move, which begins to take shape only as we move towards it, and in the light of which, as we move forward, we gradually shape our interpretation of the past. This is

---

*Editor's Note: See *What is History?*, pp. 137-43. Carr uses the example of the death of Robinson in an automobile accident to illuminate relevant and irrelevant causes of historical events.

[17]Butterfield: *The Whig Interpretation of History* (New York: Norton; 1965), p. 58. Compare the more elaborate statement in Alfred von Martin: *The Sociology of the Renaissance* (London: Routledge & Kegan Paul; 1945), p. i: "Inertia and motion, static and dynamic, are fundamental categories with which to begin a sociological approach to history. . . . History knows inertia in a relative sense only: the decisive question is whether inertia or change predominates." Change is the positive and absolute, inertia the subjective and relative, element in history.

the secular truth behind the religious myth that the meaning of history will be revealed in the day of judgment. Our criterion is not an absolute in the static sense of something that is the same yesterday, today, and for ever: such an absolute is incompatible with the nature of history. But it is an absolute in respect of our interpretation of the past. It rejects the relativist view that one interpretation is as good as another, or that every interpretation is true in its own time and place, and it provides the touchstone by which our interpretation of the past will ultimately be judged. It is this sense of direction in history which alone enables us to order and interpret the events of the past—the task of the historian—and to liberate and organize human energies in the present with a view to the future—the task of the statesman, the economist, and the social reformer. But the process itself remains progressive and dynamic. Our sense of direction, and our interpretation of the past, are subject to constant modification and evolution as we proceed.

Hegel clothed his absolute in the mystical shape of a world spirit, and made the cardinal error of bringing the course of history to an end in the present instead of projecting it into the future. He recognized a process of continuous evolution in the past, and incongruously denied it in the future. Those who, since Hegel, have reflected most deeply on the nature of history have seen in it a synthesis of past and future. Tocqueville, who did not entirely free himself from the theological idiom of his day and gave too narrow content to his absolute, nevertheless had the essence of the matter. Having spoken of the development of equality as a universal and permanent phenomenon, he went on:

> If the men of our time were brought to see the gradual and progressive development of equality as at once the past and the future of their history, this single discovery would give that development the sacred character of the will of their lord and master.[18]

An important chapter of history could be written on that still unfinished theme. Marx, who shared some of Hegel's inhibitions about looking into the future, and was principally concerned to root his teaching firmly in past history, was compelled by the nature of his theme to project into the future his absolute of the classless society. Bury described the idea of progress, a little awkwardly, but clearly with the same intention, as "a theory which involves a

18Alexis de Tocqueville: Preface to *Democracy in America*.

synthesis of the past and a prophecy of the future."[19] Historians, says Namier in a deliberately paradoxical phrase, which he proceeds to illustrate with his usual wealth of examples, "imagine the past and remember the future."[20] Only the future can provide the key to the interpretation of the past; and it is only in this sense that we speak of an ultimate objectivity in history. It is at once the justification and the explanation of history that the past throws light on the future, and the future throws light on the past.

What, then, do we mean when we praise a historian for being objective, or say that one historian is more objective than another? Not, it is clear, simply that he gets his facts right, but rather that he chooses the right facts, or, in other words, that he applies the right standard of significance. When we call a historian objective, we mean, I think, two things. First of all, we mean that he has a capacity to rise above the limited vision of his own situation in history—a capacity which is . . . partly dependent on his capacity to recognize the extent of his involvement in that situation, to recognize, that is to say, the impossibility of total objectivity. Secondly, we mean that he has the capacity to project his vision into the future in such a way as to give him a more profound and more lasting insight into the past than can be attained by those historians whose outlook is entirely bounded by their own immediate situation. No historian today will echo Acton's confidence in the prospect of "ultimate history." But some historians write history which is more durable, and has more of this ultimate and objective character, than others; and these are the historians who have what I may call a long-term vision over the past and over the future. The historian of the past can make an approach towards objectivity only as he approaches towards the understanding of the future.

When, therefore, I spoke of history . . . as a dialogue between past and present, I should rather have called it a dialogue between the events of the past and progressively emerging future ends. The historian's interpretation of the past, his selection of the significant and the relevant, evolves with the progressive emergence of new goals. To take the simplest of all illustrations, so long as the main goal appeared to be the organization of constitutional liberties and political rights, the historian interpreted the past in constitutional and political terms. When economic and social ends began to replace

[19]Bury: *The Idea of Progress*, p. 5.
[20]Namier: *Conflicts* (London: Macmillan & Co.; 1942), p. 70.

constitutional and political ends, historians turned to economic and social interpretations of the past. In this process, the sceptic might plausibly allege that the new interpretation is no truer than the old; each is true for its period. Nevertheless, since the preoccupation with economic and social ends represents a broader and more advanced stage in human development than the preoccupation with political and constitutional ends, so the economic and social interpretation of history may be said to represent a more advanced stage in history than the exclusively political interpretation. The old interpretation is not rejected, but is both included and superseded in the new. Historiography is a progressive science in the sense that it seeks to provide constantly expanding and deepening insights into a course of events which is itself progressive. This is what I should mean by saying that we need "a constructive outlook over the past." Modern historiography has grown up during the past two centuries in this dual belief in progress, and cannot survive without it, since it is this belief which provides it with its standard of significance, its touchstone for distinguishing between the real and the accidental. Goethe, in a conversation towards the end of his life, cut the Gordian knot a little brusquely:

> When eras are on the decline, all tendencies are subjective; but on the other hand when matters are ripening for a new epoch, all tendencies are objective.[21]

Nobody is obliged to believe either in the future of history or in the future of society. It is possible that our society may be destroyed or may perish of slow decay, and that history may relapse into theology—that is to say, a study not of human achievement, but of the divine purpose—or into literature—that is to say, a telling of stories and legends without purpose or significance. But this will not be history in the sense in which we have known it in the last two hundred years.

I have still to deal with the familiar and popular objection to any theory which finds the ultimate criterion of historical judgment in the future. Such a theory, it is said, implies that success is the ultimate criterion of judgment, and that, if not whatever is, whatever will be, is right. For the past two hundred years most historians have not only assumed a direction in which history is moving, but have

[21]Quoted in J. Huizinga: *Menand Ideas* (New York: Meridian Books; 1959), p. 50.

consciously or unconsciously believed that this direction was on the whole the right direction, that mankind was moving from the worse to the better, from the lower to the higher. The historian not only recognized the direction, but endorsed it. The test of significance which he applied in his approach to the past was not only a sense of the course on which history was moving, but a sense of his own moral involvement in that course. The alleged dichotomy between the "is" and the "ought," between fact and value, was resolved. It was an optimistic view, a product of an age of overwhelming confidence in the future; Whigs and Liberals, Hegelians and Marxists, theologians and rationalists, remained firmly, and more or less articulately, committed to it. For two hundred years it could have described without much exaggeration as the accepted and implicit answer to the question: What is history? The reaction against it has come with the current mood of apprehension and pessimism, which has left the field clear for the theologians who seek the meaning of history outside history, and for the sceptics who find no meaning in history at all. We are assured on all hands, and with the utmost emphasis, that the dichotomy between "is" and "ought" is absolute and cannot be resolved, that "values" cannot be derived from "facts." This is, I think, a false trail. Let us see how a few historians, or writers about history, chosen more or less at random, have felt about this question.

Gibbon justifies the amount of space devoted in his narrative to the victories of Islam on the ground that "the disciples of Mohammed still hold the civil and religious sceptre of the Oriental world." But, he adds, "the same labour would be unworthily bestowed on the swarms of savages who, between the 7th and 12th centuries, descended from the plains of Scythia," since "the majesty of the Byzantine throne repelled and survived these disorderly attacks."[22] This seems not unreasonable. History is, by and large, a record of what people did, not of what they failed to do: to this extent it is inevitably a success story. Professor Tawney remarks that historians give "an appearance of inevitableness" to an existing order "by dragging into prominence the forces which have triumphed and thrusting into the background those which they have swallowed up."[23] But is not this in a sense the essence of the historian's job? The historian must not underestimate the opposition; he must not

[22]Gibbon: *The Decline and Fall of the Roman Empire*, Ch. iv.
[23]R. H. Tawney: *The Agrarian Problem in the Sixteenth Century* (London: Longmans, Green & Co.; 1912), p. 177.

represent the victory as a walk-over if it was touch-and-go. Sometimes those who were defeated have made as great a contribution to the ultimate result as the victors. These are familiar maxims to every historian. But, by and large, the historian is concerned with those who, whether victorious or defeated, achieved something. I am not a specialist in the history of cricket. But its pages are presumably studded with the names of those who made centuries rather than of those who made ducks and were left out of the side. Hegel's famous statement that in history "only those peoples can come under our notice which form a state,"[24] has been justly criticized as attaching an exclusive value to one form of social organization and paving the way for an obnoxious state-worship. But, in principle, what Hegel is trying to say is correct, and reflects the familiar distinction between pre-history and history; only those peoples which have succeeded in organizing their society in some degree cease to be primitive savages and enter into history. Carlyle, in his *French Revolution,* called Louis XV "a very World Solecism incarnate." He evidently liked the phrase, for he embroidered it later in a longer passage:

> What new universal vertiginous movement is this: of institutions, social arrangements, individual minds, which once worked co-operative, now rolling and grinding in distracted collision? Inevitable; it is the breaking-up of a World Solecism, worn out at last.[25]

The criterion is once more historical: what fitted one epoch had become a solecism in another, and is condemned on that account. Even Sir Isaiah Berlin, when he descends from the heights of philosophical abstraction and considers concrete historical situations, appears to have come round to this view. In a broadcast delivered some time after the publication of his essay on *Historical Inevitability,* he praised Bismarck, in spite of moral shortcomings, as a "genius" and "the greatest example in the last century of a politician of the highest powers of political judgment," and contrasted him favourably in this respect with such men as Joseph II of Austria, Robespierre, Lenin, and Hitler, who failed to realize "their positive ends." I find this verdict odd. But what interests me at the moment is the criterion of judgment. Bismarck, says Sir Isaiah, understood the material in which he was working; the others were led away by abstract theories which failed to work. The moral is that

---

[24]*Lectures on the Philosophy of History* (Eng. transl., 1884), p. 40.
[25]T. Carlyle: *The French Revolution* (New York: Modern Library; 1934), I, i, Ch. 4; I, iii, Ch. 7.

"failure comes from resisting that which works best . . . in favour of some systematic method or principle claiming universal validity."[26] In other words, the criterion of judgment in history is not some "principle claiming universal validity," but "that which works best."

It is not only—I need hardly say—when analysing the past that we invoke this criterion of "what works best." If someone informed you that he thought that, at the present juncture, the union of Great Britain and the United States of America in a single state under a single sovereignty was desirable, you might agree that this was quite a sensible view. If he went on to say that constitutional monarchy was preferable to presidential democracy as a form of government, you might also agree that this was quite sensible. But suppose he then told you that he proposed to devote himself to conducting a campaign for the reunion of the two countries under the British crown; you would probably reply that he would be wasting his time. If you tried to explain why, you would have to tell him that issues of this kind have to be debated on the basis not of some principle of general application, but of what would work in given historical conditions; you might even commit the cardinal sin of speaking of history with a capital H and tell him that History was against him. The business of the politician is to consider not merely what is morally or theoretically desirable, but also the forces which exist in the world, and how they can be directed or manipulated to probably partial realizations of the ends in view. Our political decisions taken in the light of our interpretation of history are rooted in this compromise. But our interpretation of history is rooted in the same compromise. Nothing is more radically false than to set up some supposedly abstract standard of the desirable and condemn the past in the light of it. For the word "success," which has come to have invidious connotations, let us by all means substitute the neutral "that which works best.". . .

But acceptance of the criterion of "what works best" does not make its application either easy or self-evident. It is not a criterion which encourages snap verdicts, or which bows down to the view that what is, is right. Pregnant failures are not unknown in history. History recognizes what I may call "delayed achievement": the apparent failures of today may turn out to have made a vital contribution to the achievement of tomorrow—prophets born be-

[26]Broadcast on "Political Judgment" in the Third Programme of the B.B.C., June 19, 1957.

fore their time. Indeed, one of the advantages of this criterion over the criterion of a supposedly fixed and universal principle is that it may require us to postpone our judgment or to qualify it in the light of things that have not yet happened. Proudhon, who talked freely in terms of abstract moral principles, condoned the *coup d'état* of Napoleon III after it had succeeded; Marx, who rejected the criterion of abstract moral principles, condemned Proudhon for condoning it. Looking back from a longer historical perspective, we shall probably agree that Proudhon was wrong and Marx right. The achievement of Bismarck provides an excellent starting-point for an examination of this problem of historical judgment; and, while I accept Sir Isaiah's criterion of "what works best," I am still puzzled by the narrow and short-term limits within which he is apparently content to apply it. Did what Bismarck created really work well? I should have thought that it led to an immense disaster. This does not mean that I am seeking to condemn Bismarck who created the German Reich, or the mass of Germans who wanted it and helped to create it. But, as a historian, I still have many questions to ask. Did the eventual disaster occur because some hidden flaws existed in the structure of the Reich? or because something in the internal conditions which brought it to birth destined it to become self-assertive and aggressive? or because, when the Reich was created, the European or world scene was already so crowded, and expansive tendencies among the existing Great Powers already so strong, that the emergence of another expansive Great Power was sufficient to cause a major collision and bring down the whole system in ruins? On the last hypothesis, it may be wrong to hold Bismarck and the German people responsible, or solely responsible, for the disaster: you cannot really blame the last straw. But an objective judgment on Bismarck's achievement and how it worked awaits an answer from the historian to these questions, and I am not sure that he is yet in a position to answer them all definitively. What I would say is that the historian of the 1920's was nearer to objective judgment than the historian of the 1880's, and that the historian of today is nearer than the historian of the 1920's; the historian of the year 2000 may be nearer still. This illustrates my thesis that objectivity in history does not and cannot rest on some fixed and immovable standard of judgment existing here and now, but only on a standard which is laid up in the future and is evolved as the course of history advances. History acquires meaning and objectivity only when it establishes a coherent relation between past and future.

Let us now take another look at this alleged dichotomy between fact and value. Values cannot be derived from facts. This statement is partly true, but partly false. You have only to examine the system of values prevailing in any period or in any country to realize how much of it is moulded by the facts of the environment. In an earlier lecture I drew attention to the changing historical content of value-words like liberty, equality, or justice. Or take the Christian church as an institution largely concerned with the propagation of moral values. Contrast the values of primitive Christianity with those of the mediaeval papacy, or the values of the mediaeval papacy with those of the Protestant churches of the nineteenth century. Or contrast the values promulgated today by, say, the Christian church in Spain with the values promulgated by the Christian churches in the United States. These differences in values spring from differences of historical fact. Or consider the historical facts which in the last century and a half have caused slavery or racial inequality or the exploitation of child labour—all once accepted as morally neutral or reputable—to be generally regarded as immoral. The proposition that values cannot be derived from facts is, to say the least, one-sided and misleading. Or let us reverse the statement. Facts cannot be derived from values. This is partly true, but may also be misleading, and requires qualification. When we seek to know the facts, the questions which we ask, and therefore the answers which we obtain, are prompted by our system of values. Our picture of the facts of our environment is moulded by our values, *i.e.* by the categories through which we approach the facts; and this picture is one of the important facts which we have to take into account. Values enter into the facts and are an essential part of them. Our values are an essential part of our equipment as human beings. It is through our values that we have that capacity to adapt ourselves to our environment, and to adapt our environment to ourselves, to acquire that mastery over our environment, which has made history a record of progress. But do not, in dramatizing the struggle of man with his environment, set up a false antithesis and a false separation between facts and values. Progress in history is achieved through the interdependence and interaction of facts and values. The objective historian is the historian who penetrates most deeply into this reciprocal process.

A clue to this problem of facts and values is provided by our ordinary use of the word "truth"—a word which straddles the world of fact and the world of value and is made up of elements of both.

Nor is this an idiosyncrasy of the English language. The words for truth in the Latin languages, the German *Wahrheit,* the Russian *pravda,*[27] all possess this dual character. Every language appears to require this word for a truth which is not merely a statement of fact and not merely a value judgment, but embraces both elements. It may be a fact that I went to London last week. But you would not ordinarily call it a truth: it is devoid of any value content. On the other hand, when the Founding Fathers of the United States in the Declaration of Independence referred to the self-evident truth that all men are created equal, you may feel that the value content of the statement predominates over the factual content, and may on that account challenge its right to be regarded as a truth. Somewhere between these two poles—the north pole of valueless facts and the south pole of value judgments still struggling to transform themselves into facts—lies the realm of historical truth. The historian . . . is balanced between fact and interpretation, between fact and value. He cannot separate them. It may be that, in a static world, you are obliged to pronounce a divorce between fact and value. But history is meaningless in a static world. History in its essence is change, movement, or—if you do not cavil at the old-fashioned word—progress.

I return therefore in conclusion to Acton's description of progress as "the scientific hypothesis on which history is to be written." You can, if you please, turn history into theology by making the meaning of the past depend on some extra-historical and super-rational power. You can, if you please, turn it into literature—a collection of stories and legends about the past without meaning or significance. History properly so-called can be written only by those who find and accept a sense of direction in history itself. The belief that we have come from somewhere is closely linked with the belief that we are going somewhere. A society which has lost belief in its capacity to progress in the future will quickly cease to concern itself with its progress in the past. . . . Our view of history reflects our view of society. I now come back to my starting-point by declaring my faith in the future of society and in the future of history.

---

[27]The case of *pravda* is especially interesting since there is another old Russian word for truth, *istina.* But the distinction is not between truth as fact and truth as value; *pravda* is human truth in both aspects, *istina* divine truth in both aspects—truth about God and truth as revealed by God.

PETER GAY

On Optimism

LUCIAN: Your sense of modernity, Voltaire, as a mixture of light and darkness has inspired me to invent an ancient Greek myth. Long, long ago, before there were any cities, before there was writing, when men lived much like the animals of the fields, there was little intercourse between gods and mortals. Driven by lust or tedium, Zeus or Aphrodite would come down to earth to seek some favorite partner, and the consequences of those encounters were always the same: another demigod, to enrich the natural order and to complicate divine family life. One evening in that distant time, when Zeus happened to be bored with adultery, and Hera with berating him for it, these two gods sat down together peaceably and had one of their rare conversations. They looked at the earth stretched out below them, and their talk turned to that most unsatisfactory, most contradictory, of creatures—man. "There he is," said Zeus, musing. "So godlike in appearance, so appealing in his exceptional physical specimens, yet so beastly in his ignorance, his filth, his total lack of cultivation. How tedious is man." Hera, glad of Zeus' unaccustomed company, agreed. "Let us do something about him," Zeus said. "Let us find some young man, as handsome as Ganymede, and some young woman, as beautiful as . . . er . . . you, bring them to Olympus and teach them that there is more to life than eating, sleeping, and fornicating. Let us give them curiosity—about us, about themselves, about the world in which they live. Let us teach them how to read and write, to adorn themselves and their surroundings, to play, to congregate with others in orderly assemblies, and to store up wisdom."

Hera complied. After some search, she found a strapping young shepherd and a lovely young shepherdess, and took them to the dwelling of the gods. With the aid of the other gods, each imparting his special knowledge, she taught them arts, sciences, and literature. The young couple were apt, quick-witted pupils, and before long they were godlike in more than appearance, though always conscious of the gulf between them and their preceptors—more conscious, indeed, than they had been before they had begun their education. Before, they had not thought of death; now they became aware of the weight of mortality. But this made them only more thoughtful than ever. When they began to spin myths, often of surprising originality, about life and death, about the meaning of existence, and even about the birth of the gods, Zeus and Hera judged that the lessons were ended. They sent their pupils back to earth, and watched them, with pleasure, as they founded a family, gathered a society, and started a dynasty, as they built a city and a culture, complete with efforts at natural science and local history.

Then something strange happened. The couple were so responsible, and so intelligent, that the gods, with their unchecked sensuality, their stupid drinking bouts, their acrimonious quarrels, seemed actually inferior to what they had fondly described to themselves as their creatures. Feeling uncomfortable, and in some way tricked, the gods became jealous. The creature, it was painfully obvious, had somehow outstripped its creator. Of course that one ineluctable point of superiority of gods over man always remained: they were immortal, he mortal. Man could deny the gods, but not destroy them; the gods could destroy man. And Zeus and Hera, no longer bored but profoundly uneasy, decided to rid themselves of the couple they had singled out for education with such ambiguous success. They invited them up to Olympus and sat them down to a sumptuous feast in the company of all the gods. Then, with divine distance, Zeus announced to them their imminent end.

The woman was resigned. "Let death come," she said, "it must come to us anyway. At least let us bear it well. It is not everyone to whom the gods pay such personal attention as to us." But her husband was more rebellious. Having made up some philosophy for himself, he determined to use it in this critical hour. "You made us what we are today," he told the gods. "We are your greatest handiwork precisely because we are no longer acting as your handiwork. Your world is full of slaves. Thanks to you, we are free men. To kill us is to kill the best in you, to kill something you need to keep from dying of ennui in your eternity: we have become the only animal that is really interesting."

The gods are jealous—this is one of their few stable traits—but it also amuses them to display their compassion . . . sometimes. Zeus was moved, and even partly persuaded, by the shepherd's plea, and announced that he would spare his pupils' lives. But what punishment, then, should be meted out to mortals who had made the gods feel just a little silly? After some discussion, Zeus found the appropriate sentence. The thing to do was to deprive these humans of what they had learned at Olympus and then fashioned on earth, and to restore them to their old condition, to their former rustic stupidity.

This was promptly done, and for a short while shepherd and shepherdess vegetated as they had done before, steeped in filth and bestiality, seeking their pleasures in the open air. But then another strange thing happened. The gods may be powerful, but they are not omnipotent. What they had made, it turned out, they could not wholly unmake; the appetite for work, learning, and beauty they had awakened in these miserable humans continued to flicker, like a tiny flame, in shepherd and shepherdess. At first, they were only uneasy; soon they became unhappy, feeling some great loss and some great need. With painful effort—as men who have broken their limbs learn to walk again as if they were small children—they came to recognized that they had been robbed of some very precious things. Slowly, with many false starts and after many disheartening moments, they succeeded in reconstructing what had happened. And so they went to Zeus and begged him to give them back their learning, that they might again exercise their intelligence. Zeus heard them out with unaccustomed gravity, and then warned them, just as gravely, that he might give them what they wanted—to their eternal regret. "Nothing will come easily to you," he said. "You will find responsibility a heavy burden on you. You will find that every bright new invention has its shadow side; that your conquests will often enough be illusory; that you will know more only to feel less, permit yourselves greater hopes only to experience greater disappointments. Just as we discovered that we could not restore your original innocence, but merely give you back your ignorance without your peace of mind, you will discover that the innocence and ignorance you long for will no longer be possible to you, no matter how hard you try."

Shepherd and shepherdess listened politely, patiently, but their minds were made up. They insisted that civilization was worth the cost, and the gods gave them their wish. The couple departed from Olympus hand in hand, safe, yet laden down with their knowledge. And ever since then every advance has meant a retreat, all progress has caused new, hitherto unimagined difficulties, all that is good in life on earth has been bought at an exorbitant price. The historical work of the Enlightenment, with its achievements and its failures, illustrates the truth of my myth.

ERASMUS: A charming fable with a worthy moral. It might

have done the philosophes some good; it might have made them a little less naïve, a little less optimistic, than they were.

VOLTAIRE: We philosophes optimistic! This is the oldest, and remains the most persistent, slander against the Enlightenment. If we were optimists at all, we were not fatuous ones. Have you ever read the *Lettres Persanes* of Montesquieu? or the essays of Hume? or the political dialogues of Wieland—even those he wrote before the French Revolution which so frightened poor little Gibbon? or the essay on progress by my unfortunate young friend Condorcet? He was, I suppose, the greatest optimist among us all—his hopes were swollen and, I fear, a little unphilosophical—but even he had a keen eye for the sufferings of the past, the inadequacies of the present, and the inescapable limitations on the future. Have you, for that matter, read *me*? "If this is the best of all possible worlds, what are the others like?" is, among all my remarks, my favorite.

ERASMUS: You will never persuade me that you and your Enlightenment are innocent of fathering the pernicious theory of progress—

LUCIAN: Fathering? The idea of progress was an invention of Christian dreamers; there were, through the centuries, Christian optimists who saw the course of man's life as a progress toward redemption. Only we pagans knew how to be true pessimists.

ERASMUS: Well, if not fathering, at least encouraging: the theory of progress made progress only in the Enlightenment. After two thousand years of sensible and appropriate seriousness— broken occasionally by mystical exaltation—the Enlightenment turned men's minds to foolish notions of original innocence, foolish confidence in man's capacity to reform himself and his institutions, in a word, foolish optimism. I have long enjoyed your *Candide,* Voltaire, like everyone else—have I not told you? I much admire your fictions—but you cannot make me believe that the despairing cry you put into Candide's mouth represents a dominant, or even prominent, mood in your movement, or even in yourself. If we were to take responsibility for everything we make our dramatic creations say, there would be an end to literature.

VOLTAIRE: I would feel easier about your ambiguous compliment to my fictions if you did not insist on classifying as fictions what I offered as objective reporting or truthful history. I need hardly tell you that, like you, I reject the vulgar kind of reading that identifies the literary creator with his creatures. But, unlike you, I am sure that what we believed—like the original innocence of man—was not foolish; and what was foolish—like the theory of inevitable progress—we did not believe. If I did not exclaim over your delightful fable, Lucian, that was not because I did not enjoy it, but because it taught me nothing new. Lucian's fable—and other stories, like the myth of Prometheus, and Herodotus' story about King Croesus—illustrates in dramatic form something that we, in the Enlightenment, firmly believed about the way of the world. Let me call it, for want of a better term, the law of compensation. We all believed, more or less strongly, that culture reaches a certain peak and then inevitably declines.

LUCIAN: Don't tell me you believed in the historical cycles we ancients believed in. I should have thought that you would have scorned them as just another antique superstition.

VOLTAIRE: We did not have a theory of historical cycles—we really had no historical theories of that kind at all. We simply saw an ebb and flow in experience. "Everything has its limits," I said. "Genius has but one century; after that, everything must degenerate." And Hume said, "No advantages in this world are pure and unmixed." And Montesquieu said it before us all: "Almost all the nations of the world travel this circle: to begin with, they are barbarous; they become conquerors and civilized nations; this civilization permits them to grow, and they become refined; refinement enfeebles them, and they return to barbarism." Do you want more? I could quote Condillac, or Wieland—by the hour—or Kant on the heavy price of progress, on the dubious quality of all advances, on the slowness and difficulty with which every step toward civilization must be fought for, and on the ease with which civilization retreats. But I think I have made my point.

ERASMUS: Your quotations are impressive but not convincing. After all, you did get the reputation of being optimists—you yourself call it the oldest and most persistent slander against you—and you cannot explain away the near-unanimity of your critics as partisanship, malice, or sheer ignorance.

LUCIAN: Erasmus is right, Voltaire. So many readers cannot be simply, certainly not wholly, wrong.

VOLTAIRE: But the evidence I gave you cannot be simply, or wholly, wrong either.

ERASMUS: I accept it for what it is worth. I only doubt that it is worth much. You conveniently forgot to quote the philosophe—our friend Gibbon—who said that it is unlikely that civilization will ever relapse into its original barbarism, or the philosophe—your friend

Diderot—who said that culture might change countries but would never decline, or the philosophes—and there were many—who said that ultimately reason and humanity would win out.

VOLTAIRE: Lucian anticipated my answer: the Enlightenment did not believe in cycles. We believed, with Lucian's shepherd and shepherdess, that progress is slow and hard, but that it is possible and always worth working for. We understood that the pace, the quality, of progress have varied from time to time and from place to place, and that there were decades, sometimes long centuries, when there was no progress at all. We knew that even when there *was* progress, it was never the automatic working of fate, or a gift of the gods, or a chimera dangling before men's infatuated eyes, but the fruit of labor and of thought. In fact, it was philosophies like ours that made progress possible—it is precisely this conviction that gave our thought its energy. In general, we in the Enlightenment did not subscribe to theories of progress at all—Turgot and Condorcet, often called representative, were exceptions—but we saw enough progress in history to give us heart; and we expected progress in the future, provided that men followed our methods and adopted our goals. If you must call us optimists, call us moderate, skeptical optimists.

LUCIAN: Well, be candid: looking back on your time from the perspective of two centuries and with the detachment of an immortal, do you find that even in your "moderate, skeptical optimism" you were, so to speak, not moderate enough?

VOLTAIRE: I confess I am torn between what I now see and what I still hope. I take comfort in the implausibility of truth. Does not science teach us to distrust the reports of our senses, and our observation? Common sense shows that the sun moves round the earth, science demonstrates that common sense is wrong. Observation shows that the world today is a miserable pile of mud, a sink of stupidity and crime, a wearisome catalogue of missed opportunities, but may not the sciences of man and society eventually prove this observation wrong? What we are witnessing in the twentieth century may be an aberration, the panicked response to overly rapid change, the detour that will eventually lead to the straight way, the last supreme effort by the mortally wounded beast of unreason.

ERASMUS: Your faith in progress remains as touching today as it was two hundred years ago. Admit it: the most thoughtful are rejecting your facile philosophy of hope and taking on the heavy burden of despair.

VOLTAIRE: I see nothing heavy in that burden—it is not a sign of insight but a symptom of self-indulgence. It is always easier to despair than to hope. Despair is a form of laziness.

LUCIAN: That is shallow psychology; say, rather, laziness is a form of despair. Inaction is the appropriate response to a hopeless situation. If we were pessimists in antiquity, that was because we lived in circumstances in which the world had power over us, and we little power over the world. If men in the twentieth century are pessimists once again—and doubly pessimists, having in their memories the fair shape of hope—it is for the same reason.

VOLTAIRE: But just as you were pessimists because your time would let you be nothing else, we were men of good hope because our time urged hope upon us. We were cheered by progress in science, in manners, in humaneness, in knowledge, and by what appeared to progress in medicine. Best of all, as men of letters we took the improvement in the condition of literary men—we were freer, wealthier, more respectable than our predecessors—as indicative of a general improvement. For us in the Enlightenment, progress was an experience before it became a program. And this, just by the way, confirms the claim we have always made: we were realistic interpreters of our time.

LUCIAN: Even if that were true, you were in any case unsuccessful prophets. Moderate as you were, you made at least three miscalculations: You thought that, no matter how slowly, reason would eventually triumph. You thought that science, reason's favorite offspring, would be used for man's benefit. And you thought that when science was so used, whenever ignorance and superstition and disease were conquered, men would be happier than they had been before.

VOLTAIRE: When I was a boy and first learned about government and the state, I thought that laws were like repairs on a watch, or corrections in a drawing; they were ways of perfecting the imperfect in obedience to a static model. And I thought in my innocence that the need for laws and lawmakers would steadily diminish, and eventually disappear, once all the flaws had been eliminated, all the distortions corrected. It was only much later that the essentially dynamic, forever unfinished nature of social life dawned on me. Then I came to see the perpetual need for legislative action, the perpetual need for social criticism, in a word, the perpetual need for philosophes.

ERASMUS: However you twist it, the predictions you made, or

your followers made on the basis of your writings, have on the whole not been confirmed. The decline of superstition has resulted not in the diminution of unreason but in its shift to other fields; unreason has found new forms of expression—nationalism, imperialism, fascism, bolshevism. Unreason has taken its revenge on you men of reason by becoming cannier and more bloodthirsty than ever before.

VOLTAIRE: I wish humanity well enough to wish that I could crush you with my reply. But sadly I must concede that you are right. Reason has moved more slowly, and conquered fewer areas, than we thought it would. But we never equated knowledge with virtue.

ERASMUS: You didn't? I thought that this was precisely what you did.

VOLTAIRE: Not at all. Diderot said—

ERASMUS: Very well. Spare me your quotations.

VOLTAIRE: We thought that knowledge and virtue were friends, not synonyms. We knew enough about science to know that learning can be abused by an exclusive caste to its own advantage—even Condorcet knew that. We knew enough about statesmanship to know that knowledge can be pressed into the service of the most evil designs—Montesquieu, Bentham, and, I feel compelled to add, Gibbon analyzed the stratagems of rulers at length and with great subtlety.

ERASMUS: Perhaps. But you did not really expect that the natural sciences, of which you were so enamoured, would be systematically employed for the sake of private profit or general destruction; or that the social sciences, in which you placed such extravagant hopes, would be systematically employed to induce men to want what they did not need, choose what would do them harm, reward their exploiters and cheer their oppressors.

VOLTAIRE: True, we did not really expect that—though I must insist that it was only to the extent that the natural and the social sciences departed from our critical principles that they became instruments of evil. But I must admit that we underestimated man's obtuseness, his perversity, his positive love of disaster.

ERASMUS: And you were just as wrong about man's happiness. Look about you. At your prompting, modern reformers liberated merchants and manufacturers from those hateful medieval constraints—as you called them—and to what end? Freedom only gave them unprecedented opportunities to enrich themselves, to exploit their workingmen, to corrupt the officials appointed to watch over them, and to drown the world in shoddy goods. High-minded public servants—your followers!—built houses for the poor, only to see the new dwellings degraded into hovels as horrible as the old tenements. Humanitarians freed the slaves, and freedmen riot in the streets. Liberal empires gave independence to countries they had grown ashamed of oppressing—it was your philosophy, you know, that made them ashamed—and the new nations have used their independence to demonstrate a frightful ferocity and a total incapacity to govern themselves. Well-meaning educators constructed schools, printed books, forced education on everyone, disseminated culture and information in attractive and unprecedented ways, all in quantities wholly unimaginable in my, and even in your, day—all in vain. The plebs continue to prefer trash to quality, vulgarity to refinement, the fashionable to the enduring, and they have committed crimes by the books their teachers had taught them to read. Statesmen learned—you taught them!—to be humane to criminals and lenient with children. What happened? Criminals have remained criminals, and children have become delinquents; ideas like responsibility, hard work, and self-respect have suffered ridicule, and almost disappeared from the world. Look at the cities: all the ingenuity employed to make cities—the glory, the repository, of civilization!—more delightful has made them into uninhabitable rabbit warrens, where the water is disgusting, the air lethal, and the street unsafe. It is not that progress has exacted its cost: progress has made life intolerable. Scientists have improved men's diet, physicians have lengthened men's lives, inventors have lightened men's labor, men of good will have ensured men more leisure than they have ever had in history. But while the quantity of life on earth has grown—when it is not being decimated by modern mass war—the quality of life has deteriorated. And could you, in your most oppressive nightmares, have dreamt of the Nazis, who applied all the resources of scientific cunning to degrade, torment, and finally to murder men—and women and children as well—by the millions, in the most revolting ways, compelling hapless men to select their friends for slaughter, and mothers to point out their children to executioners, depopulating villages and cities through large-scale reprisals for single acts of rebellion, through bestial medical experiments, diabolical tortures, until many of their victims would die of sheer heartbreak standing in their own excrement?

VOLTAIRE: No: I could not have dreamt it. The Marquis de

Sade, that madman who mouthed our slogans and defiled our ideas, could have dreamt it, but not I. You overwhelm me. Much of what you say is untrue: you do not really suppose, do you, that your cities were any safer, any healthier, any more civilized than the cities of the twentieth century? Much of what you say is unjust: the unwashed are not incapable of instruction—I saw that even in my own day; and we must be patient with the freedmen—we gave them much to riot about. But you are right about modern barbarism, barbarism all the more appalling because it followed upon such high hopes—hopes that we were not alone to harbor! Still, not even the Nazis could kill the spirit of decency, indignation, and courage. There were Jews who rebelled, Dutchmen and Danes who helped them; there were even a few decent Germans.

ERASMUS: To say, as you just have, that there is some good in man, and to find very little more to say, is to join the company of Christians. Four and a half centuries ago, I chronicled man's folly; imagine how much more material I would have now. Man is not the rational but the insatiable animal: satisfy one of his desires, and ten dissatisfactions arise. Deprive him of what he wants, and he will be miserable; give him what he wants, and he will be miserable still. Seneca's Medea is not a caricature of humanity but its fitting representative: man, as she said, sees the better and chooses the worse.

VOLTAIRE: And do you suppose that we did not know, or did not wholly accept, Seneca's famous line? Diderot said—

ERASMUS: Yes, yes. You honored the saying in words, but you did not really understand it. If you had understood it, you would not have raised men's hopes with your philosophy; you have only plunged him into despair. You aroused expectations that could not be fulfilled—the very height of irresponsibility.

VOLTAIRE: While you Christians prevent men from exercising their powers—the very height of wickedness.

ERASMUS: No: it would have been cheaper and more charitable to do nothing; it would have been better by far to keep alive in men's hearts the consolations of true faith. Gibbon was right to complain of those who deprived men of religion, wrong only to include me among the destroyers of celestial hope—I only tried to clear away the weeds, that true religion might blossom. Men are by all accounts as confused, as irrational, as bored—in a word, as unhappy—as ever. Consider that strange modern phenomenon: the revolt of the prosperous.

VOLTAIRE: There is still plenty of poverty to go around.

ERASMUS: True, but the revolt of the wretched is not surprising, nor is it a difficulty for your philosophy. The misery of those who have enough *is* a difficulty. You thought that once you give men enough, they will be happy. You were wrong. And that proves the ineradicable contradictions in man, conflicts that no amount of new inventions, better food, or critical thinking can resolve, the unappeasable hunger that is the consequence of original sin.

VOLTAIRE: The revolt of the prosperous, as you call it, is neither a mystery to me nor a difficulty for the philosophy of the Enlightenment. They do not have enough—by definition.

ERASMUS: Because God has left their lives, and, with Him, purpose. That is why man needs religion: to keep sane, not merely in a terrifying universe, but amidst a mad species—his own. Lucian said that you miscalculate. You did far worse: the philosophy of the Enlightenment was a false philosophy from beginning to end, a tower of self-deception built on the swamp of rationalism. No wonder it has come crashing down about our ears, and yours.

VOLTAIRE: The twentieth century has its miseries. Every century has its miseries. We never doubted that it was so, and we never promised that the day would come when it would not be so. Yes: we underestimated man's capacity for diabolical ingenuity, but for the rest, our philosophy made room for fallibility, for stupidity and viciousness. We all said so—I said so over and over again. Is it my fault that my laments were not taken seriously just because I was witty about them? My wit, if I may say so, was a sign not of callousness but of courage. We were far from insensitive to man's need for consolation and the difficulties of enforcing social discipline. That, in fact, is why we took so much interest in social religion, that catalogue of noble lies which most of us thought essential for the illiterate—most of us, for we argued about this matter as we argued about practically everything. One thing we agreed on: we were too self-reliant, too grown up, to need lies for ourselves. Yes: there were times when we felt exceedingly gloomy and would say the kind of thing you just said. But, as reasonable men, we grew ashamed of our self-pity and went back to work. You know, when George Bernard Shaw wanted to give expression to views like yours, he put them into the mouth of the devil, for they are seductive and pernicious. To find nothing but evil in man's unaided efforts, and to see nothing but prospects for further gloom unless man sells himself into slavery or prays himself into a second childhood, is to invite passivity and make future disasters inevitable. We erred in our predictions, but if erroneous predictions damn a philosophy, every philosophy and theology alike would be damned— though all would not be damned alike. True: some of the preachers' predictions have been fulfilled: there have been war and pestilence and misery. But their prophecies were self-fulfilling prophecies. If we predicted that men would be happy yet they are not happy, I am sorry about it, for their sake, but I cannot accept responsibility for it—it is not our fault. Preachers predicted that men would be unhappy, and they saw to it that they would be right. For misery has come not from our philosophy but from that of our adversaries. We fought with all our strength, all our lives, the cruelty and irrationality that we saw around us. At most you can accuse us of ineffectuality, but of nothing more.

ERASMUS: You are making too much of what I said. No one here is accusing you of the crimes of the twentieth century.

VOLTAIRE: There are those who do. There are those who accuse us of fathering modern totalitarianism. I told you: we have been called fanatics, and the fathers of fanatics. It is not true! When the Nazis occupied Paris, they melted down my statue. I suppose they needed the metal to make guns, but I like to think that they could not bear the spirit of the Enlightenment.

ERASMUS: Confess it! These attacks are actually very convenient for you. By dwelling on unreasonable criticisms you divert attention from reasonable criticisms. You cannot evade us so easily. Your failure to foresee the course of events is not a casual failure; it reflects back on your philosophy as a whole, and suggests a profound lack of vision.

LUCIAN: Precisely. The point is not that your hopes have by and large not been realized. The point is that your hopes were in themselves unreasonable. And when I put it this way, I think, we have reached the core of the problem of optimism: reason, and its powers, played a far too prominent role in your philosophy.

VOLTAIRE: Contrary to its reputation, the Enlightenment was not an Age of Reason but a Revolt against Rationalism.

ERASMUS: A slogan, no more. You dare not deny that reason was your final arbiter, your greatest hope, your highest ideal.

VOLTAIRE: Why should I deny what I am proud to affirm? Our revolt against rationalism was not a revolt against reason. It was a revolt against the Scholastics' love of words and the metaphysicians' love of vast constructions. We attacked reason in the name of reason. The kind of reason we cherished was in touch with reality, it lived on things rather than words, sought accuracy rather than neatness. It was scientific method: searching, self-critical, modest, effective. And it was not hostile to the passions—on the contrary, we philosophes recognized the power and admired the work of the passions—

LUCIAN: Within reason—

VOLTAIRE: If you like: within reason. When Hume said that reason is, and ought to be, the slave of the passions, he put it a little strongly, but he was making our case. Diderot said—

LUCIAN: Yes. For all of that, you misjudged the tenacity of unreason—its pervasiveness, its persistence, its imperviousness to rational control. The course of modern history should prove that empirically.

ERASMUS: And the findings of modern psychology have proved it scientifically.

VOLTAIRE: Are you speaking of Sigmund Freud?

ERASMUS: I am. The man is positively Christian in his pessimism. He has shown conclusively that man is inherently a sinner filled with murderous thoughts, a fallen creature whose most profound ideas and feelings are inaccessible to him, and hence incorrigible by good intentions or rational will. The whole corpus of his work is one large Praise of Folly. And it exposes your philosophy to be naïve, shallow, wholly out of date.

VOLTAIRE: That's larceny! You are stealing our man!

LUCIAN: You did anticipate him, of course: the study of dreams, the Oedipus complex, the sexual origins of moral notions . . .

VOLTAIRE: True. But as I said before: I do not like to rest my case on anticipations. Freud belongs to the family of philosophes not because we anticipated him but because, whatever he discovered, he discovered with our methods, within the range of our intellectual style. His view of man, like ours, was secular; his explanations of man's aggressiveness drew not on some fairy tale about man's disobedience to God but on purely natural causes; his system was not metaphysics but science.

ERASMUS: But is not Freud's notion of aggression merely a secularized version of original sin?

VOLTAIRE: It is not, it is the fruit of clinical observation. He studied dreams, he was not a dreamer.

LUCIAN: Perhaps. But why, of all twentieth-century figures, concentrate on Freud?

VOLTAIRE: You brought him up, not I. Though I am pleased that you did. For Freud, whom you take to be the nemesis of the philosophes, was, in fact, our most distinguished representative in the twentieth century. To grasp this is to grasp not merely the meaning of Freud but the meaning of the Enlightenment. Those who invoke Freud without reading him forget that his *attitude* toward reason coincides with ours, even if his *estimation* of it rather differed from ours. And they forget that he concentrated on unreason not to celebrate but to defeat it.

LUCIAN: He dredged up many awful mysteries: the unconscious, the sexual wishes of children.

VOLTAIRE: Not to wallow in them, but to understand them. He believed, as we did, and, I'll admit, with sounder evidence, that reason is weak and divided, but he wished to strengthen and to unify it. He believed, as we did (if I may cite the New Testament), that we should know the truth, and that the truth would make us free. "Science is no illusion," he said. "But it would be an illusion to suppose that we could get anywhere else what it cannot give us." If this is not Enlightenment thinking, I do not know what is.

LUCIAN: Yet he was convinced that love and aggression would always tear man apart and make him, as long as he lives, at best uneasy, at worst miserable.

VOLTAIRE: He denied that complete happiness is possible. So did we. Neither he nor we ever asked for immobile serenity. We asked for the happiness of activity, of enjoyment amidst the risks of life. Freud said: Where id was, there shall ego be. We put it differently. We said: Men can learn to reconcile freedom and discipline and to reduce their sufferings. Do you know, Lucian, when you were telling us your fable, I kept thinking of Freud? He would have liked it, for the same reason that I liked it: he knew, as we knew, that civilization is a burden; that it demands self-denial for the sake of self-fulfillment, the capacity to postpone gratifications and to moderate one's desires. But he also knew, as we know, that it is a glorious burden, a destiny that man must accept if he wants to be a man. He wanted to reduce the burdens of civilization, to identify and eliminate those that had been imposed by false moral and religious notions, but he never for a moment believed that all burdens were unnecessary. Yet while we thought that total, infantile contentment was both unattainable and undesirable, we thought that we must never cease to reduce suffering. We believed that to feed someone who is hungry is to make him happy, if only for an hour; to free someone from a superstition is to lift an oppression from his shoulders, if only one among many; to exercise one's mind and gratify one's body freely is better than to be chained to timidity and asceticism. To say that all these things do not make men ultimately happy is not to say that their pursuit is not worthwhile, or that their absence would not make men even less happy. To turn away from reform because it does not make men perfect is like hating your parents because you have discovered that they are not omnipotent. These are simple truths, incomprehensible only to jaded voluptuaries, disillusioned radicals, or gloomy fanatics. No, no: if the Enlightenment had never existed, the world, miserable as it is, would be far more miserable still.

ERASMUS: This is precisely what I find it impossible to believe. You keep telling us that you philosophes were realists, yet we have compelled you to admit that history has proved you wrong over and over again. No: you were not realists at all: you were Utopians.

VOLTAIRE: I know how much it irritates you when I convert a criticism into a commendation, but at the risk of annoying you once again, let me say that I accept the charge of Utopianism with pleasure, though I interpret the term in my own way. I need not tell you—were you not, after all, Thomas More's friend?—that there are many reasons for Utopianism. Some Utopias, to be sure, read like fancies and wishes in the form of a story; they are like the little fairy tales a child tells himself to still the terror of the dark. But there are other kinds of Utopias, far more earthbound than these, the offspring not of night but of day. These Utopias describe conditions that, though they are not yet real, may become real—they show the potential as actuality. They are social criticisms or social programs pleasingly disguised as Oriental tales or adventures in imaginary kingdoms. Our Utopianism was of this second kind—shall I call it realistic Utopianism? No reformer can do without this kind of Utopian thinking; to do without it is to be like Pangloss, to hold that what is must be and need not—no, cannot—be improved. That kind of complacency is simply another form of despair.

I am reminded of an old story—not freshly invented like Lucian's fable, but a tale told many times. Once there was a prosperous farmer who had three sons. He lived long and worked hard, and when time came for him to die, he gathered his sons around and told them that he was leaving them all his land and all his savings—a large chest filled with gold coins buried on his property. Then he died, without telling them where the chest lay buried. The three sons began to search for it. They turned over the ground with great care, as they had always done, but more diligently, more thoroughly, than they had ever done before. They searched and searched, dug and dug, and they never found the legacy their father promised them. But, as you have guessed by now, there was no chest; there were no gold coins; there was only the fertile land. And in the course of digging for this imaginary treasure, the sons gathered up a very real treasure, for with their incessant labor they magnificently cultivated the soil and produced richer crops than ever. Thus the unattainable may serve as a guide and a goad to the attainable. We must cultivate our garden, even if it is only the garden of hope.

III History and Purpose

The following four essays deal with a variety of advantages and disadvantages to the study of history. They range from G. R. Elton's attack on Carr and Plumb for arbitrary adherence to the idea of progress to Page Smith's call for a universal history which would serve the moral purpose of giving mankind a sense of unity, a sense of belonging to the same family. Elton, while rejecting the idea of progress, finds value in the study of history because it gives the historian and his reader "emotional and intellectual satisfaction." In addition, the historian plays a part in promoting the general culture of the society in which he works and lives. History also teaches us about human behavior and, most importantly, it trains the human mind in that noble enterprise, the seeking of truth.

David Hackett Fischer writes that history by providing us with background can help us to understand better the problems of today and to predict to some extent the trends and directions of the future. Perhaps he is thinking of books like Robert Heilbronner's *The Future as History,* which weaves past, present, and future together in such a way that we begin to perceive the nature of the world in which we will live out our lives. Fischer also sees history contributing to the development of social science theory and helping people learn about men whose life styles are different from their own.

This section includes Herbert Butterfield's essay on the dangers of studying history. Butterfield is worried about what Arthur Schlesinger has recently called the tyranny of the past. So often the historical record reveals how men have been trapped by false analogies, by "frozen" history that hampers creative thinking about the problems of the present. Butterfield's cure for "frozen history" is a deeper and continuing study of the past that transmutes the record of man's triumphs and failures into "wisdom and experience."

G. R. ELTON
The Purpose of History

SAVING THE SOCIAL SCIENTIST from himself (and society from the social scientist) may be a worthy reason for studying history, but not many historians are likely to regard themselves simply as specialized nursemaids and Samaritans. Some feel that they must discover that in the past which will help men to understand their present and future. The words, "the purpose of history," have strictly two meanings: they can refer either to the purpose of the historical process or to the purpose to be served by the historian in studying it. In practice, however, the meanings are close to each other and tend to merge. The historian who thinks that he has discerned the future towards which the past is moving conceives it his duty to instruct his readers accordingly. It becomes the purpose of his study to elucidate and demonstrate the purposes of the historical process. At the same time, it is true that even historians who do not claim to see anything significant in the way things have happened are bound to have had a purpose in mind when they entered upon their studies. No one reads or writes history in a fit of total absentmindedness, though a fair amount of history has been written by people whose minds seem in part to have been on other things.

Is there a purpose in history? Mr. Carr grows very scornful at the expense of an honest man like H. A. L. Fisher, who in a famous sentence explained that he could see none.[1] Mr. Carr is surely right to denounce the theory of the pure accident, the theory that history is just one damn thing after another. Though in a sense, of course, the sequence of events is just that, it becomes history only when marshalled by the interpretative human intelligence. This is not to overlook the importance of accidents, which do happen (though Mr. Carr would seem to suppose that they can be written out of history), but to stress that in the understanding of the past the accident is just another point to be explained, considered and accommodated. Accidents may affect the course of events, but the historian, in his analysis, must not be accident-prone. No historian, including Fisher, has in fact ever treated his subject as though it were entirely without

[1]E. H. Carr, *What is History?* (Penguin edition, 1964), 43, 100.

From *The Practice of History* by G. R. Elton, (New York: Thomas Y. Crowell Company, 1967), pp. 39-50. Reprinted by permission of Sydney University Press.

meaning; if he had, he would have been unable to write. What is really at issue is whether one may discern a larger purpose, whether things produce effects that are continuous and, up to a point, predictable. When Mr. Carr, and others, seek a purpose in history, they are trying to fill the vacuum created when God was removed from history. Even historians who hold that God reveals himself in history would not today feel entitled to use him by way of explanation, but the temperament which demands a certain guidance from the past by way of illumination for the future—the religious temperament—continues to exist among historians and produces theories of the course of history which seek this prophetic purpose.

There are in the main two ways of subordinating history to prophecy, the circular and the linear; and both have an ancient, respectable, and largely pre-professional history. The first supposes that societies grow and decay, to be replaced by others which follow much the same pattern. The other view supposes that the sum total of the past moves in a straight line of progress; though it will often allow that lapses, back-trackings, and lateral movements may interrupt the main line of advance, it nevertheless insists that such a main line can be discovered and plotted. Linear theories are not necessarily optimistic, but their vocabulary (progress, advance) tends to inculcate a conviction that things not only move along a line but move towards an improvement.

Today's best known cyclical theory is that developed by A. J. Toynbee, and it is not necessary at this date to demonstrate once again how little his vast edifice has to do with the facts of the past.[2] Linear theories are certainly commoner, and Mr. Carr as well as Professor J. H. Plumb have recently entered eloquent pleas for a return to the allegedly discredited notion of progress, the notion that things get better in sum, however much the detail may get worse at times.[3] They both want historians to write to this purpose because they seem to regard it as the scholar's function not only to describe change but also to advocate it; the historian should be the prophet of

---

[2]E.g. Pieter Geyl, *Debates with Historians* (The Hague, 1954), chs. 5-8. Toynbee may have contributed something useful to the study of history when he directed attention to areas and times little studied by the ordinary English historian. Even this is not altogether certain; as for his interpretative scheme and his treatment of evidence, they do nothing but harm to those who allow themselves to regard them with respect.

[3]Carr, *What is History?*, ch. 5; J. H. Plumb, ed., *Crisis in the Humanities* (Harmondsworth, 1964), 24 ff.

an intelligent radicalism. Both abominate nostalgia about the past and wish to use history to teach men reliance on their powers to better themselves and their world. Mr. Carr seems to think this right because he believes that this is the lesson of history; Dr. Plumb adds a fear that unless historians will attend to this task of propaganda they will cease to be read and cease to play any part in their societies. Both manifestly confuse the problem of why men should be made to learn about history with the problem of the meaning of the past; or rather, to them only the particular meaning they extract from the past justifies the pursuit of history as an activity of the scholar and teacher.[4]

Let it be said at once that the underlying convictions behind these demands are in part sound. Historians cannot exist in a vacuum; they live in the society of men, influence it whether they like it or not, and should therefore be conscious of what they are about. But they should also be conscious of the dangers they run. It is all very well to regret the day when history was "philosophy teaching by example," the day when historians thought themselves the moral preceptors of a ruling class and, aping Plutarch, used their science to instil high principles in their pupils. We cannot return to the attitude which produced a *Mirror for Magistrates* to show, by using historical instances, how those who offend against the divine order always come to a bad end;[5] and if we could return to it I doubt if many of us would. Yet such schoolmasterly ambitions are at the back of Dr. Plumb's mind. When we take our more sophisticated history into the market place and the pulpit, we assume a task of some danger and must be almost pedantically careful of our integrity. Few, I daresay, would wish to deride the conviction, expressed by that not uneminent American historian, Conyers Read, who some years ago told the American Historical Association that "the social responsibilities of the historian" involved him in the defence of "values."[6] But how many would agree with him that those values must be those of American civilization and democracy, that the historian plays a part in "total war"? Since no man in society, said Read, can escape some form of social control, the historian must "accept and endorse such

---

[4]Plumb, *Crisis in the Humanities*, 43: historians' "explanations of the past should lead to an explanation of it for their time and generation, so that, by explaining, man's control over his future may be increased."

[5]*The Mirror for Magistrates* (best edition by Lily B. Campbell, Oxford, 1938), a collection of cautionary tales mostly in verse, first published in 1559.

[6]*American Historical Review*, 1v (1949-50), 275 ff.

controls as are essential for the preservation of our way of life." Calling, in a fiery peroration, for the suppression of inconvenient facts, he cried that if the historian will not offer "assurance that mankind's present position is on the highway and not on some dead end, then mankind will seek for assurance in a more positive alternative, whether it be offered from Rome or from Moscow."

Conyers Read was expressing too frankly what others might wish to think, though it should be recorded that he was fully and firmly answered by a fellow-historian from a sounder American tradition.[7] Yet he was neither fool nor knave, and he had thought as hard about his professional purpose as Dr. Plumb, with his more radical predilections, has done. Read's case makes plain that the historian's function in society cannot be reduced to that of a preacher, whether he preaches the excellence of all that is, or the necessity of reform, or the desirability of revolution. If he is to be a good preacher he must rest his case upon a faith; but if he is to be a good historian he must question his own faith and admit some virtue in the beliefs of others. If he allows the task of choosing among the facts of the past to deteriorate into suppression of what will not serve the cause, he loses all right to claim weight for his opinions. An historian may be an ex-businessman, as Read was, or like Gibbon an ex-captain of grenadiers, but when he pronounces upon economics or strategy we have a duty to judge him as an historian, and only as an historian. And there the simplicities of the preacher's call at once collapse.

The trouble with all these theories about "the meaning of history" is twofold: the great range of contemporaneous events and the shortness of historical time permit of no convincing demonstration one way or the other. It is never difficult to see purpose or direction in a sequence of historical events if one confines oneself sufficiently, especially if one limits one's gaze to the winners in any conflict. Take the seventeenth century in England: few collections of years have had more "purpose" inflicted upon them. If one looks at the struggles of the Stuart kings with their Parliaments, one readily writes the century's history as the story of growing liberty. If one concentrates on the problems of production and distribution, one sees the age as one of expanding trade (decline of liberty) for certain sectors of the population. If one looks at men's minds, one comes up with an explanation based on the secularization of thought

[7]Howard K. Beale, "The Professional Historian: His Theory and His Practice," *Pacific Historical Review*, xxii (1953), 227 ff.; see esp. 254 f.

and the development of the scientific approach. There is no obvious or provable connection between these lines of "progress," and the historian who proceeds to make one—who, for instance, argues that political liberty was a precondition of intellectual advance and economic enterprise—can no more prove his case than the historian who refuses to see any such links. Moreover, he would be ignoring other things, such as the influence of the Reformation or the central position of land-ownership. And then there is seventeenth-century France where political liberty on the whole declined, scientific thought flourished in different conditions and in its own, quite different, fashion, and economic life followed a different line towards increasing wealth as well as increasing strain. There is the rest of seventeenth-century Europe, not to mention Moghul India, Ch'ing China, or the kingdoms of tropical Africa. How can one possibly bring these varieties of experience into a scheme depending on a single line of progress? One can do it only by seizing on some development in subsequent history and elevating that to the sole significant position. This is not the legitimate activity of selecting the meaningful; it is the idle activity of forgetting the inconvenient. As for the shortness of historical time, I have already pointed out that recorded history amounts to no more than about two hundred generations. Even if there is a larger purpose in history, it must be said that we cannot really expect so far to be able to extract it from the little bit of history we have.

Still, Mr. Carr and Dr. Plumb claim to be able to discern it. They deny that they have fallen victim to the cruder fallacies of progress doctrines, those that identify what is with what must be, see in the past only the triumph of the present, and thus guarantee that high degree of self-satisfaction which was characteristic of whig historiography in England. Historians who adhere to a belief in progress are always liable to lapse from description into approval, to condemn the losers as blind or wicked, and to set the judicious garland of historical necessity on the victor's head. Mr. Carr and Dr. Plumb try to remember the variety of the past and claim that they give it due weight in the story. They both assert that they are not determinists in the simple sense of believing that the processes of history could not have worked out differently from the way they did. In this respect, however, it is difficult to treat them as companions. Dr. Plumb seems less concerned with the question whether progress is really the lesson to be learned from history than with his demand that it should be the lesson taught by historians to their own age, in order that the age may feel usefully optimistic. He trembles on the precipice which swallowed up Conyers Read. Mr. Carr wishes to assert that an event like the Russian Revolution not only happened in some measure necessarily (to him, the logic of history brought it about) but in its happening testifies to the necessary improvement of mankind. That is to say, both concede a measure of determinism in their thinking, but Dr. Plumb is not aware that it is there. Both are good enough historians to avoid the more obvious traps of biased selectivity and conditioned prejudice. In Mr. Carr's attitude to the Russian Revolution, and in Dr. Plumb's account of social amelioration, there is not only doctrine but also much sound historical learning. Where they err is not in their history but in their propaganda, in their insistence that only their kind of interpretation will do.

Progress in history is in great part a matter of value judgment, a personal matter, and though every competent historian can discover a measure of necessity in events, none can prove that they are truly determined.[8] If our authors see progress and necessity in history, they are justified in saying so and in trying to persuade others to agree with them. They are not justified in supposing that no one can honestly see things in any other way than in the light of their simplifying handtorch, and I object to their claim that history *must* be understood and proclaimed in their single fashion. For myself, I believe that they are wrong to concentrate so exclusively on the progressive and deterministic elements in the story. All talk about progress, if it does not simply mean change, rests on the assumption that the historian can tell what is better and what worse; but one man's better is usually another man's worse. I agree with Mr. Carr and Dr. Plumb that twentieth-century technology has greatly improved material life. I agree that in England, at least, social attitudes have in many ways grown better, that the nation is less given to violence and cruelty than once it was. I should, however, hesitate before supposing this to be a universal experience; and though, like Dr. Plumb, I am temperamentally hostile to the school of thought which sentimentalizes the past and worships a chocolate-box substitute for the reality, I cannot forget that material progress has often been linked with deterioration, even material deterioration, in the

[8]Cf. Isaiah Berlin, *Historical Inevitability* (London, 1954).

quality of life[9], and that the decline in active cruelty has been accompanied by a decline in active indignation against despotism and arbitrary rule. I do not pretend here to make an assessment or strike a balance, a thing each man must do for himself though the historian can assist him by illuminating the past; I only wish to point out that progress and necessity are doctrines which cannot be derived from, can only be superimposed upon, the study of history. And above all, I do not see why there should be only historians like Mr. Carr and Dr. Plumb, *laudatores temporis futuri,* why they should claim authority for their manifestly highly selective history, and why other points of view should be not so much controverted as despised and condemned.

Does this then mean that there is no very positive purpose in studying history, that it really is only a matter of the student's private satisfaction? Are there no standards by which one may call historians good or bad, adequate or inadequate, right or wrong? I think there are, but they cannot be discovered if the purpose of history is approached from outside the discipline itself. The sort of arguments put forward by Mr. Carr and Dr. Plumb do not arise from their concern with history but from their personal involvement in the present and future of their own society.[10] This is comprehensible and can be creditable, but it in no way helps to explain the purpose of studying history, and it begs the question of what history means. Mr. Carr and Dr. Plumb are, at heart, "whigs," looking into the past for reassurance; they begin with the assumption of a social purpose stated (that the historian must offer to society a demonstration of its power to advance itself) and they then eliminate any use of history which does not contribute to this purpose. For this reason they do fall into the deterministic error of choosing from the variety of history the line of events and detail which leads to their own present position, their preconceived end; everything else, if they do not ignore it, they explain away. The right approach would surely start from the other end. We must first explain in what manner the past can truly be studied—that is, we must accept the despised tenet that

[9]Mr. Carr *(What is History?,* 143 ff.) comes very close to identifying technical progress with the expansion of true reason. One does not have to be a sentimentalist to regard this as a crude and misleading point of view.

[10]I do not, of course, mean to deny that at other times they are also very much concerned with history.

the past must be studied for its own sake—and then enquire whether this study has any contribution to make to the present.

In short, we are once again faced with the autonomy of history: the study of history is legitimate in itself, and any use of it for another purpose is secondary. That secondary use will be laudable or deplorable in proportion as the autonomous purpose has been served well or ill. If I have rather more respect for the progress doctrines of Dr. Plumb or Mr. Carr than I have for the historical racialism of Rosenberg or the historical inevitabilities of Marxism, it is because I think their history better; if I have my reservations about their preferred interpretations, and especially about their prescriptions to other historians, it is because in my view they still ignore far too much about the past. The task of history is to understand the past, and if the past is to be understood it must be given full respect in its own right. And unless it is properly understood, any use of it in the present must be suspect and can be dangerous. One cannot use a corrupt means to a worthy end. And the creation of the sound instrument involves not only obvious things like doing the serious work of study, avoiding anachronism both in interpretation and judgment, devoting attention to the defeated as well as to the victors; it involves, above all, the deliberate abandonment of the present. The historian studying the past is concerned with the later event only in so far as it throws light on the part of the past that he is studying. It is the cardinal error to reverse this process and study the past for the light it throws on the present.

However, it does not in the least follow from this that the study of history, treated as autonomous and justified within itself, has no contribution to make beyond its frontiers. In the first place, let it be remembered that this pursuit of history in its own right is not only morally just but also agreeable. A good many people simply want to know about the past, for emotional or intellectual satisfaction, and the professional historian fulfils a useful "social" function when he helps them to know better. He is also, of course, satisfying his own desire for knowledge, and he also is, after all, a part of society. This might be supposed to reduce the historian to a mere entertainer, but in fact it gives him a cultural role: he contributes to the complex of non-practical activities which make up the culture of a society. When he stimulates and satisfies the imagination he does not differ essentially from the poet or artist, which is not to say that he should be picturesque. There is an emotional satisfaction of a high order to be gained from extending the comprehending intelligence to include the past.

Next, it would certainly be untrue to suppose that history can teach no practical lessons. It enlarges the area of individual experience by teaching about human behaviour, about man in relationship to other men, about the interaction of circumstances and conditions in their effect upon individual and social fortunes. Its lessons are not straightforward didactic precepts, either instructions for action (the search for parallels to a given situation) or universal norms (history teaches that everything progresses, history teaches the triumph—or futility—of moral principles); there is far too much variety about the past, far too much confused singularity about the event, to produce such simple results. Nevertheless, a sound acquaintance with the prehistory of a situation or problem does illumine them and does assist in making present decisions; and though history cannot prophesy, it can often make reasonable predictions. Historical knowledge gives solidity to the understanding of the present and may suggest guiding lines for the future.

Yet these emotional and practical uses of history are not its main contribution to the purposes of man. The study of history is an intellectual pursuit, an activity of the reasoning mind, and, as one should expect, its main service lies in its essence. Like all sciences, history, to be worthy to itself and beyond itself, much concentrate on one thing: the search for truth. Its real value as a social activity lies in the training it provides, the standards it sets, in this singularly human concern. Reason distinguishes man from the rest of creation, and the study of history justifies itself in so far as it assists reason to work and improve itself. Like all rational activities, the study of history, regarded as an autonomous enterprise, contributes to the improvement of man, and it does so by seeking the truth within the confines of its particular province, which happens to be the rational reconstruction of the past. In this larger purpose it has no sort of monopoly, for this it shares with every form of intellectual investigation, but it happens to have certain advantages in that it attracts a wide variety of intelligences, can do its work without too much demand on technical specialization in the learner, and can rest its capacity to train on its capacity to entertain.

In these advantages, which it possesses over both the natural and the social sciences, lie its temptations and perils: absence of technical specialization can lead to lack of rigour, entertainment to meretricious superficiality, variety of appeal to bias and propaganda. But the dangers do not deny the advantages; the possibility of corruption does not cast out the possibility of excellence. Integrity, resting on professional training and professional attitudes, is the safeguard. All historical work which satisfies the conditions of professional competence and integrity fulfils the historian's very important social duty; none that falls short of that standard can be trusted to fulfil any social duty safely, however conscious it may be of its obligations or however earnestly it may preach progress, the goodness of man, or the inevitability of revolutions. The quality of an historian's work must, as I have said, be judged purely by intellectual standards; the same is true of his contribution to society, though moral consequences may well flow from adherence to these principles of the reasoning capacity. It is not the problems they study or the lessons they teach that distinguish the historical sheep from the goats, but only the manner of their study, the precision of their minds, and the degree to which they approximate to the ultimate standards of intellectual honesty and intellectual penetration. *Omnia veritas.*

DAVID HACKETT FISCHER
The Uses of History

> History is not only a particular branch of knowledge, but a particular mode and method of knowledge in other branches.
> —Lord Acton

ANY SERIOUS ATTEMPT to answer the question "What is good history?" leads quickly to another—namely, "What is it good for?" To raise this problem in the presence of a working historian is to risk a violent reaction. For it requires him to justify his own existence, which is particularly difficult for a historian to do—not because his existence is particularly unjustifiable, but because a historian is not trained to justify existences. Indeed, he is trained not to justify them. It is usually enough for him that he exists, and history, too. He

From pp. 307-318 from *Historians' Fallacies: Toward a Logic of Historical Thought* by David Hackett Fischer. Copyright © 1970 by David Hackett Fischer. Reprinted by permission of Harper & Row, Publishers, Inc.

is apt to be impatient with people who doggedly insist upon confronting the question.

Nevertheless, the question must be confronted, because the answer is in doubt. In our own time, there is a powerful current of popular thought which is not merely unhistorical but actively antihistorical as well. Novelists and playwrights, natural scientists and social scientists, poets, prophets, pundits, and philosophers of many persuasions have manifested an intense hostility to historical thought. Many of our contemporaries are extraordinarily reluctant to acknowledge the reality of past time and prior events, and stubbornly resistant to all arguments for the possibility or utility of historical knowledge.

The doctrine of historical relativism was no sooner developed by historians that it was seized by their critics and proclaimed to the world as proof that history-as-actuality is a contradiction in terms, and that history-as-record is a dangerous delusion which is, at best, an irrelevance to the predicament of modern man, and at worst a serious menace to his freedom and even to his humanity. A few of these people even believe, with Paul Valéry, that

> History is the most dangerous product which the chemistry of the mind has concocted. Its properties are well known. It produces dreams and drunkenness. It fills people with false memories, exaggerates their reactions, exacerbates old grievances, torments them in their repose, and encourages either a delirium of grandeur or a delusion of persecution. It makes whole nations bitter, arrogant, insufferable, and vainglorious.[1]

These prejudices have become a major theme of modern literature. Many a fictional protagonist has struggled frantically through six hundred pages to free himself from the past, searching for a sanctuary in what Sartre called "a moment of eternity," and often finding it in a sexual embrace.[2]

In Aldous Huxley's *After Many a Summer Dies the Swan,* Mr. Propter is made to say, "After all, history isn't the real thing. Past time is only evil at a distance; and of course, the study of past time is itself a process in time. Cataloguing bits of fossil evil can never be more than an ersatz for eternity."[3] In the same author's *The Genius*

---

[1] Paul Valéry, *Regards sur le Monde Actuel* (Paris, 1949), p. 43.
[2] Jean Paul Sartre, *The Reprieve* (New York, 1947), p. 352.
[3] Aldous Huxley, *After Many a Summer Dies the Swan,* Harper & Row ed. (New York, 1965), p. 81.

and the Goddess, John Rivers compares history to a "dangerous drug" and dismisses it as a productive discipline of knowledge:

> God isn't the son of memory: He's the son of Immediate Experience. You can't worship a spirit in spirit, unless you do it now. Wallowing in the past may be good literature. As wisdom, it's hopeless. Time Regained is Paradise Lost, and Time Lost is Paradise Regained. Let the dead bury their dead. If you want to live at every moment as it presents itself, you've got to die at every other moment. That's the most important thing I learned.[4]

Some entertaining errors of the same sort appear in John Barth's splendid picaresque novel, *The Sot-Weed Factor,* where, in sixty-five chapters, Clio is ravished as regularly as most of the major characters. In an epilogue, the author writes,

> Lest it be objected by a certain stodgy variety of squint-minded antiquarians that he has in this lengthy history played more fast and loose with Clio, the chronicler's muse, than ever Captain John Smith dared, the Author here posits in advance, by way of surety, three blue-chip replies arranged in order of decreasing relevancy. In the first place be it remembered, as Burlingame himself observed, that we all invent our pasts, more or less, as we go along, at the dictates of Whim and Interest. . . . Moreover, this Clio was already a scarred and crafty trollop when the Author found her; it wants a nice-honed casuist, with her sort, to separate seducer from the seduced. But if, despite all, he is convicted at the Public Bar of having forced what slender virtue the strumpet may make claim to, then the Author joins with pleasure the most engaging company imaginable, his fellow fornicators, whose ranks include the noblest in poetry, prose and politics; condemnation at such a bar, in short, on such a charge, does honor to artist and artifact alike.[5]

Other literati have set their sights on historians, rather than history. Virginia Woolf asserted, "It is always a misfortune to have to call in the services of any historian. A writer should give us direct certainty; explanations are so much water poured with the wine. As it is, we can only feel that these counsels are addressed to ladies in

---

[4]Aldous Huxley, *The Genius and the Goddess,* Bantam Books ed. (New York, 1956), p. 4.

[5]John Barth, *The Sot-Weed Factor,* Grosset and Dunlap ed. (New York, 1964), p. 793.

hoops and gentlemen in wigs—a vanished audience which has learnt its lesson and gone its way and the preacher with it. We can only smile and admire the clothes."[6] Similar sentiments are cast as characterizations of historians in Sartre's *Nausea,* Kingsley Amis's *Lucky Jim,* George Orwell's *1984,* Aldous Huxley's *Antic Hay,* Wyndham Lewis's *Self-Condemned,* Anatole France's *Le Crime de Silvestre Bonnard,* Edward Albee's *Who's Afraid of Virginia Woolf?,* Stanley Elkin's *Boswell,* and Angus Wilson's *Anglo-Saxon Attitudes.* "It's so seldom that Clio can aid the other muses," says one character in the latter work. "Bloody fools, these historians," growls another.[7]

The antihistorical arguments of our own time have infected historians themselves, with serious results. Historical scholarship today is dominated by a generation (born, let us say, between 1900 and 1940) which has lost confidence in its own calling, lost touch with the world in which it lives, and lost the sense of its own discipline. Historians have failed to justify their work to others, partly because they have not even been able to justify it to themselves. Instead, when academic historians explain why they do history, there is a narrow parochialism and petty selfishness of purpose which surpasses rational belief. I have heard five different apologies for history from academic colleagues—five justifications which are functional in the sense that they permit a historian to preserve some rudimentary sense of historicity, but only at the cost of all ideas of utility.

First, there are those who claim that history is worth writing and teaching because, in the words of one scholar, "It is such fun!"[8] But this contemptible argument, which passes for wisdom in some professional quarters, is scarcely sufficient to satisfy a student who is struggling to master strange masses of facts and interpretations which are suddenly dumped on him in History I. It is unlikely to gratify a graduate student, who discovers in the toil and loneliness of his apprenticeship the indispensable importance of a quality which the Germans graphically call *Sitzfleisch.* It will not be persuasive to a social scientist who is pondering the pros and cons of a distant journey to dusty archives. It cannot carry weight with a general

---

[6]Virginia Woolf, "Addison," *Essays,* 4 vols. (London, 1966), 1:87.

[7]Angus Wilson, *Anglo-Saxon Attitudes* (London, 1956), pp. 11, 364.

[8]Fritz Stern, ed., *Varieties of History: From Voltaire to the Present* (New York, 1956), p. 30.

reader, who is plodding manfully through a pedantic monograph which his conscience tells him he really ought to finish. Nor will it reach a public servant who is faced with the problem of distributing the pathetically limited pecuniary resources which are presently available for social research. And I doubt that it has even persuaded those historiographical hedonists who invoke it in defense of their profession.

For most rational individuals, the joys of history are tempered by the heavy labor which research and writing necessarily entail, and by the pain and suffering which suffuses so much of our past. Psychologists have demonstrated that pleasure comes to different people in different ways, including some which are utterly loathesome to the majority of mankind. If the doing of history is to be defended by the fact that some historians are happy in their work, then its mass appeal is likely to be as broad as flagellation. In all seriousness, there is something obscene in an argument which justifies the pedagogic torture inflicted upon millions of helpless children, year after year, on the ground that it is jolly good fun for the torturer.

Another common way in which historians justify historical scholarship is comparable to the way in which a mountain-climbing fanatic explained his obsession with Everest—"because it is there." By this line of thinking, history-as-actuality becomes a Himalayan mass of masterless crags and peaks, and the historian is a dauntless discoverer, who has no transcendent purpose beyond the triumphant act itself. If the object is remote from the dismal routine of daily affairs, if the air is thin and the slopes are slippery, if the mountain is inhabited merely by an abominable snowman or two, then all the better! If the explorer deliberately chooses the most difficult route to his destination, if he decides to advance by walking on his hands, or by crawling on his belly, then better still! By this convenient theory, remoteness is a kind of relevance, and the degree of difficulty is itself a defense.

This way of thinking is a tribute to the tenacity of man's will but not to the power of his intellect. If a task is worth doing merely because it is difficult, then one might wish with Dr. Johnson that it were impossible. And if historical inquiry is merely to be a moral equivalent to mountaineering for the diversion of chairborne adventurers, then historiography itself becomes merely a hobbyhorse for the amusement of overeducated unemployables.

A third common justification for history is the argument that there are certain discrete facts which every educated person needs to know. This view has been explicitly invoked to defend the teaching of required history courses to college freshmen, and to defend much research as well. But it is taxonomic in its idea of facts and tautological in its conception of education. What it calls facts are merely the conventional categories of historians' thought which are reified into history itself. And what it calls education is merely the mindless mastery of facts—a notion not far removed from the rote learning which has always flourished in the educational underworld but which no serious educational thinker has ever countenanced.

There are *no* facts which *everyone* needs to know—not even facts of the first historiographical magnitude. What real difference can knowledge of the fact of the fall of Babylon or Byzantium make in the daily life of anyone except a professional historian? Facts, discrete facts, will not in themselves make a man happy or wealthy or wise. They will not help him to deal intelligently with any modern problem which he faces, as man or citizen. Facts of this sort, taught in this way, are merely empty emblems of erudition which certify that certain formal pedagogical requirements have been duly met. If this method is mistaken for the marrow of education, serious damage can result.

Fourth, it is sometimes suggested that history is worth doing because it is "an outlet for the creative urge."[9] Undoubtedly, it is such a thing. But there are many outlets for creativity. Few are thought sufficient to justify the employment of thousands of highly specialized individuals at a considerable expense to society.

Tombstone rubbing is a creative act. So is the telling of tall stories. If history is to be justified on grounds of its creative aspect, then it must be shown to be a constructive, good, useful, or beautiful creative act. Most people who use this argument seem to be thinking in aesthetic terms. But if aesthetic principles become a justification for history, then surely 99 percent of the monographs which have appeared in the past generation are utterly unjustified. Most historians publish a single book in their lifetime—usually their doctoral dissertation. I cannot remember even one of these works which can be seriously regarded as a beautiful creative act. There have been a good many manifestoes for creative history in the past several

---

[9]Norman Cantor and Richard I. Schneider, *How to Study History* (New York, 1967), p. 3. For a more extended argument, see Emery Neff, *The Poetry of History* (New York, 1947).

decades, and more than a few essays which fulsomely describe the potential of history as art. But the number of modern histories which are worth reading on any imaginable aesthetic standard can be reckoned on the fingers of one hand. Painful as the fact may be, historians must face up to it—literary history as a living art form is about played out. In an earlier generation, it was otherwise. But today this tradition is either altogether dead or sleeping soundly. An awakening has been confidently predicted from time to time, but with every passing decade the anticipated date has been postponed. Historians, for the past several generations, have been moving squarely in the opposite direction. There is nothing to suggest a change, and there are a good many hints of continuity in years to come. Until there is a reversal, or some sort of revival, or even a single serious and successful creative act, history as it actually is today, and as it is becoming, must be justified by another argument.

A fifth justification for history is cast in terms of the promise of future utility. I have heard historians suggest that their random investigations are a kind of pure research, which somebody, some-day, will convert to constructive use, though they have no idea who, when, how, or why. The important thing, they insist, is not to be distracted by the dangerous principle of utility but to get on with the job. It is thought sufficient for an authority on Anglo-Saxon England to publish "important conclusions that all Anglo-Saxonists will have to consider."[10] If enough historians write enough histories, then something—the great thing itself—is sure to turn up. In the mean-time we are asked to cultivate patience, humility, and pure research.

This argument calls to mind the monkeys who were set to typing the works of Shakespeare in the British Museum. So vast is the field of past events, and so various are the possible methods and interpretations, that the probability is exceedingly small that any single project will prove useful to some great social engineer in the future. And the probability that a series of random researches will become a coherent science of history is still smaller.

A comparable problem was studied by John Venn, some years ago. He calculated the probability of drawing the text of *Paradise Lost* letter by letter from a bag containing all twenty-six signs of the alphabet—each letter to be replaced after it is drawn, and the bag thoroughly shaken. Assuming that there were 350,000 letters in the

[10] *The American Historical Review* 71 (1966): 529.

poem, Venn figured the odds at 1 in $26^{350,000}$, which if it were written out, would be half again as long as the poem itself.

This operation is in some ways analogous to the method of historians who hope to construct a science of history by reaching into the grab bag of past events and hauling out one random project after another. The analogy is not exact—the probability of success in history is even more remote than Venn's. If A is the number of possible methods (a large number), B is the number of possible topics (even larger), C is the number of possible interpretations (larger still), and D is the length of a sufficient series, then the odds are 1 in $(ABC)^D$. Now D may be as small as 1, but A, B, or C may equal infinity. If any one of them does, then the odds are infinitely improbable, in the sense of an infinite regression toward zero. In this context, infinite improbability will serve as a working definition of practical impossibility.

A series of researches can be expected to yield a coherent result only if they are *not* random. If a historian hopes that his work will promote some future purpose, then he must have some idea of what that purpose might be. The question cannot be postponed to another day. It must be faced now. And yet historians who justify their work as "pure research" deliberately avoid it. Their lives are wasted in aimless wanderings, like those which Bertrand Russell remembers from his childhood. "In solitude," he writes, "I used to wander about the garden, alternately collecting birds' eggs and meditating on the flight of time."[11] When grown men carry on in this way, the results are not amusing but pathetic.

All five of these justifications for history are functional to historical scholarship, but only in the sense that they serve to sustain a rough and rudimentary historicity in the work of scholars who have lost their conceptual bearings. But these attitudes are seriously dysfunctional in two other ways. First, they operate at the expense of all sound ideas of social utility. Secondly, they stand in the way of a refinement of historicity, beyond the crude level of contemporary practice.

Academic historians have been coming in for a good deal of abuse lately, and with a great deal of justification. There is a rising chorus of criticism which is directed principally against the sterility and social irrelevance of their scholarship. Only a few professional pollyannas would assert that these complaints are without cause.

[11]Bertrand Russell, *Autobiography, 1872-1914* (Boston, 1967), p. 14.

But the reform proposals that accompany these protests are worse than the deficiencies they are designed to correct. Historians of many ideological persuasions are increasingly outspoken in their determination to reform historical scholarship, and often exceedingly bitter about the willful blindness of an alleged academic establishment which supposedly stands in their way. But these reformers are running to an opposite error.

Historians are increasingly urged to produce scholarship of a kind which amounts to propaganda. There is, of course, nothing new in this idea. It appeared full-blown in the work of James Harvey Robinson and other so-called New Historians more than fifty years ago.[12] There was much of it after the Second World War, in the manifestoes of conservative anti-Communist scholars such as Conyers Read,[13] and in the monographs of liberal activists during the 1950's. There is still a great deal of it today in Eastern Europe, where more than a few historians imagine that they are "scholar-fighters," in the service of world socialism. Today, in America and Western Europe, this idea is being adopted with increasing fervor by young radical historians, who regard all aspirations to objectivity as a sham and a humbug, and stubbornly insist that the real question is not whether historians can be objective, but which cause they will be subjective to.

These scholars[14] are in quest of something which they call a "usable past." But the result is neither usable nor past. It ends merely in polemical pedantry, which is equally unreadable and inaccurate.

There have always been many historians who were more concerned that truth should be on their side than that they should be on the side of truth. This attitude is no monopoly of any sect or generation. But wherever it appears in historical scholarship, it is hateful in its substance and horrible in its results. To make historiography into a vehicle for propaganda is simply to destroy it. The problem of the utility of history is not solved but subverted, for what is produced by this method is not history at all. The fact that earlier

[12]James Harvey Robinson, *The New History* (New York, 1912).

[13]See David Hackett Fischer, *Historians' Fallacies, Toward a Logic of Historical Thought* (New York, 1970), p. 86.

[14]For a discussion of their work, see Irwin Unger, "The 'New Left' and American History," *The American Historical Review* 72 (1967): 1237-63. For a sample, see Barton J. Bernstein, *Towards a New Past: Dissenting Essays in American History* (New York, 1968).

generations and other ideological groups have committed the same wrong does not convert it into a right.

Moreover, the "usable" history which is presently being produced by historians of the "New Left" is not objectionable because it is substantively radical but rather because it is methodologically reactionary. Radical historians today, with few exceptions, write a very old-fashioned kind of history. They are not really radical *historians.* A good many new procedural devices are presently in process of development—devices which may permit a closer approximation to the ideal of objectivity. But one rarely sees them in radical historiography, which is impressionistic, technically unsophisticated, and conceptually unoriginal—old conceptions are merely adjusted in minor respects.

If history is worth doing today, then it must *not* be understood either in terms of historicity without utility, or of utility without historicity. Instead, both qualities must be combined. The trouble with professional historians is that they are not professional enough—and not historians enough. If they are to be useful as historians, then they must do so by the refinement of their professional discipline and not by its dilution.

History can be useful, as history, in several substantive ways. It can serve to clarify contexts in which contemporary problems exist—not by a presentist method of projecting our own ideas into the past but rather as a genuinely empirical discipline, which is conducted with as much objectivity and historicity as is humanly possible. Consider one quick and obvious example—the problem of Negro-white relations in America. It is surely self-evident that this subject cannot be intelligently comprehended without an extended sense of how it has developed through time. Negro Americans carry their history on their backs, and they are bent and twisted and even crippled by its weight. The same is true, but less apparent, of white Americans, too. And precisely the same thing applies to every major problem which the world faces today. Historians can help to solve them, but only if they go about their business in a better way—only if they become more historical, more empirical, and more centrally committed to the logic of a problem-solving discipline.

Historical inquiry can also be useful not merely for what it contributes to present understanding but also for what it suggests about the future. A quasi-historical method is increasingly used, in many disciplines, for the purpose of forecasting—for establishing trends and directions and prospects. Historians themselves have had nothing to do with such efforts, which many of them would probably put in a class with phrenology. Maybe they should bear a hand, for they have acquired by long experience a kind of tacit temporal sophistication which other disciplines conspicuously lack—a sophistication which is specially theirs to contribute.

Third, history can be useful in the refinement of theoretical knowledge, of an "if, then" sort. Econometric historians have already seized upon this possibility, and political historians are not far behind. What, for example, are the historical conditions in which social stability, social freedom, and social equality have tended to be *maximally* coexistent? No question is more urgent today, when tyranny, inequality, and instability are not merely disagreeable but dangerous to humanity itself. This is work which a few historians are beginning to do. Maybe it is time that more of them addressed such problems, more directly.

Fourth, historical scholarship can usefully serve to help us find out who we are. It helps people to learn something of themselves, perhaps in the way that a psychoanalyst seeks to help a patient. Nothing could be more productive of sanity and reason in this irrational world. Historians, in the same way, can also help people to learn about other selves. And nothing is more necessary to the peace of the world. Let us have no romantic humbug about brotherhood and humanity. What is at stake is not goodness but survival. Men must learn to live in peace with other men if they are to live at all. The difficulties which humanity has experienced in this respect flow *partly* from failures of intellect and understanding. Historical knowledge may help as a remedy—not a panacea, but a partial remedy. And if this is to happen, professional historians must hold something more than a private conversation with themselves. They must reach millions of men, and they will never do so through monographs, lectures, and learned journals. I doubt that they can hope to accomplish this object by literary history or by the present forms of popular history. Instead, they must begin to exploit the most effective media of mass communication—television, radio, motion pictures, newspapers, etc. They cannot assign this task to middlemen. If the message is left to communications specialists, it is sure to be garbled in transmission. All of these uses of history, as history, require the development of new strategies, new skills, and new scholarly projects.

In addition to these four substantive services which historians can hope to provide, there is another one which I regard as even more important. Historians have a heavy responsibility not merely to teach people substantive historical truths but also to teach them how to think historically. There is no limit to the number of ways in which normative human thinking is historical. Nobody thinks historically all the time. But everybody thinks historically much of the time. Each day, every rational being on this planet asks questions about things that actually happened—questions which directly involve the logic of inquiry, explanation, and argument which is discussed in this book.

These operations rarely involve the specific substantive issues that now engage the professional thoughts of most historians. They do not touch upon the cause of the First World War, or the anatomy of revolutions, or the motives of Louis XIV, or the events of the industrial revolution. Instead, this common everyday form of historical thought consists of specific inquiries into small events, for particular present and future purposes to which all the academic monographs in the world are utterly irrelevant.

Historical thought ordinarily happens in a thousand humble forms—when a newspaper writer reports an event and a newspaper reader peruses it; when a jury weighs a fact in dispute, and a judge looks for a likely precedent; when a diplomat compiles an *aide-memoire* and a doctor constructs a case history; when a soldier analyzes the last campaign, and a statesman examines the record; when a householder tries to remember if he paid the rent, and when a house builder studies the trend of the market. Historical thinking happens even to sociologists, economists, and political scientists in nearly all of their major projects. Each of these operations is in some respects (not all respects) historical. If historians have something to learn from other disciplines, they have something to teach as well.

The vital purpose of refining and extending a logic of historical thought is not merely some pristine goal of scholarly perfection. It involves the issue of survival. Let us make no mistake about priorities. If men continue to make the *historical* error of conceptualizing the problems of a nuclear world in prenuclear terms, there will not be a postnuclear world. If people persist in the *historical* error of applying yesterday's programs to today's problems, we may suddenly run short of tomorrow's possibilities. If we continue to pursue the ideological objectives of the nineteenth century in the middle of the twentieth, the prospects for a twenty-first are increasingly dim.

These failures—failures of historical understanding—exist everywhere today. Frenchmen, in pursuit of their venerable vision of Gallic grandeur, combine a *force de frappe* with the fallacy of anachronism—a lethal combination. Arabs cry up a *jihad* against the infidels, as if nothing had changed in nine hundred years but the name of the enemy. On the other side of the Jordan River, Jews nurse their bitter heritage of blood and tears, without any apparent sense of how the world has changed. In Moscow and in Washington, in London and in Bonn, in Peking and New Delhi, statesmen and citizens alike are unable to adjust their thoughts to the accelerating rate of changing realities.

That people will learn to see things as they are—that they will understand the world as it is, and is becoming—that they will become more rational and empirical in their private thoughts and public policies—that these things will come to pass, is not what Damon Runyon would have called a betting proposition. He might have figured the most favorable odds at six to five, against. But if people continue to commit their fatal fallacies at something like the present rate, the odds for their survival will become a long shot.

Responsible and informed observers have estimated that by the 1990's as many as forty-eight nations may possess nuclear weapons.[15] As the number of these arsenals increases arithmetically, the probability of their use grows in geometric ratio. Biological and chemical weapons of equal destructive power and even greater horror are already within the reach of most sovereign powers, and many private groups as well.

Natural scientists have helped to create this deadly peril; now it is the business of social scientists to keep it in bounds. Here is work for historians to do—work that is largely educational in nature—work that consists in teaching men somehow to think reasonably about their condition. Reason is indeed a pathetically frail weapon in the face of such a threat. But it is the *only* weapon we have.

---

[15]Sir John Cockcroft, "The Perils of Nuclear Proliferation," in Nigel Calder, ed., *Unless Peace Comes* (New York, 1968), p. 37.

HERBERT BUTTERFIELD
The Dangers of History

IN SPITE OF the development of technical historical enquiry
during the seventeenth century, and the recognised importance of
historical study in the systems of eighteenth-century thought, it
would seem to be true that the modern rage for history was born out
of the morbidities and nostalgias of the Romantic Movement. It was
assisted by the reaction against the French Revolution, which in
England—particularly in the teaching of Edmund Burke—tended to
confirm the nation in its attachment to its own past and its belief that
the liberties of the country went back to times immemorial. Englishmen have particularly prized the continuity of their history, and
have found something rich and fruitful in the very fact of continuity;
all of which was to have its effect on our interpretation of our
national story. In Germany, on the other hand, during the Romantic
Movement, men were particularly conscious of the tragic political
situation of the country in modern centuries and they tended to
contrast it with the glories of the Holy Roman Empire of medieval
times.

In general, we see in the nineteenth century one of the most
important movements in the whole story of European thought:
namely, the great development of history and of historical thinking.
Not only did history become a principal branch of study, but it
affected all other departments of mental activity. As an English
writer once said, in the nineteenth century human thought in every
field seemed to run to history; and this was true for example of
philosophy in Hegel and of a great deal of Protestant theology. The
movement was one in which Germany held the intellectual leadership. Furthermore, it is chiefly to Germany that we owe the great
advance which was achieved in the development of a more scientific
study of the past, the evolution of a higher and more austere form of
scholarship; all of which made it a much more serious matter than it
had ever been before to write about past events. Partly because
Germany was so large a country, she was able to reach a higher
degree of impartiality than most other people. If she had some
historians who were inclined to support Prussia, for example, there

would be other historians in different parts of the country who were opposed to Prussia; and somewhere or other in Germany both sides of the question would be stated, and the truth was more carefully tested as a result. In the development of high and austere standards of scholarship English students in particular set out to be the disciples of the great German writers of history, so producing what for a long time was a remarkable intellectual alliance. Lord Acton once suggested that this German historical movement in the nineteenth century was a more fateful step in the story of European thought than even the famous Italian Renaissance of the fifteenth century. It seems to me that we must agree with this view, for the Renaissance did not add a new ingredient to our Western civilisation in the way that the historical movement of the nineteenth century was able to do.

The twentieth century has not been so happy for the historical sciences, and these sciences are gravely injured by two things which have turned out to be the great plagues of our time—namely, wars and revolutions. In all countries the very interest that governments have come to have in history—government patronage of historical study—has proved to carry with it hidden dangers. The very popularity of history amongst new classes of people (who are sometimes lazy readers, sometimes unaware of the necessity for the older critical canons, and sometimes unconscious of the way in which wishful thinking operates in the study of history) has produced many new embarrassments, especially in a world where men have learned how powerful history can be for purposes of propaganda. The establishment of many new nation-states since 1918 has also proved to be not always a good fortune for historical study in Europe. New nations are particularly sensitive about their historical past, particularly jingoistic in their national pride. And it seems that small nations, especially if they are new nations too, are liable to be more intense and local in their prejudices—they are sometimes more narrowly self-concentrated than the greater ones. It is going to need a harder struggle everywhere to keep up the standards of academic scholarship in [the] future than it did before 1914.

We are now in a position to survey the influence which something like a hundred and fifty years of historical study has exercised on the development of modern Europe. It is not clear that as yet we have learned all that there is to learn from this particular aspect of the history of historical science, or fathomed all the effects that the study of the past has itself had on nations and their policies.

Concerning historians as interpreters and guides in the affairs of their own generation, I have read some severe things that Englishmen have written about German scholars, and there are similar things that the Germans have said about us. But the world still waits for the wag who will scientifically examine the nineteenth and twentieth-century writers of history and show us how far their studies and researches really did raise them above the fevers and prejudices of their time—how far in reality it is plausible to argue that historians are wiser then the rest of their contemporaries on political matters. And a more scientific age than ours may even find materials for an analytical treatment of associated questions; for, to take one example, it would be interesting to see it demonstrated whether it is always prudent to rely for political advice on the kind of "expertness" which the "regional historian" possesses—at any rate the one who, through the knowledge of one of the obscurer languages has happened to acquire something approaching a monopoly in his field, without having to face any great clash of scholarship in his own country. And if we say that a given expert on Ruritania must be right provided he is accepted by the Ruritanians themselves, the history of historiography will be able no doubt to raise a debate even on this issue.

At any rate it is possible even now to make certain comments on the part which historical reflection has played in the development of the errors that have been so tragic for the twentieth century. And in this connection there is one law which makes itself apparent if we examine the events of the last one hundred and fifty years; and that is the paradox that a great deal of what people regard as the teaching or the lessons of history is really an argument in a circle. In reality the historian is in the habit of inserting some of his present-day prejudices into his reconstructions of the past; or unconsciously he sets out the whole issue in terms of some contemporary experience—he has what we might call the modern "set-up" in his mind. In this way English writers once tended to see the ancient Greeks as modern Whigs; the Germans would read something of modern Prussia even into ancient Rome. Magna Carta would be interpreted in the nineteenth century in the light of modern English constitutional problems. Those who dealt with the medieval Holy Roman Empire too often envisaged it with the nineteenth-century conflict of Austria and Prussia in their minds. Sometimes there has been a tendency to project the prejudices of the present day into the structure of the past as it was envisaged in long periods and in general terms—the tendency for the British to say, when France was the enemy, that France had been the "eternal enemy of mankind." In England the view once prevailed that German history was particularly the history of freedom, for it was a story that comprised federation, parliament, autonomous cities, Protestantism, and a law of liberty carried by German colonists to the Slavonic east. In those days it was the Latin States which were considered to be congenial to authoritarianism, clinging to the Papacy in Italy, the Inquisition in Spain and the Bonapartist dictatorships in militaristic France. The reversal of this view in the twentieth century, and its replacement by a common opinion that Germany had been the aggressor and the enemy of freedom throughout all the ages, will no doubt be the subject of historical research itself some day, especially as it seems to have coincided so closely with a change in British foreign policy. The historian, then, can even deepen and magnify present-day prejudices by the mere fact that he so easily tends to throw them back and project them on to the canvas of all the centuries. And the more the historian seeks to please his generation or serve his government or support any cause save that of truth, the more he tends to confirm his contemporaries in whatever they happen to want to believe, the more he hardens the age in its favourite and fashionable errors.

Before 1919 I was taught a kind of history which saw in the sovereignty of national states the culmination of the progress of centuries—the very end towards which history was moving. I remember how the Reformation itself would be applauded for having released the nation-states from "the fetters of international-ism"; and it was the custom to show that history, especially in the nineteenth century (the "Holy Alliance," for example), had demon-strated the folly and futility of attempts to form anything like a League of Nations. From 1919, however, one saw the teaching of history reorganised and text-books rewritten—the events of the past now marshalled to serve a different purpose, and in particular the course of nineteenth-century European history reshaped—this time for the purpose of proving that all the centuries had been pointing to a different kind of consummation altogether, namely the League of Nations. I am not concerned with the question which of these views was the true one. But I should have been more impressed if on both those occasions the historian had not been so inclined to ordain and dispose his subject-matter, and lay out the whole course of cen-turies, for the purpose of ratifying the prejudice that already prevailed for other reasons at the time. It can easily be seen, therefore, that the historian who most desires to please his age—the historian whom we most applaud because he chimes in with our views—may be betraying us, and may rob us of one of the possible benefits of historical study, namely the advantage of an escape from merely contemporary views and short-range perspectives. On the other hand, Burckhardt and Acton gave the nineteenth century certain warnings which the lapse of time has proved to be of great significance. It appears, however, that a generation does not take much notice of a message that it happens to dislike.

The things which happened in England have taken place in the historiography of all other countries; and of course the Englishman sees the error when German historians make it, and the German sees the error in the foreigner too, but none of us seem able to jump out of our own skins and to see our own position with a certain relativity. And for the most part there is much too little disposition even to attempt the task. Sometimes historical students take tremendous trouble with the details of their researches, but when they come to the important point where they build up the larger framework of their story or draw their final conclusions, or pretend to extract from the narrative its teaching value, they are liable to become very casual and to be totally unaware of the processes that are taking place in their minds. They do not realise that very often they are smuggling into history the things they eventually imagine themselves to be extracting from it—the penny that they draw out of the slot-machine is the very penny that they first put in. Even after the historian has collected data and sifted his materials with industry and discrimination, a very minute addition of wishful thinking may deflect the whole organisation of the results. A desire for self-justification may set the historian at a slightly wrong angle; and the extension of the lines of the picture may mean that this apparently small deflection will ultimately have the effect of carrying him far away from the central course. Indeed, history can be very dangerous unless it is accompanied by severe measures of self-discipline and self-purification—unless we realise that there is something that we must do with our personalities. Let us note, then, that historians have developed a remarkable scientific apparatus for the discovery, handling and sifting of historical evidence. They have not always remembered that this leaves vast areas of historical reconstruction and historical thinking which have not yet been brought under the same scientific control, though the history of historiography may enable us to make further advances even here.

The situation is more serious than anything that has so far been stated, however; for I think it is true to say that in the European politics of the last two centuries certain errors are discoverable which were born out of historical reflection as such—errors which would not have been made if people had not been so interested in the past and so concerned with it. The influence of historical study in the nineteenth century led to the creation of what we can only regard as new kinds of myths—things which came with the mysterious halo of religion about them and were almost made to serve as substitutes for religion. Amongst these I should put the myth of romantic nationalism, the modern religion of exaggerated nationalism, which is a perversion of such principle of nationality as had existed hitherto. That myth had historians as its high priests while its prophets were a particular type of student of the past who enquired into the history of languages and interested themselves in early folk-literature. Moreover, ideas which are introduced into historical scholarship at a high level soon become degraded into myths. Instead of being developed in a flexible manner with the passage of time, they are repeated with rigidity, dragged into different contexts, tossed to and fro in the market-place, and generally hardened and coarsened in the rough-and-tumble of the world's affairs. Historical memories, especially in Eastern Europe—and also in Ireland—have engendered much of the national animosity of modern times. In a far wider sense than this the over-stressing of the historical argument in modern European politics has been unfortunate both for historical study and for diplomacy. One must wonder sometimes whether it would not have been better if men could have forgotten the centuries long ago, and thrown off the terrible burden of the past, so that they might face the future without encumbrances. And above all, when history has been accompanied by a tendency to regard the past as an independent source of rights, or when it has been accompanied by a tendency to worship the primitive stages of one's national culture and the uniqueness of a national mentality, it has made its contribution even to that serious drift of the modern world in the direction of irrationalism—the flight from the old ideal of a universal human reasonableness.

It would seem that history possesses certain initial attractions which will prevent it from being overlooked in any consideration of a scheme of general education. It is one of the subjects which purport to produce a "well-informed mind," and it answers many of the requirements of ordinary curiosity. It is capable of easy discussion across a table without necessary resort to any long-term intellectual system. It gives an extension to the material which the mind can gather for the purpose of manufacturing into experience. And it imparts the kind of knowledge which throws light on the problems of the present day, and which can be used to broaden our consciousness of citizenship, whether in a nation or in the world.

On the other hand, against mathematics (for example), it has the disadvantage that mere progress from one chapter to another—the mere perusal of a larger area of the subject-matter—does not in itself constitute or impose an intellectual discipline. The mere reading of history, the mere process of accumulating more information in this field, does not necessarily give training to a mind that was initially diffuse. For this reason it is not wise to learn history by a hasty accumulation of information, so that the mass of data clutters up the memory and the growth of knowledge too greatly outstrips the general development of the mind. Furthermore, in the case of mathematics we start with our feet on the hard earth, learning the simplest things first, firmly establishing them at each point before we go any further, and making our argument good and watertight at each step of the way. In other words, we begin with strong foundations of concrete, and we gradually build our skyscrapers on the top of this. In the case of history, on the other hand, we start up in the clouds, at the very top of the highest skyscraper. We start with an abridged story, seen in the large and constructed out of what in reality are broad generalisations. It is only much later, when we reach the actual work of research, that we really come down to earth and arrive at the primary facts and primary materials. Only at the end of many years of training do we come to know what it means genuinely to establish the assertions that we make. For this reason, history is dangerous as an educational subject; and the best kind of history-teacher is not the one who tells us most clearly what to believe—not the one who seeks merely to transfer a body of knowledge from his head into the heads of his pupils. The best kind of history-teacher is the one who realises the danger of the subject itself and construes it as his function to redeem and rescue it as far as possible.

If our Western civilisation were to collapse even more completely than it has done, and I were asked to say upon which of the sins of the world the judgment of God had come in so signal a manner, I should specify, as the most general of existing evils and the most terrifying in its results, human presumption and particularly intellectual arrogance. There is good reason for believing that none of the fields of specialised knowledge is exempt from this fault; and I know of no miracle in the structure of the universe that should make me think even archbishops free of it. But it is the besetting disease of historians, and the effect of an historical education seems very often actually to encourage the evil. The mind sweeps like the mind of God over centuries and continents, churches and cities, Shakespeares and Aristotles, curtly putting everything in its place. Any schoolboy thinks that he can show that Napoleon was foolish as a statesman, and I have seen Bismarck condemned as a mere simpleton in diplomacy by undergraduates who would not have had sufficient diplomacy to wheedle sixpence out of a college porter. I do not know if there is any other field of knowledge which suffers so badly as history from the sheer blind repetitions that occur year after year, and from book to book—theses and statements repeated sometimes out of their proper context, and even sometimes when they have not been correctly understood; and very supple and delicate ones turned by sheer repetition and rigidity of mind into hard dogmatic formulas. I have seen historians condemn the Middle Ages for their blindness in quoting and requoting earlier authorities and so perpetuating an original error; when it was in fact these self-same historians who were doing just that very thing—repeating judgments at second-hand—in the very act of stating that particular case. I do not personally feel that in modern times technical history, in spite of all the skill that has gone to the making of it, has ever been taken up by a mind that I should call Shakespearean in its depth and scope, save possibly in the remarkable case of Ranke. I think that, compared with the novelists, the historians have even been coarse-fingered and too lacking in subtlety in their handling of human nature; so that, if he had only the novelists and the historians to judge from, a visitor from another planet would think that they were talking about two different kinds of substance.

In any case, though we had an Aristotle or a Shakespeare as an historian, the best that any of us can do at a given moment only represents the present state of knowledge in respect of the subject with which we are dealing. There is a profound sense in which all histories—like all scientific interpretations of the universe—are only interim reports; and in history the discovery of a small fact that may be pivotal is calculated to produce a drastic reshaping of the whole field of study. It is not so much the concrete facts—like the date of the battle of Waterloo—that are liable to such drastic revision, but rather the whole organisation of the story. In other words, the effect of the revision falls most of all on that region where our moral lessons, our teaching-conclusions and our verdicts have their roots. In a manner that we cannot imagine or quite foretell our historical conclusions are liable to be transformed and wrenched into a different shape when for fifty years English, German, French and American scholars have co-operated in the gigantic task of historical revision. Professor Trevelyan said in his Inaugural Lecture in Cambridge that the world would be liable to be plunged into bloodshed if teachers and students disseminated wrong history. There can be no doubt of this; but any generation that looks back to any previous generation can hardly close its eyes to the fact that wrong history is being taught in all countries, all the time, unavoidably. Research is being constantly conducted by thousands of people over the globe for the purpose of correcting it. And the corrections—especially in the case of comparatively recent history—are often very surprising and disconcerting.

History, in fact, is so dangerous a subject—and so often it is the sinister people like a Machiavelli or a Napoleon or a Lenin who learn "tricks of the trade" from it, before the majority of people have thought of doing so—that we might wonder whether it would not be better for the world to forget all of the past, better to have no memories at all, and just to face the future without ever looking back. We must teach history, however, precisely because so much bad history exists in the world already. Bad history is in the air we breathe, and even those who do not pretend to know any history behind the days of their grandfathers are dangerous sometimes, for they too are the slaves of unconscious assumptions or concealed perversities on the subject of the past. From one point of view we must say that none of us learns history—none of us ever attains a final understanding or the kind of knowledge in which he can safely rest. From another point of view, however, we may say that there is great need for history all the same, provided we conceive it as a process of unlearning. Something can be achieved if we can sweep away only a single layer of the tremendous crust of error that already has the world under its grip. Perhaps we may say that we sweep away one layer of error from our minds when we are at school; another layer when we study history at the university; and a further layer still if we reach so far as actual research. Indeed, supposing we continue the study of history all our lives we may sweep away a further layer of this crust of error every ten years, if we can keep our freshness of mind. But we do not complete the process. We do not reach the stage when we can say that we comprehend a particular subject in a final manner. For this reason it is better that men, when they leave the university, should forget the history of Louis XIV as they learned it there, unless they are prepared to continue the process of "unlearning." It is better that they should not allow the knowledge to freeze in their minds, while the world changes, and historical science changes—better that they should not thirty years later be holding too rigidly in their memory the things learned so long before. For historical knowledge is valuable only while it is, so to speak, liquid—it is worse than lumber if it freezes and hardens in the mind. We may say, then, that it is better for men to forget what they have actually learned of Louis XIV and cling rather to the experience they gained in the study of history and in historical exercises. History is more useful when transmuted into a deeper wisdom that melts into the rest of experience and is incorporated in the fabric of the mind itself.

The dangers of history are liable to become much greater if we imagine that the study of this subject qualifies us to be politicians or provides us with patterns which we can immediately transpose into the context of contemporary politics. It is not even clear that English people are wise in teaching a knowledge of Tudor government if their ultimate objective is to show young people how their country is governed in the twentieth century. I once read a detective story written with the intention of showing precisely the movements and operations that take place at Scotland Yard after a murder has been reported. If our object is to show future voters how the wheels of government work, some such method applied to the Cabinet or any other part of the constitutional system would seem to me to be more appropriate than the study of history, as the Schools Section of the B.B.C. have [sic] apparently discovered.

The argument that history qualifies men for the practice of politics is one which had a certain relevance and validity when it was used by the aristocrats who ruled England in the eighteenth century; but they were thinking of history as an additional acquirement for people who were supposed to have had their real education already. In any case, those English gentlemen of the eighteenth century were brought up from their very childhood to be rulers and politicians. They saw the practice of administration, heard political discussion, learned the arts of management in their local estates and observed the conduct of public affairs at first hand from their earliest days—they were being educated all the time in the actual practice of politics. For these people history came in its proper context—it was the one additional thing which would widen their horizon. Since they knew so much about the practical working of current affairs they were politicians already, and the study of history was calculated to make them better ones precisely because it broadened their horizon. I should seriously question the validity of a parallel argument for the modern democratic world and our modern educational system. We are wrong to think that the study of history itself is sufficient to turn us into competent politicians. And it is perhaps a tragedy that nowadays so many people—even if unconsciously—are in reality building up their political outlook from what they have read in books.

Some of the best diplomatic historians I ever met were almost the worst diplomats in the world when it came to transacting business in real life. It is often said in England that history is useful, and that it qualifies people to take part in politics, because it enables them to see how such things as politics and diplomacy work. I once had to induce the governing body of my college in Cambridge to try to come to an agreement on the colour of a carpet for a college library. A person who has had to undertake such a task and who has discovered all the maneuverings, all the delicate tactics, the persuasions, the whole science of give-and-take, that are necessary to get twelve men to agree on the colour of a carpet—such a person may be said to have had his first lesson in diplomacy. A person who merely reads a life of Bismarck is liable to be deceived a hundred times over, owing to the sheer fact of unavoidable abridgements, even if for no other reason. In our condensed version of the story a host of little shiftings and successive adjustments and minute maneuverings made by Bismarck over the course of a number of weeks get compressed and telescoped together—so that they cake and solidify into one big thing, a mighty instantaneous act of volition, a colossal piece of Bismarckism. My teacher, Professor Temperley, once reminded us in Cambridge that when the research student goes to manuscript sources, to the original diplomatic correspondence, for example, he does not go merely in order to have a scoop and to uncover some surprising secret; he goes to the sources primarily in order that by an actual day-to-day study of the whole correspondence he shall learn the way in which diplomacy works and decisions are arrived at. Only the research student really studies things at close enough quarters to understand the complexity of these processes.

Indeed, abridged history—through the mere fact that it is necessarily so abridged—is having the effect of leaving the world with so many serious misconceptions. By foreshortening the picture and making Bismarckian strokes of policy more trenchant than they really were, abridged history gives men a greater appearance of sovereignty over events than they actually possess; and it tends to magnify the controlling power of governments over the next stage in the story. With the decline of religion, and in the absence of anything else that seems authentic, men and nations rely on the abridged history they have learned to give them their impression of their place in the sun, their purposeful intent, and their idea of what they can do with their destiny. They acquire an academic dream-impression of what statesmen can do in the world, what governments achieve, what their national .mission is, and what can be brought about by sheer self-assertion and will.

In any case, the world rarely remembers to what a degree the pretended "lessons" which are extracted by politicians from history are judgments based on the assumption that we know what would have happened if some statesman in the past had only acted differently. When historians so often assert that the Congress of Vienna made a mistake in neglecting the "principle of nationality," we may wonder whether they have really faced for a single moment the question: What would have happened in Europe if the Congress of Vienna had followed the twentieth-century view? There was much talk in 1919 of the necessity of "avoiding the mistakes of 1815"; and when a person has been fed with the apparently self-evident verdicts of abridged history, it is difficult to convince him that in any event this is a fallacious formula for policy. What you have to avoid in 1919 are not the mistakes of 1815 but the mistakes of 1919. What you have to avoid is too blind an immersion in the prejudices of your own time. Those who talked of "avoiding the mistakes of 1815" were using history to ratify the prejudices they had already. In any case, men are slow to count their blessings and quick to see the faults and shortcomings of the world into which they are born, and in 1919 it was the general cry that Europe must not be saddled with the burden of a settlement as unsatisfactory as that of the Congress of Vienna. It took our knowledge of the difficulties, weaknesses and ephemerality of the Versailles settlement to make us realise that the state of the question is entirely different. What we want to learn now is why the Congress of Vienna was so much more successful than we have known how to be.

Not only do historical judgments rest so often on an assumption concerning what would have happened if a certain statesman had acted differently—if only Metternich had done *the other thing,* for example—but there is a rigidity that occurs in our treatment of the possible alternatives, for we so often imagine that there was only one alternative, when in reality there was a great range of them. We overlook, therefore, the complexity of the mathematics that will be required to work out the displacements which a different event would have produced, as in the case of the problem of what would have happened if Napoleon had won the battle of Waterloo. So from an armchair every Tom, Dick and Harry in England can conduct a facile course of reasoning which will satisfy him that he could easily have thwarted Hitler at an earlier point in the story, because he, for his part, would have done *the other thing;* as though in such a case a man like Hitler would not have done something different too at the next remove, and a host of other factors would have to be altered, the historical process quickly complicating all the calculations that require to be made. Indeed, history adds to the errors of a rigid mind and only serves us when we use it to increase our elasticity.

Over a quarter of a century ago Paul Valéry produced a serious criticism of historical study, and it is not clear that his main charge has been answered—his criticism is certainly applicable to that kind of historical education which is directed merely to the "learning" of history, the acquisition of the sort of knowledge which is examined in memory tests. He put his finger on a critical point, indeed on what perhaps is the very crux of the matter, when he suggested that the effect of historical study was to produce a certain lack of mental elasticity. This, as he showed, was liable to be particularly harmful in a world where changes were coming in such rapid cascades that the mind could hardly be expected to move quickly enough to catch up with them. I believe it is true to say that many people in England in 1919 looked back upon the previous hundred years of European history, and saw that during that period events had been moving in a certain curve—moving in the direction of "liberalism" and "nationality," for example. Too easily and unconsciously they assumed that in the coming years the course of history would continue that curve: so that their knowledge of the past, especially of the very recent past, robbed them of a certain flexibility. They would have been better equipped to meet the developments of the succeeding decades if they had studied in ancient history the deeper processes that political bodies have been observed to undergo over long periods.

When Norway was invaded in 1940 the view was put forward in English official quarters that Hitler had broken one of the laws of history, in that he had conducted an invasion across water without possessing the command of the sea. Again the rigidities to which historical thinking are liable were the cause of deception. Even if a thing has never proved possible in the past we are not justified in inferring directly that history has proved such a thing to be impossible. When France collapsed in 1940 many Englishmen regarded it as self-evident that that country had made a tragic mistake in preparing only for defensive warfare and putting her trust in the Maginot Line. A French statesman said, however, that he, for his part, regretted not the construction of the Maginot Line but the failure to continue something of the sort to the sea. Other alternatives still were open, for the explanation of the downfall of France—including the possibility that her armies had made the reverse of the mistake generally imputed to them, by rushing with too great *élan* into Belgium when hostilities were opened in that region. On occasion it might require very subtle calculation and a microscopic sifting of evidence to decide the choice between the alternative interpretations that are possible in a situation of this kind. Few people take this trouble, and it is exactly in choices of this type that a very slight insertion of "wishful thinking" carries the majority of men to what is apparently a self-evident conclusion. One of the dangers of history lies in the ease with which these apparently self-evident judgments can be extracted from it, provided one closes one's eyes to certain facts. The person who is incapable of seeing more than one thing at once—incapable of holding two factors in his mind at the same time—will reach results all the more quickly and will feel the most assured in the judgments that he makes.

I imagine that if we wish to study the effect of historical study on the actual conduct of affairs, one of the appropriate fields in which we can pursue the enquiry is that of military strategy. In general, it is not possible to have a war just for the purpose of training the leaders of an army, and it has been the case that the teaching of strategy was for a long time carried on by means of historical study—for a hundred years by a continual study of the methods of Napoleon. Since the time when Machiavelli inaugurated the modern science of war there have been grave misgivings about this use of history. Machiavelli himself was open to the reproach that since he required the detailed imitation of the methods of the Romans, he refused to believe in artillery. Similarly, it would appear to be the case that if men shape their minds too rigidly by a study of the last war, they are to some degree unfitting themselves for the conduct of the next one. If a nation decides conversely that it will set out with the particular purpose of avoiding the mistakes of the last war, it is still liable to be the slave of history and to be defeated by another nation that thinks of new things. Historical study, therefore, has sometimes had a deadening effect on military strategists; and it has often been a criticism of them that they were too prone to conduct the present war on the method of the previous one, forgetting how times had changed.

It seems true, however, that many of the errors which spring from a little history are often corrected as people go on to study more and more history. If a man had a knowledge of many wars and of the whole history of the art of war, studying not merely the accounts of battles and campaigns, but relating the weapons of a given period to the conditions of the time, relating policies to circumstances, so that he came to have an insight into the deep causes of things, the hidden sources of the changes that take place—if he allowed this knowledge not to lie heavily on his mind, not to be used in a narrow and literal spirit, but to sink into the walls of his brain so that it was turned into wisdom and experience—then such a person would be able to acquire the right feeling for the texture of events, and would undoubtedly avoid becoming the mere slave of the past. I think he would be better able to face a new world, and to meet the surprises of unpredictable change with greater flexibility. A little history may make people mentally rigid. Only if we go on learning more and more of it—go on "unlearning" it—will it correct its own deficiencies gradually and help us to reach the required elasticity of mind.

PAGE SMITH

Unity of History

To DISTINGUISH BETWEEN existential and symbolic history is not enough to preserve the historian from error and futility. Since World War II dozens of new nations, the great majority of them former colonies of European powers, have come into formal, if extremely precarious, existence. This fact of history has had its effect upon historical study in the colleges and universities of the nation. American institutions of higher learning have perhaps been especially responsive to the problems posed by "emergent nations." Dozens of institutes have been established to sponsor post-doctoral work in Near and Far Eastern History, in the histories of Africa, Latin America, and Southeast Asia. This is all commendable. Honest and systematic efforts are being made to study the social, political, and economic problems of these nations, so new and so tenuous. But the emphasis, not unnaturally, is contemporary, as indeed it must be, since many of these countries have very little history in the sense in which the Western world has used the word.

In the emergent nations themselves, native historians have already begun to write histories; histories of the colonial period are popular in countries which, like the Latin American nations, are far enough removed from their beginnings so that their colonial past has taken on an aura of glamour and adventure and where, as a general rule, the dominant class is descended from the settlers sent out by the colonizing power.

More popular in the recently emerged nations are histories of an ancient golden age before the appearance of the European invaders. That this golden age is generally illusory is less important than that the new nations need such a fabricated history to define themselves as a people. Certainly the West should not be surprised at this development, for it was the West which, in the nineteenth century, discovered this means of self-identification. As much myth as fact was mixed into the early histories of the nation states of Europe. Yet the history of the European states in the last century—armored with an aggressive arrogance which was based, in part at least, upon spurious history—does not make us wish to see the experiment repeated by a host of new nations.

If there is an overriding theme for the century ahead, it is the unity of mankind. Such a goal cannot be served by the production of particularistic histories in which truth is submerged in legend. The new nations need, above all, to see themselves and their neighbors as free as possible of illusion and gross error. But the problem is not easily dismissed. The Western nations, confident and poised, are able to affect considerable sophistication about their respective histories. They have shown a commendable rigor in reducing overblown histories to their proper proportion, in separating myth from fact, in criticizing their own excesses of nationalistic zeal. With all this, their histories are still cast in an essentially nationalistic and parochial mold. They can hardly be surprised (nor should they be supercilious) that new nations which are struggling desperately to achieve some sense of national identity employ the means invented by their former colonial overlords. Most of the new nations have been propelled out of pre-history into history by the West. The experience has been traumatic and irreversible (unless indeed the whole world is to return to barbarism, an eventuality which is by no means to be ruled out). However primitive, crude, naïve, or presumptuous these newcomers may be, they must be integrated into the community of nations. The alternative is chaos.

It is we who have burdened the primitive and traditional cultures of the world with "the terror of history." Most of them have evaded history for thousands of years by means of the techniques Mircea Eliade has described—astral analogies, archetypes, repetition, cosmogonies of creation, and so on. They have been wrenched out of the womb of the eternal present or, as in the case of India, out of a complex but consoling cosmogony, and delivered raw and naked into a historical world. It is not surprising that Marxism, which offers a prospective release from history, should have great appeal for them; that it does not have more is due less to its attractiveness than to the fact that a vast majority of these newly modern peoples still cling to remnants of their anti-historical theologies. Certainly their very tentative acceptance of a historical world in the Western sense may be withdrawn at any time, particularly if the tragedies of history place too heavy a burden on psyches ill-prepared to cope with them. Moreover, we should remember that in the United States the millennial Protestant sects, with their expectation of Christ's more or less imminent reign on earth, offer a tempting avenue of escape within the framework of fundamentalist Christianity. These forces, so different in origin, may combine to overwhelm the historic consciousness of twentieth-century man if we fail to recover and then dramatize the human meaning and relevance of history, thus using history as a means of creating the true unity of mankind.

In this primary task (one shared, incidentally, by Russia), historians must surely take part. As we have noted, institutes have been established on many university campuses to carry on research in the problems of the emergent nations. But these programs will not satisfy the deeper needs of the new countries for a place in the family of nations. If the avenue to national respectability seems to lie in an insistence upon a unique and glorious history, they will, inevitably, follow this path. Western historians can forestall such intellectually disreputable and politically dangerous enterprises by emerging from their national preserves and writing universal history; that is to say, the common history of mankind in which new nations and old nations take their proper place. It is entirely conceivable that the citizens of newly independent Nigeria will be satisfied to see themselves as part of the general history of the human race; that they and their sister states will then waive their rights to particularistic and largely mythical histories. The experiment is worth trying—the more so since national histories are, in any event, obsolete. Unfortunately, the idea of historians in England, France, Germany, and, above all, the United States, abandoning their primarily nationalistic orientation is, on the face of it, wildly Utopian. It runs counter to all the tendencies and prejudices of our day. Specialization and compartmentalization are everywhere in the ascendency. The Toynbees are viewed with suspicion or contempt; the monograph reigns supreme and virtually unchallenged.

Yet suppose the notion that the sum total of monographs with each passsing year can come closer and closer to the truth; suppose this notion, in which we have in fact lost faith, should suddenly fall to the ground. Suppose that, like the one-horse shay, it were to disintegrate before the astonished eyes of the onlookers. What would then occupy the attention of historians?

To take another tack, let us consider the number of Ph.D.'s in institutions of higher learning in the United States who are engaged in research in American history. The vast majority of historians who have received the doctorate in this country since 1873 have concentrated on American history. There are between five and six thousand Ph.D.'s in history in the United States, and the ranks are growing at the rate of some three hundred a year. Of these, approximately fifty-five per cent—or between twenty-five hundred and three thousand—are working in the field of American history. And perhaps seventy-five per cent are specialists in some aspect of the so-called national period—roughly the hundred and seventy-three years since the formation of the Federal Constitution. In other words, there are about fifteen trained and presumably productive scholars for every year of our history as a nation. And as the passage of time adds about a hundred and fifty Ph.D.'s a year for every additional year of our history, the "historian explosion" has rather serious implications. Technological unemployment may be as much of a threat to American historians as to the assembly-line workers of Detroit.

Despite the fond expectations and periodic exhortations of department chairmen, colleagues, and deans, most of these Ph.D.'s produce very little in the way of so-called scholarly work. And that, under the circumstances, is a blessing. Nonetheless, there are so many productive historians and so few years to cover that the same field is constantly being replowed. This is known as offering "new interpretations," and each new interpretation, hopefully, brings us nearer the truth. In earlier chapters I have suggested that this is too optimistic an expectation. Often the new interpretations are fleeting indeed and do more to confuse than to enlighten the undergraduate students to whom they are revealed immediately by instructors anxious to "keep up" with the latest scholarship. One cannot but wonder what this consists of. A Rip Van Winkle student familiar with David Ramsay's interpretation of the causes of the American Revolution who subsequently fell asleep and awoke a hundred and seventy years later would find the Revolution being interpreted very much as it had been in Ramsay's day. This would be reassuring to him until he discovered that at least three quite different interpretations had been considered "true" before the contemporary view once again prevailed.

We have reached the point of diminishing returns in the research and writing of American history.[1] If anyone doubts this, he has only to compare the quality of articles which appeared in the early years of the *American Historical Review* with those of, say, the last decade. We have better training, more resources, more monographs, more historians, and, generally speaking, worse history. American historians need a new concept of their task. They have trampled around in their own back yard too long, stumbling over one another and working and reworking an increasingly arid soil. It may thus be

---

[1]It might be well to recall Burckhardt's warning about the dangers of national history: "Bias . . . is particularly prone to make its appearance in the guise of patriotism, so that true knowledge finds its chief rival in our preoccupation with the history of our own country. . . . There are certainly things in which the history of a man's own country will always take precedence, and it is our bounden duty to occupy ourselves with it. Yet it should always be balanced by some other great line of study, if only because it is so intimately interwoven with our desires and fears, and because the bias it imparts to our mind is always towards intentions and away from knowledge." *Force and Freedom* (New York: Pantheon Books; 1943), p. 88.

hoped that they will be favorably inclined toward a new orientation.

All they need to do is to recapture the generous and cosmopolitan spirit of the first generation of American historians. The word *universal* came readily to the minds of these gentlemen. Jedediah Morse wrote a *Universal Geography* with special emphasis on the United States of America, and David Ramsay, at the time of his death, was at work on a *Universal History; or, an Historical View of Asia, Africa, Europe, and America, from their Earliest Records to the Nineteenth Century; with a Particular Reference to the State of Society, Literature, Religion, and Form of Government, in the United States of America.* In the years after the Revolution, Americans were very conscious of their relation to the rest of the world. Nationalistic zeal had not yet caused them to become provincial, to speak with increasing stridency of American this and American that, of American wealth and power, American wisdom and virtue, American uniqueness and American rectitude.

With a United Nations and a European Economic Community, it is perhaps not too much to hope that historians might once more become part of a world community. Of course, when one speaks of universal history to a scholar who has spent the better part of his life mastering a decade of American history or a generation of European history, one arouses the profoundest anxieties and suspicions. And, indeed, it might properly be asked: Is everyone suddenly to start writing universal history? Is the historian who feels incapable of encompassing a decade to be asked to venture into the broad stream of time which includes all human societies? Such a notion is inconsistent with all the canons of conscientious scholarship, and we are not naïve enough to recommend it. What is involved, essentially, is a new frame of mind in which the historian's study of a single period or event in a single nation is broadened to include the whole spectrum of similar events in other nations. We might well recall the words spoken in 1890 by Herbert Baxter Adams, the dean of American historical studies. He wanted, Baxter declared, "a fair field for comparative studies in Church and State and the Institutes of Education, without being regarded as an American provincial." A review of the statements and the scholarship of this generation of historians will disclose a much greater concern for the history of man in general than is found among their present-day heirs. It is this spirit, deepened and extended, which we would call universal history. The historian will still have his specialty, but it will be related to problems common to segments of society larger than his own nation.[2]

In an age when astronauts orbit the earth in little more than an hour and by doing so give dramatic emphasis to the common destiny of man, it is an anachronism for historians to confine themselves to an intellectual orbit that fails to carry them beyond the borders of their own nation. What is demanded as the price for this wider range is that the historian do what by the nature of his craft he has been most reluctant to do, that is, distinguish between that which is important and that which is unimportant. The monograph, which includes everything of any conceivable relevance to its subject, is the model of indiscriminate history and involves the abdication of the process of selection and arrangement that is the essence of good history.

C. Vann Woodward has enumerated some of the specific tasks with which modern history has presented the historian. These are, primarily, tasks imposed or suggested by the manifestly in-terdependent relationship of the nations of the world: military and diplomatic history, the history of science and technology, the relation of America to Europe, etc.[3] All these are relatively new fields for investigation. In addition, epic political history, which has been the backbone of all history, will doubtless reassert itself. In the fields of social and intellectual history, as indeed of what we have called symbolic history, work of considerable insight and sophistica-tion is being done. Such work only needs, in most instances, to be broadened to yield enormously fruitful results. It is concerned, generally, with analysis and needs to be balanced by better existen-tial history.

Science claims to be predictive. Indeed, if it is not, it is not science. The historian's desire to work toward prediction or to attain the power of prediction is a measure of his longing to share in the

---

[2]C. Wright Mills has written: "You cannot understand or explain the major phases through which any modern Western nation has passed, or the shape that it assumes today, solely in terms of its own national history. I do not mean merely that in historical reality it has interacted with the development of other societies; I mean also that the mind cannot even formulate the historical and sociological problems of this one social structure without understanding them in contrast and in comparison with other societies." *The Sociological Imagination* (New York: Oxford University Press; 1959), p. 151.

[3]C. Vann Woodward: *The Age of Interpretation* (Washington, D.C.: Service Center for Teachers of History; 1961), No. 35.

dazzling nimbus of the scientist. But the yearning has deeper roots. The historian, as we have suggested, is vitally concerned with the future. In fact, it is his concern for the future which induces him to turn his attention to the past. The future can only take place when that portion of the past which must be preserved has been distinguished from that portion which must be abandoned, and this can only be done by reference to a future which commands the deepest faith and the highest aspiration of the present. For this reason, history is important; for this reason, we pay heed to it. As science, as antiquarianism, as history-for-history's sake, it is quite unimportant. As a means of survival, as a means of making possible a decent future for all mankind, it must be told and must be heard. Santayana has said that the nation which will not remember its history has to repeat it. Historians are the custodians of the common memories of mankind. In a very real sense it is upon their wisdom and resolution that the destiny of man depends. The Hebrews discovered history; the Christians made it the heritage of all men. The secular mind of the Western world put it in the service of modern nation states without at the same time destroying its power to unify mankind through its ability to evoke the universality of man. This is its present task. The yearning of many historians to make history a predictive science degrades the prophetic power of history. History is not concerned with predicting: the ability to predict would mean a closed and determined universe or, perhaps worse, a managed one. And if we know anything from our observation of the drama of history, it is that history is open, full of extraordinary potential and inexplicable turns and changes.

Egon Friedell, writing in 1920 of the future, professed to find "just these five possibilities: that (1) America will triumph materially, which would mean world-domination by the United States and, at the end of this interim empire, the fall of the West through over-technicalization; (2) America will triumph spiritually by becoming sublimated, this implying the rebirth of Germany, whence alone this sublimation could be derived; (3) the East will triumph materially, bringing about world-Bolshevism and the interim reign of anti-Christ; (4) the East will triumph spiritually, reviving Christianity through the Russian soul; and (5) the fifth eventuality is—chaos. These five possibilities present themselves and no others, whether political, ethical, or psychological. It will, however, be clear, we hope, to the intelligent reader that none of these eventualities will materialize, for world history is not an equation, not even one with several solutions. Its only real possibility is the unreal, and its only causality irrationality. It is made by a higher mind than the human."[4].

When we say that the proper role of history is prophetic, we use the word in its Old Testament sense. The prophets of the Hebrews did not try to predict the future from any position "outside" their tribe or kingdom. They called their people to judgment because they loved them only less than they loved the Lord and they were, in consequence, compelled to remind the people constantly of what they wished to forget: the requirements of Jehovah. The responsibility of the modern historian, like that of the prophets of Israel, is to speak of those things which must continue to claim our loyalties and engage our faith (Robert Frost has defined faith as our power to dream the future into existence); the future is given shape by our faith, or condemned to drift and disaster by our indifference.[5]

The relativism which has so distressed present-day historians and which most of them have come to accept finally as an unfortunate but inescapable fact of their human condition might be better translated as *commitment*. Because the historian is himself involved in history, or should be; because he is a participant in the struggles and crises that now quite clearly shape man's common destiny, his history is relative—which is not only as it must be, but as it should be. In this context, *relative* might also be translated *relevant*. It is only by being relevant to his day and age that the historian has the remotest chance of being relevant to any future day. All his whoring after objectivity is a death wish in disguise—disguised as a desire for a kind of immortality to be won, hopefully, by escaping from history, by getting "outside" and thus being as true tomorrow as today, by being, in other words, like God Himself. But such an expectation is the vanity of all vanities. Out of the vast legions of the past, the few souls who have won earthly immortality—whether in history or in literature—have done so because of their power to universalize the particular, to involve themselves so deeply and

[4]*Cultural History of the Modern Age* (New York: Alfred A. Knopf; 1932), III, p. 478.

[5]"History, without qualification, is the process of the civilizing of mankind. It is world history, always something more than a collection of stories of independent states and nations, or collations of these. History is mankind expressed over time, inching on in the production of a single civilization where men flourish in peace and justice fulfilling themselves together as wills, bodies, minds and persons." Paul Weiss: *History: Written and Lived,* p. 130.

percipiently in their own time or in an earlier time that they transcend time by the power of their love. Their passion speaks with such accuracy and insight of the men and events that moved them that others are equally moved and stand in spirit with them at the pass of Thermopylae or at the ruins of Carthage.

The historian must recognize that history is not a scientific enterprise but a moral one. It is the study of human beings involved in an extraordinary drama, and its dramatic qualities are related to the moral values inherent in all life. History is in large part the story of the men and women who have suffered and sacrificed to create the world in which we live. In this sense, it is selective rather than democratic. In history, all men are *not* created equal. The general is more important than the private; the king, in most instances, is more important than his subject. History is concerned with the actions of individuals and social groups, and since such action almost invariably has been undertaken in the name of certain values and ideals, the historian must make judgments on the actors and their actions. He must discriminate, furthermore, between that which must be preserved and that which must be discarded. If he is dealing with the American Civil War, for instance, he must implicitly or explicitly take a position on slavery. And this position will have very little to do with objectivity; it will be based on certain moral assumptions about the nature of involuntary servitude. And so on, throughout history. Sometimes the values will be, as we are so fond of saying, "relative," but they will nonetheless be present. Judgment is a continual part of the dialogue of the historian—although, if he is true to his muse, he will temper his judgment with understanding and compassion. There is nothing more irritating than the complacent and insensitive boor who tramps through the past, meting out praise and blame with a heavy and dogmatic hand. It is this type that is so ready to indict an individual or an age for failing to be as enlightened in its social, political, or religious practices as he is. To abuse the Founding Fathers for favoring suffrage based on property, for example, is not only stupid but gratuitous. On the other hand, we should hardly be inclined to propose such a basis for suffrage as a panacea for present-day political ills.

Historians have hotly debated the question of "present-mindedness" as opposed to "history-mindedness"—whether the historian should exploit the past in behalf of the present, or whether his primary responsibility is to try to detach himself from the present and immerse himself in the past. Either course, pursued single-mindedly, invites disaster. Present-mindedness may result in the most superficial and jejune treatment of the individuals and events of earlier ages—in adapting the past, as Nietzsche expressed it, "to present trivialities." These are the "thoughtless folk who write history in the naïve faith that justice resides in the popular view of their time, and that to write in the spirit of the times is to be just."[6]

History-mindedness may equally well result in antiquarianism, in a stultifying devotion to the imagined charm and quaintness of the past. The truth lies somewhere between. Almost inevitably, the historian's attention is directed to those aspects of the past which are relevant to his own day. Once that assumption is granted, it must be said with equal emphasis that the historian is under the heaviest obligation to extend his own sympathy and understanding to those who, in other times, loved and aspired, believed and fought, suffered and died—actors, like the historian himself, in the universal drama of mankind.

Above all, the historian must cease to think of himself on the one hand as standing "outside" history, as explaining to youthful and immature minds the "way things happened," and on the other hand as carrying on an esoteric conversation with his colleagues about the finer points of interpretation. The historian is existentially involved in history, or he is nothing. His task is to awaken the minds of his students and to inspire them with a vision of the future which will make sense of the past.

[6]Peter Geyl, *The Use and Abuse of History* (New Haven: Yale University Press; 1955), p. 44.

IV History and Commitment

Howard Zinn has become one of the leading proponents of history designed to help us resolve the problems of today. In spite of Zinn's allegiance to professional standards, there is a danger that the historian following his approach will cross the thin line that separates history from propaganda. The dominant strain in Zinn's writings is social utility, and pursuit of that goal may lead the historian to ignore or suppress some unpleasant truths about man's history. Should we dismiss, for example, the possibility that slavery may have been a step forward in the history of mankind? Perhaps, as one writer has suggested, victors in wars no longer slaughtered their prisoners when they found they could use them to perform certain menial tasks. Yet historical examples of the advantages of slavery have little social utility in today's racially tense climate. Should we ignore the unpleasant possibility that warfare may have been one of the prime contributors to the health, the vigor, and the advance of western civilization? This "fact" has little social utility in an age of nuclear weapons. Ignoring the role of public opinion in sanctioning past wars may be a serious distortion of history even though in our time it may be more useful to concentrate on the power of decision-making elites.

Martin Duberman's thoughtful essay leaves us with the impression that history has very little social utility for those who are interested in attacking the evils of our time. It may be good for the individual in a variety of ways, but, unlike Zinn, Duberman expresses doubts that the historian *qua* historian can contribute much to solving the great problems that face us today.

The essays by J. H. Hexter and Siegfried Kracauer are in marked contrast to those of Duberman and Zinn, who are as noted for social and political activism as for their historical works. Kracauer is acutely aware of how present interests can corrupt the historian and lead him to write bad history, i.e., history that does violence to what actually happened in the past. Hexter explains why he knows more about the sixteenth century than the twentieth, and he directly challenges the unabashed relativism of those historians who feel that since we cannot escape from present concerns, we might as well admit our biases and write history for particular causes.

HOWARD ZINN
History as Private Enterprise

LET US TURN NOW from scholars in general to historians in particular. For a long time, the historian has been embarrassed by his own humanity. Touched by the sight of poverty, horrified by war, revolted by racism, indignant at the strangling of dissent, he has nevertheless tried to keep his tie straight, his voice unruffled, and his emotions to himself. True, he has often slyly attuned his research to his feelings, but so slyly, and with such scholarly skill, that only close friends and investigators for congressional committees might suspect him of compassion.

Historians worry that a deep concern with current affairs may lead to twisting the truth about the past. And indeed, it may, under conditions which I will discuss below. But nonconcern results in another kind of distortion, in which the ore of history is beaten neither into plowshare nor sword, but is melted down and sold. For the historian is a specialist who makes his living by writing and teaching, and his need to maintain his position in the profession tends to pull him away from controversy (except the polite controversy of academic disputation) and out of trouble.[1]

The tension between human drives and professional mores leads many to a schizophrenic separation of scholarly work from other activities; thus, research on Carolingian relations with the Papacy is interrupted momentarily to sign a petition on civil rights. Sometimes the separation is harder to maintain, and so the specialist on Asia scrupulously stays away from teach-ins on Vietnam, and seeks to keep his work unsullied by application to the current situation. One

---

[1] The historian of the eighteenth and nineteenth century was not a professional, and so tended more often to write partisan history, although his very independence in wealth and stature in society (Henry Adams, George Bancroft) meant his partisanship was most often of behalf of national or upper class interests. In any case, his writing had the tang of life and combat so often missing in the professional historian. This is not to close out the occasional transcendence of narrow interest as by Richard Hildreth, who wrote in the early national period, "unbedaubed with patriotic rough" (as he described himself), while Bancroft wrote with nationalist fervor. Hildreth was relatively obscure, Bancroft immensely popular.

From *The Politics of History,* pages 15-34, by Howard Zinn. Copyright © 1970 by Howard Zinn. Reprinted by permission of Beacon Press.

overall result is that common American phenomenon—the secret radical.

There is more than a fifty-fifty chance that the academic historian will lose what vital organs of social concern he has in the process of acquiring a doctorate, where the primary requirement of finding an untouched decade or person or topic almost assures that several years of intense labor will end in some monstrous irrelevancy. And after that, the considerations of rank, tenure, and salary, while not absolutely excluding either personal activism or socially pertinent scholarship, tend to discourage either.

We find, of course, oddities of academic behavior: Henry Steele Commager writing letters to the *Times* defending Communists; Martin Duberman putting the nation's shame on stage; Staughton Lynd flying to Hanoi. And to the rule of scholarly caution, the exceptions have been glorious:

Beard's *An Economic Interpretation of the Constitution* was muckraking history, not because it splattered mud on past heroes, but because it made several generations of readers worry about the working of economic interest in the politics of their own time. The senior Arthur Schlesinger, in an essay in *New Viewpoints in American History,* so flattened pretensions of "states' rights" that no reader could hear that phrase again without smiling. DuBois' *Black Reconstruction* was as close as a scholar could get to a *demonstration,* in the deepest sense of that term, puncturing a long and destructive innocence. Matthew Josephson's *The Robber Barrons* and Henry David's *History of the Haymarket Affair* were unabashed in their sympathies. Walter Millis' *The Road to War* was a deliberate and effective counter to romantic nonsense about the First World War. Arthur Weinberg's *Manifest Destiny* quietly exposed the hypocrisy of both conservatives and liberals in the idealization of American expansion. Richard Hofstadter's *The American Political Tradition* made us wonder about *now* by brilliantly deflating the liberal heroes—Jefferson, Jackson, Wilson, the two Roosevelts. And C. Vann Woodward gently reminded the nation, in *The Strange Career of Jim Crow,* that racism might be deeply embedded, yet it could change its ways in remarkably short time. There are many others.

But with all this, the dominant mood in historical writing in the United States (look at the pages of the historical reviews) avoids direct confrontation of contemporary problems, apologizes for any sign of departure from "objectivity," spurns a liaison with social action. Introducing a recent collection of theoretical essays on American history,[2] historian Edward N. Saveth asserts that the social science approach to history "was confused" by "the teleology of presentism." (In the space of three pages, Saveth uses three variations of the word "confusion" to discuss the effect of presentism.)

What is presentism? It was defined by Carl Becker in 1912 as "the imperative command that knowledge shall serve purpose, and learning be applied to the solution of the problem of human life." Saveth, speaking for so many of his colleagues, shakes his head: "The fires surrounding the issues of reform and relativism had to be banked before the relationship between history and social science could come under objective scrutiny."[3]

They were not really fires, but only devilishly persistent sparks, struck by Charles Beard, James Harvey Robinson, and Carl Becker.[4] There was no need to "bank" them, only to smother them under thousands of volumes of "objective" trivia, which became the trade mark of academic history, revealed to fellow members of the profession in papers delivered at meetings, doctoral dissertations, and articles in professional journals.

In *Knowledge for What?*, Robert S. Lynd questioned the relevance of a detailed analysis of "The Shield Signal at Marathon" which appeared in the *American Historical Review* in 1937. He wondered if it was a "warranted expenditure of scientific energy." Twenty-six years later (in the issue of July 1965), the lead article in the *American Historical Review* is "William of Malmesbury's Robert of Gloucester: a Reevaluation of the *Historia Novella.*" In 1959, we find historians at a meeting of the Southern Historical Association (the same meeting which tabled a resolution asking an immediate end to the practice of holding sessions at hotels that barred Negroes) presenting long papers on "British Men of War in Southern Waters, 1793-1802," "Textiles: A Period of Sturm und Drang," and "Bampson of Bampson's Raiders."

As Professor Lynd put it long ago: "History, thus voyaging forth

[2]Edward N. Saveth, ed., "Conceptualization of American History," *American History and the Social Sciences,* Free Press, 1964.
[3]Ibid., p. 8.
[4]See James Harvey Robinson's *The New History*, MacMillan, 1912; Carl Becker's *Everyman His Own Historian*, Appleton-Century-Crofts, 1935. See also the discussion of Beard's activism in Richard Hofstadter, *The Progressive Historians: Turner, Beard, Parrington*, Knopf, 1968, especially pp. 170-181.

with no pole star except the objective recovery of the past, becomes a vast, wandering enterprise." And in its essence, I would add, it is *private* enterprise.

This is not to deny that there are many excellent historical studies only one or two degrees removed from immediate applicability to crucial social problems. The problem is in the proportion. There is immense intellectual energy in the United States devoted to inspecting the past, but only a tiny amount of this is deliberately directed to the solution of vital problems: racism, poverty, war, repression, loneliness, alienation, imprisonment. Where historical research has been useful, it has often been by chance rather than by design, in accord with a kind of trickle-down theory which holds that if you only fill the libraries to bursting with enough processed pulpwood, something useful will eventually reach a society desperate for understanding.

While scholars do have a vague, general desire to serve a social purpose, the production of historical works is largely motivated by profit (promotion, prestige, and even a bit of money) rather than by use. This does not mean that useful knowledge is not produced (or that what is produced is not of excellent quality in its own terms, as our society constructs excellent office buildings while people live in rattraps). It does mean that this production is incidental, more often than not. In a rich economy, not in some significant degree directed toward social reform, waste is bound to be huge, measured in lost opportunities and misdirected effort.

True, the writing of history is really a mixed economy, but an inspection of the mixture shows that the social sector is only a small proportion of the mass.[5] What I am suggesting is not a totalistic direction of scholarship but (leaving complete freedom and best wishes to all who want to analyze "The Shield Signal at Marathon" or "Bampson of Bampson's Raiders") an enlargement of the social sector by encouragement, persuasion, and demonstration.

I am not directing my criticism against those few histories which are works of art, which make no claim to illuminate a social problem, but instead capture the mood, the color, the reality of an age, an incident, or an individual, conveying pleasure and the warmth of genuine emotion. This needs no justification, for it is,

---

[5]"In sheer bulk," John Higham points out in *The Reconstruction of American History,* "the product equals or surpasses the historical literature of any modern nation." Harper (Torchbook edition), 1962, p. 10.

after all, the ultimate purpose of social change to enlarge human happiness.

However, too much work in history is neither art nor science. It is sometimes defended as "pure research" like that of the mathematician, whose formulas have no knowable immediate use. But the pure scientist is working on data which open toward infinity in their possible future uses. This is not true of the historian working on a dead battle or an obscure figure. Also, the proportion of scientists working on "pure research" is quite small. The historian's situation is the reverse; the proportion working on applicable data is tiny. Only when the pendulum swings the other way will the historian be able justly to complain that pure research is being crowded out.

Enlarging the social sector of historiography requires, as a start, removing the shame from "subjectivity." Benedetto Croce undertook this, as far back as 1920, reacting against the strict claims of "scientific history": what von Ranke called history "as it actually was," and what Bury called "simply a science, no less and no more." Croce openly avowed that what he chose to investigate in the past was determined by "an interest in the life of the present" and that past facts must answer "to a present interest."[6] In America, James Harvey Robinson said: "The present has hitherto been the willing victim of the past; the time has now come when it should turn on the past and exploit it in the interest of advance."[7]

But this confession of concern for current problems made other scholars uneasy. Philosopher Arthur O. Lovejoy, for instance, said the aims of the historian must not be confused with those of the "social reformer," and that the more a historian based his research on problems of "the period in which he writes" then "the worse historian he is likely to be." The job of the historian, he declared (this was in the era of the Memorial Day Massacre, Guernica, and the Nuremberg Laws) is "to know whether . . . certain events, or sequences of events, happened at certain past times, and what . . . the characters of those events were." When philosophers suggest this is not the first business of a historian, Lovejoy said, "they merely tend to undermine his morals as a historian."

At the bottom of the fear of engagement, it seems to me, is a confusion between ultimate values and instrumental ones. To start

---

[6]Benedetto Croce, quoted in Hans Meyerhoff, ed., *The Philosophy of History in Our Time,* Doubleday (Anchor edition), 1959.

[7]James Harvey Robinson, *The New History,* Free Press (paper edition), 1965, p. 24.

historical enquiry with frank adherence to a small set of ultimate values—that war, poverty, race hatred, prisons, should be abolished; that mankind constitutes a single species; that affection and cooperation should replace violence and hostility—such a set of commitments places no pressure on its advocates to tamper with the truth. The claim of Hume and his successors among the logical positivists, that no *should* can be proved by what *is,* has its useful side, for neither can the moral absolute be disproved by any factual discovery.[8]

Confusion on this point is shown by Irwin Unger, in his article "The 'New Left' and American History,"[9] where he says:

> If there has been no true dissent in America; if a general consensus over capitalism, race relations, and expansionism has prevailed in the United States; if such dissent as has existed has been crankish and sour, the product not of a maladjusted society but of maladjusted men—then American history may well be monumentally irrelevant for contemporary radicalism.

Unger seems to believe that a radical historian who is opposed to capitalism *must* find such opposition to capitalism in the American past in order to make the study of history worthwhile for him; the implication is that if he does not find such opposition he may invent it, or exaggerate what he finds. But the factual data need not contain any premonition of the future for the historian to advocate such a future. The world has been continually at war for as long as we can remember; yet the historian who seeks peace, and indeed who would like his research to have an effect on society in behalf of peace, need not distort the martial realities of the past. Indeed, his recording of that past and its effects may itself be a very effective

[8]If our ultimate aim is human happiness and particular arrangements of the races in residential patterns are *means,* then the fact that integration of the races in a particular situation did not prove a happy solution need not be hidden for fear it might hurt our ultimate values. That fact would show us that integration in itself is not sufficient to produce happiness—it may set us to look for other factors—and we would even keep our minds open to the possibility that integration could produce unhappiness, either in certain situations or conceivably in all situations. I present this illustration not for its factual accuracy, but as an example of how honesty is not foreclosed by "subjectivity" if one keeps the ultimate values distinct from the instrumental ones.

[9]Irwin Unger, "The 'New Left' and American History," *American Historical Review,* July 1967.

way of reminding the reader that the future needs kinds of human relationships which have *not* been very evident in the past.

(Unger continues to make the same mistake in this essay when, discussing William A. Williams' *The Contours of American History,* he notes that it shows general American acceptance of private property and says "*The Contours* proves a constant embarrassment to the younger radical scholars.")

For an American historian with an ultimate commitment to radical equality there is no compulsion to ignore the facts that many slaveholders did not use whips on their slaves, that most slaves did not revolt, that some Negro officeholders in the Reconstruction period were corrupt, or that the homicide rate has been higher among Negroes than whites. But with such a commitment, and more concerned to shape the future than to recount the past for its own sake, the historian would be driven to point out what slavery meant for the "well-treated" slave; to explain how corruption was biracial in the 1870's as in all periods; to discuss Uncle Tomism along with the passivity of Jews in the concentration camps and the inertia of thirty million poor in an affluent America; to discuss the relationship between poverty and certain sorts of crime.[10]

Unyielding dedication to certain *instrumental* values, on the other hand—to specific nations, organizations, leaders, social systems, religions, or techniques, all of which claim their own efficacy in advancing the ultimate values—creates powerful pressures for hiding or distorting historical events. A relentless commitment to his own country may cause an American to glide over the elements of brutality in American "diplomatic history" (the term itself manufactures a certain aura of gentility). Compare, for instance, James Reston's pious column for Easter Sunday, 1965, on the loftiness of American behavior toward other countries, with Edmund Wilson's harsh, accurate summary of American expansionism in his introduction to *Patriotic Gore.*

It was rigid devotion to Stalin, rather than to the ultimate concerns of a humane Marxism, that led to fabrication of history in the Soviet Union about the purges and other things. After 1956, a shift in instrumental gods led to counter-fabrication. With the advent of the

---

[10]The problem of *lying* is not the most serious one. If a historian lies, someone will soon find him out. If he is irrelevant, this is harder to deal with. We have accepted truth as criterion, and we will rush to invoke it, but we have not yet accepted relevance.

cold war, the United States began to outdo the Soviet Union in the large-scale development of government-supported social science research which assumed that an instrumental value—the nation's foreign policy—was identical with peace and freedom.

Thus, teams of social scientists under contract to the armed forces took without question the United States government's premise that the Soviet Union planned to invade Western Europe, and from this worked out all sorts of deductions for policy. Now it turns out (and we are told this by the same analysts) that premise was incorrect. This is replaced not by the overthrow of dogma itself, but by substituting a new assumption—that Communist China intends to take over all of Asia and eventually the world—and so the computers have begun to click out policy again. The absolutization of an instrumental value—in this case, current U.S. foreign policy (in other cases, Soviet policy or Ghanaian policy or whatever) distorts the results of research from the beginning.[11]

Knowing that commitments to instrumental values distort the facts often leads scholars to avoid commitment of any kind. Boyd Schafer, reporting for the American Historical Association on the international congress of historians held in Vienna in the summer of 1965, notes an attempt at one session to introduce the question of Vietnam. The executive body of the Congress "firmly opposed the introduction of any current political question," saying the organization "had been and could only be devoted to scientific historical studies." Here were twenty-four hundred historians from forty nations, presumably an enormous assembly of data and insights from all branches of history; if this body could not throw any light on the problem of Vietnam, what claim can anyone make that history is studied to help us understand the present?

It testifies to the professionalization, and therefore the dehumanization of the scholar, that while tens of thousands of them gather annually in the United States alone, to hear hundreds of papers on scattered topics of varying significance, there has been no move to select a problem—poverty, race prejudice, the war in Vietnam,

---

[11]One of the contributions the historians can make is to disprove the absolute value of certain social instruments by revealing their weaknesses and failures—thus helping us guard against total approval of any particular nation, race, ideology, party. Pieter Geyl, for instance, in *Encounters in History,* Meridian, 1961, makes the point that history can prevent us from hating a whole people, a whole civilization, by the understanding it gives.

alternative methods of social change—for concentrated attention by some one conference.

But if a set of "ultimate values"—peace, racial equality, economic security, freedom of expression—is to guide our questioning, without distorting our answers, what is the source of these values? Can we prove their validity?

It is only when "proof" is identified with academic research that we are at a loss to justify our values. The experiences of millions of lives over centuries of time, relived by each of us in those aspects common to all men, *prove* to us that love is preferable to hate, peace to war, brotherhood to enmity, joy to sorrow, health to sickness, nourishment to hunger, life to death. And enough people recognize these values (in all countries, and inside all social systems) so that further academic disputation is only a stumbling block to action. What we see and feel (should we not view human emotion as crystallized, ineffable rationality?) is more formally stated as a fact of social psychology in Freud's broadest definition of Eros and in Erik Erikson's idea of "the more inclusive identity."[12]

How should all this affect the actual work of the historian? For one thing, it calls for an emphasis on those historical facts which have hitherto been obscured, and whose recall would serve to enhance justice and brotherhood. It is by now a truism that all historical writing involves a selection of facts out of those which are available. But what standards should govern this selection?

Harvard philosopher Morton White, anxious to defend "historical objectivity" against "the hurried flight to relativism," says that the "ideal purpose of history" is "to tell the whole truth."[13] But since it is impossible to have historical accounts list all that has taken place, White says the historian's job is to give a shorter, "representative" list. White values "impersonal standards" and "a neutral standpoint." The crux of this argument is based on the notion that the fundamental aim of the historian is to tell as much of the story of the past as he can.

Even if it were possible to list *all* the events of a given historical

---

[12]For an extended discussion on this point—that beyond intuitive and existential "proof" of these values there is a wealth of biological, psychological, cultural, and historical evidence to support them—see Abraham Edel, *Ethical Judgement: The Use of Science in Ethics,* Free Press, 1955.

[13]Morton White, *Social Thought in America,* Beacon (paper edition), 1947, pp. 227-228.

period, would this really capture the human reality of this period? Can starvation, war, suffering, joy, be given their due, even in the most complete historical recounting? Is not the *quality* of events more important than their quantity? Is there not something inherent in setting the past on paper which robs human encounter of its meaning? Does not the attention to either completeness or representativeness of "the facts" only guarantee that the cool jelly of neutrality will spread over it all, and that the reader will be left in the mood of the writer—that is, the mood of detached scholarship? And if this is so, does not the historian, concerned with the quality of his own time, need to work on the list in such a way as to try to restore its human content?

In a world where justice is maldistributed, historically and now, there is no such thing as a "neutral" or "representative" recapitulation of the facts, any more than one is dealing "equally" with a starving beggar and a millionaire by giving each a piece of bread. The condition of the recipient is crucial in determining whether the distribution is just.

Our best historians, whether or not they acknowledge it, take this into account. Beard's study of the making of the Constitution was hardly a representative list of the events connected with the Philadelphia Convention. He singled out the economic and political backgrounds of the Founding Fathers to illustrate the force of economic interest in political affairs, and he did it because (as he put it later) "this realistic view of the Constitution had been largely submerged in abstract discussion of states' rights and national sovereignty and in formal, logical, and discriminative analyses of judicial opinions."[14]

When C. Vann Woodward wrote *The Strange Career of Jim Crow* he chose instances of equal treatment for Southern Negroes in public facilities, voting, transportation, in the 1880's. These were certainly not "representative." But he chose to emphasize them because he was writing in a time (1954) when much of the American nation, North and South, seemed to believe that segregation was so long and deeply entrenched in the South that it could not be

[14]This larger point is often forgotten in the meticulous critiques of Beard's specific data by scholars. For instance, see Robert E. Brown, *Charles Beard and the Constitution: A Critical Analysis of an Economic Interpretation of the Constitution,* Princeton, 1956, where Brown's main correction is that the Constitution favored "middle-class property owners" whose holdings were in land as opposed to Beard's emphasis on holdings in more disposable wealth.

changed. Woodward's intent was to indicate that things have not always been the same in the South.[15]

Similarly, the "Freedom Primer," used in the deep South by the Student Nonviolent Coordinating Committee, carefully selects from the mass of facts about the Negro in America those stories of heroism and rebellion which would give a Mississippi black child a sense of pride and worth, precisely because those are the feelings which everything around him tries to crush. (Yet one should not hesitate to point out, to a black child who developed the notion that blacks could do no wrong, that history also showed some unheroic Negroes.)

The examples I have given are not "neutral" or "representative," but they are *true* to the ideal of man's oneness and to the reality of his separateness. Truth only in relation to what is or was is one-dimensional. Historical writing is most *true* when it is appropriate simultaneously to what was in the past, to the condition of the present, and to what should be done in the future. Let me give a few examples.

How can a historian portray the twenties? It was a time of glittering "prosperity," with several million unemployed. There were floods of new consumer goods in the stores, with poverty on the farm. There was a new class of millionaires, while people in city slums struggled to pay the rent and gas bills. The two hundred largest corporations were doubling their assets, but Congressman Fiorello LaGuardia, representing a working-class district in East Harlem, wrote in 1928:[16]

> It is true that Mr. Mellon, Mr. Ford, Mr. Rosenwald, Mr. Schwab, Mr. Morgan and a great many others not only manage to keep their enormous fortunes intact, but increase their fortunes every year. . . . But can any one of them improve on the financial genius of Mrs. Maria Esposito or Mrs. Rebecca Epstein or Mrs. Maggie Flynn who is keeping house in a New York tenement raising five or six children on a weekly envelope of thirty dollars . . . ?

A "comprehensive" picture of the twenties, the kind most often

---

[15]As with Robert Brown and Beard, the scholarly critics often miss Woodward's main point, which is *not* invalidated by the evidence of segregation alongside slavery, as in "Racial Segregation in Ante Bellum New Orleans," by Roger A. Fisher, *American Historical Review,* February 1969.

[16]Clipping from New York *Graphic* in *LaGuardia Papers,* New York Public Library.

found in American history textbooks, emphasizes the prosperity, along with amusing instances of governmental corruption, a summary of foreign policy, a dash of literature, and a bit on the K.K.K. and the Scopes Trial. This would seem to be "representative"; it leaves the reader with an unfocused mishmash, fogged over by a general aura of well-being. But wouldn't a history of the twenties be most true to both past facts and future values if it stressed the plight of many millions of poor behind the facade of prosperity? Might not such an emphasis on the twenties, if widespread, have hastened the nation's discovery (not made until the 1960's) of poverty amidst plenty?

There is still another flaw in the exhortation to the historian to give a "representative" account of his subject: he is not writing in an empty field; thousands have preceded him and have weighted the story in certain directions. When the Marxist historian Herbert Aptheker wrote *American Negro Slave Revolts,* he was giving heavy emphasis to a phenomenon in which only a small minority of slaves had participated. But he was writing in an atmosphere dominated by the writings on slavery of men like Ulrich Phillips, when textbooks spoke of the happy slave. Both southern and northern publics needed a sharp reminder of the inhumanity of the slave system. And perhaps the knowledge that such reminders are still necessary induced Kenneth Stampp to write *The Peculiar Institution.*

The earth has for so long been so sharply tilted on behalf of the rich, the white-skinned, the male, the powerful, that it will take enormous effort to set it right. A biography of Eugene Debs (Ray Ginger's *The Bending Cross*) is a deliberate focusing on the heroic qualities of a man who devoted his life to the idea that "while there is a lower class, I am in it; while there is a criminal element, I am of it; while there is a soul in prison, I am not free." But how many biographies of the radical Debs are there, compared to biographies of John D. Rockefeller or Theodore Roosevelt? The selection of the topic for study is the first step in the weighting of the social scales for one value or another.

Let me give one more illustration of my point that there is no such thing as any one true "representative" account of a complex phenomenon, and that the situation toward which the assessment is directed should determine the emphasis (without ignoring the counter-evidence, it is important to add). In the debate between Arnold Toynbee *(A Study of History)* and Pieter Geyl *(Encounters in History),* Geyl objects to Toynbee's emphasis on the failures of

Western civilization and suggests that the West's successes should be more heavily stressed. Behind the debate, one can see the Cold War, with Geyl reacting sharply and sensitively to any account of the world which implies more condemnation of the Western countries than of the Communist nations. But what is crucial in assessing the Geyl-Toynbee debate is not one's view of the past. All of us, Toynbee as well as Geyl, could readily agree on a list of the sins committed by the Communist nations and probably also agree on a list of sins of the West. Where would that leave us, in view of the difficulty of quantifying this situation and declaring a "winner" as if in a baseball game? The crucial element is the present and the question of what we, the receivers of any assessment, will do in the present. And since Toynbee is addressing himself to the readers of the West primarily, he is implying that for Westerners to take a more critical view of their own culture will lead to more beneficial results (for those values esteemed by critics of both East and West) than to engage in self-congratulation. Since the argument about the past is insoluble, one does better directing his judgment toward the present and future.[17]

The usual distinction between "narrative" and "interpretive" history is not really pertinent to the criterion I have suggested for writing history in the public sector. It has often been assumed that narrative history, the simple description of an event or period, is "low level" history, while the interpretation of events, periods, individuals is "high level" and thus closer to the heart of a socially concerned historian. But the narration of the Haymarket Affair, or the Sacco-Vanzetti Case, to someone with a rosy picture of the American court system, has far more powerful effect on the present than an interpretation of the reasons for the War of 1812. A factual

---

[17]Confusion on this point is shown by William Bark, reviewing Pieter Geyl's *Encounters in History* (Meridian, 1961), *History and Theory,* Vol. IV, 1964. Bark connects the desire for free enquiry into history with the defense of the West against criticism. He says: "Those who believe in unrestricted historical study believe in the civilization of which their free historical interpretations are one of the cultural products and without which there could be no such study of history. When that civilization and that history are attacked, no matter how persuasively, as being meaningless and on the verge of collapse, such historians can be expected to engage in controversial discussions. . . . " Bark makes clear the past-oriented approach which leads to Geyl's defense of the West when he says: "Geyl's great service has been his insistence on standards in the writing of history and on the proper role of history as preserver of faith in the past, therefore of health and balance" (p. 107).

recounting of the addresses of Wendell Phillips constitutes (in a time when young people have begun to be captivated by the idea of joining social movements) a far more positive action on behalf of social reform than a sophisticated "interpretation" of the abolitionists which concludes that they were motivated by psychological feelings of insecurity. So much of the newer work on "concepts" in history gives up both the forest and the trees for the stratosphere.

If the historian is to approach the data of the past with a deliberate intent to further certain fundamental values in the present, then he can adopt several approaches. He may search at random in documents and publications to find material relevant to those values (this would rule out material of purely antiquarian or trivial interest). He can pursue the traditional lines of research (certain periods, people, topics: the Progressive Period, Lincoln, the Bank War, the Labor Movement) with an avowed "presentist" objective. Or, as the least wasteful method, he can use a problem-centered approach to the American past. This approach, used only occasionally in American historiography, deserves some discussion.

The starting point, it should be emphasized, is a *present* problem. Many so-called "problem approaches" in American history have been based on problems of the past. Some of these may be extended by analogy to a present problem (like Beard's concern with economic motive behind political events of the eighteenth century), but many of them are quite dead (the tariff debates of the 1820's; the character of the Southern Whigs; Turner's frontier thesis, which has occupied an incredible amount of attention). Not that bits of relevant wisdom cannot be extracted from these old problems, but the reward is small for the attention paid.[18]

Teachers and writers of history almost always speak warmly (and vaguely) of how "studying history will help you understand our own

[18]Benedetto Croce writes: "For dead history revives, and past history again becomes present, as the development of life demands them." He says that as soon as you become *interested* in a thing of the past, it becomes contemporary. His distinction between *history* and *chronicle* is based on this present-mindedness, for history is contemporary, chronicle is the dead past, and Croce says: "First comes history, then chronicle. First comes the living being, then the corpse; and to make history the child of chronicle is the same thing as to make the living be born from the corpse." (Quoted in Hans Meyerhoff, *Philosophy of History in Our Time,* Doubleday (Anchor edition), 1959, p. 52.) His metaphor recalls the Orozco mural in the Dartmouth College library, where skeletons in academic robes bring forth baby skeletons.

time." This usually means the teacher will make the point quickly in his opening lecture, or the textbook will dispose of this in an opening sentence, after which the student is treated to an encyclopedic, chronological recapitulation of the past. In effect, he is told: "The past is useful to the present. Now you figure out how."

Barrington Moore, discussing the reluctance of the historian to draw upon his knowledge for suggestive explanations of the present, says: "Most frequently of all he will retreat from such pressures into literary snobbishness and pseudo cultivation. This takes the form of airy generalizations about the way history provides 'wisdom' or 'real understanding.' . . . Anyone who wants to know how this wisdom can be effectively used, amplified and corrected, will find that his questions usually elicit no more than irritation."[19]

To start historical enquiry with a present concern requires ignoring the customary chronological fracture of the American past: the Colonial Period; the Revolutionary Period; the Jacksonian Period; and so on, down to the New Deal, the War, and the Atomic Age.[20] Instead, a problem must be followed where it leads, back and forth across the centuries if necessary.

David Potter has pointed to the unconfessed theoretical assumptions of historians who claim they are not theorizing.[21] I would carry his point further: all historians, by their writing, have some effect on the present social situation, whether they choose to be presentists or not. Therefore the real choice is not between shaping the world or not, but between doing it deliberately or unconsciously.[22]

[19]Barrington Moore, Jr., *Political Power and Social Theory,* Harvard University, 1958.

[20]John Higham, *Reconstruction of American History,* Harper (Torchbook edition), 1962, declared concern "with the rethinking that American history has undergone in recent years," and said each of the essays "tells how a standard topic in American history was understood a generation ago and how its interpretation has altered since that time." But the freshness of new interpretation was trapped by that book inside stale and purposeless categories—the "standard" topics: Puritanism, the Revolution, the West, the Jacksonian Period, the Civil War, the Progressive Tradition, Emergence to World Power. Two of the essays it must be said, were fresh topics ("The Working Class" and "The Quest for National Character").

[21]David Potter, "Explicit Data and Implicit Assumptions in Historical Study," Louis Gottschalk, ed., *Generalization in the Writing of History,* University of Chicago, 1963.

[22]Irwin Unger's complaint that: "The young radicals' efforts are generally governed not by the natural dialogue of the discipline but by the concerns of the outside

Psychology has contributed several vital ideas to our understanding of the role of the historian. In the first place, the psychologist is not recording the events of the patient's life simply to add to his files, or because they are "interesting," or because they will enable the building of complex theories. He is a therapist, devoted to the aim of curing people's problems, so that all the data he discovers are evaluated in accord with the single objective of therapy. This is the kind of commitment historians, as a group, have not yet made to society.

Second, there is Harry Stack Sullivan's notion of the psychologist as "participant." Whether the psychologist likes it or not, he is more than a listener. He has an effect on his patient. Similarly, the historian is a participant in history by his writing. Even when he claims neutrality he has an effect—if only, with his voluminous production of irrelevant data, to clog the social passages. So it is now a matter of consciously recognizing his participation, and deciding in which direction his energies will be expended.

An especially potent way of leading the historian toward a presentist, value-directed history is the binding power of social action itself. When a group of American historians in the Spring of 1965 joined the Negroes marching from Selma to Montgomery they were performing an unusual act. Social scientists sometimes speak and write on public policy; rarely do they bodily join in action to make contact with those whose motivation comes not from thought and empathy but from the direct pain of deprivation. Such contact, such engagement in action, generates an emotional attachment to the agents of social change which even long hours in the stacks can hardly injure.

Surely there is some relationship between the relative well-being of professors, their isolation in middle-class communities, their predictable patterns of sociality, and the tendency to remain distant, both personally and in scholarship, from the political battles of the day. The scholar does vaguely aim to serve some social purpose, but there is an undiscussed conflict between problem-solving and safety for a man earning fifteen thousand dollars a year. There is no deliberate avoidance of social issues, but some quite gyroscopic

cultural and political world" ignores the point that there is no "natural dialogue" of the discipline, but only a dialogue imposed by the concerns of the outside world, whether the historian chooses to recognize this fact or not. "The 'New Left' and American History," *American Historical Review,* July 1967.

mechanism of survival operates to steer the scholar toward research within the academic consensus.

When Arthur Mann writes that: "Neither dress, style, nor accent unifies the large and heterogeneous membership of the American Historical Association," he adds immediately: "Yet most writers of American history belong to the liberal intelligentsia that voted for John F. Kennedy and, before him, for Adlai Stevenson, Harry S. Truman, Franklin D. Roosevelt, Alfred E. Smith, Woodrow Wilson, Theodore Roosevelt, and William Jennings Bryan."[23] In other words, historians have almost all fitted neatly into that American consensus which Richard Hofstadter called "The American Political Tradition." So when it is said (again, by Mann) that Richard Hofstadter is a "spectator" while Arthur Schlesinger (who wrote loving books about Jackson, FDR, Kennedy) "writes history as he votes," it is because this country only hands ballots to Republicans and Democrats, to conservatives and liberals, while yearning radicals like Richard Hofstadter are given no one to vote for in this political system. Hofstadter might well write a sequel, *The American Historical Tradition,* describing among historians the same kind of liberal consensus he found in American politics—a consensus which veers toward mild liberalism in politics, and which therefore ensures that where the historian does go beyond irrelevancy to engagement, it is a limited engagement, for objectives limited by the liberal Democratic frame. Mann shows his own entrapment inside this frame by his comment that the progressives, lauded by almost all American historians, "transformed the social Darwinian jungle of some eighty years ago into the humane capitalistic society it is today." Five years after this statement was published the urban ghettos in America were exploding in rebellion against this "humane capitalistic society."

Engagement in social action is not indispensable for a scholar to direct his scholarship toward humane concerns; it is part of the wonder of people that they can transcend their immediate circumstances by leaps of emotion and imagination. But contact with the underground of society, in addition to spurring the historian to act out his value-system, might also open him to new data: the experiences, thoughts, feelings of the invisible folk all around us. This is the kind of data so often missed in official histories, manuscript

---

[23]Arthur Mann, "The Progressive Tradition," John Higham, ed., *Reconstruction of American History,* Harper (Torchbook edition), 1962.

collections of famous personalities, diaries of the literate, newspaper accounts, government documents.[24]

I don't want to exaggerate the potency of the scholar as activist. But it may be that his role is especially important in a liberal society, where the force available for social change is small, and the paralysis of the middle class is an important factor in delaying change. Fact can only buttress passion, not create it, but where passion is strained through the Madisonian constitutional sieve, it badly needs support.

The black revolution has taught us that indignation stays alive in the secret crannies of even the most complacent society. Niebuhr was right in chiding Dewey that intellectual persuasion was not enough of a force to create a just America. He spoke (in *Moral Man and Immoral Society*) of his hope that reason would not destroy that "sublime madness" of social passion before its work was done. Perhaps reason may even help focus this passion.

Except for a scattered, eloquent, conscience-torn few, historians in America have enjoyed a long period of luxury, corresponding to that of a nation spared war, famine, and (beyond recent memory) imperial rule. But now, those peoples who were not so spared are rising, stirring, on all sides—and even, of late, in our midst. The rioting Negro poor, the student-teacher critics on Vietnam, the silent walls around state prisons and city jails—all are reminders in this, the most luxurious of nations, that here, as well as abroad, is an exclusiveness based on race, or class, or nationality, or ideology, or monopolies of power.

In this way, we are forced apart from one another, from other people in the world, and from our freedom. To study this exclusiveness critically, and with unashamed feeling, is to act in some small way against it. And to act against it helps us to study it, with more than sharpness of eye and brain, with all that we are as total human beings.

[24]Rowland Berthoff, in his essay "The Working Class" in John Higham, *The Reconstruction of American History,* says: "The egalitarianism of this country of the common man . . . is a peculiarly middle-class doctrine. . . . The historians of the poor and the disadvantaged have, therefore, ordinarily approached them as special cases. . . . Accordingly the main stream of American historiography has flowed past these social backwaters, except in so far as they have presented special problems to the middle-class commonality."

J. H. HEXTER
The Historian and His Day

FOR A GOOD WHILE now a fairly strenuous contest has been in progress between two opposed schools of historical thought. Accepting a classification suggested by Professor R. L. Schuyler, one of the keenest though most courteous of the riders in the lists, the division lies roughly between the "present-minded" and the "history-minded" historians. In the course of time many historians have joined one side or the other in the controversy with the natural consequence that there has been some sense and a good deal of nonsense talked on both sides. In general, for subtle psychological reasons that I am unable to fathom, the kind of scholar who, distrustful of ideas and theories, believes that history is all facts has tended to take the side of the history-minded historians. For more obvious reasons the chronic do-gooder, who believes that knowledge justifies itself only by a capacity to solve current problems, lines up with the present-minded position.

This peculiar alignment has frequently obscured the issues at stake. It is easy to expose the feebleness and absurdity of those who want only facts and of those who want only current problem-solving; and it is fun, too. Consequently the attacks on both sides have often been directed mainly against these vulnerable positions, and it has sometimes seemed as if the main bodies were too busy assaulting their opponents' camp followers to come to grips with one another. For, of course, there is nothing intrinsic to the history-minded position that precludes ideas or theories or, if you prefer, generalization. Nor is there anything in present-mindedness that demands an optimism as to the efficacy of history as a panacea for current social ills.

Obviously it is not fair to judge either the history-minded or the present-minded historians by the vagaries of their respective lunatic fringes. Casting off the eccentric on both sides, there remains a real and serious divergence of opinion, as yet apparently irreconcilable, maintained on both sides by scholars whose achievements entitle their views to respectful consideration. The divergence is connected

From *Reappraisals in History* by J. H. Hexter (Evanston, Illinois: Northwestern University Press, 1961), pp. 1-13. An earlier version of this essay appeared in the *Political Science Quarterly* in June 1954. Reprinted by permission of Northwestern University Press and Longman Group Ltd.

at least ostensibly with a fundamental difference in general outlook between the two parties to the argument. In a sense the present-minded are realists with respect to the study of history, the history-minded are idealists.

The approach of the latter to the problem is essentially apodictic. They say we *ought* not to intrude our contemporary value systems and preconceptions and notions into our reconstruction of the past. They insist that it is our *duty* as historians to understand the past in its terms, not in our own; and they document their thesis with some undeniably horrible examples of what has happened in the last century to historians who looked at the past with the dubious prepossessions, current in their own day, but since invalidated or replaced by other prepossessions equally dubious. Truly there is nothing quite so *passé* as the intellectual fashions of yesteryear. We find them at once especially ludicrous and especially disturbing when they are worn by men of high talents. We do not like to see the nineteenth-century present-mindedness of so perceptive a man as J. R. Green transforming the roughneck barons of Runnymede into harbingers of nineteenth-century democracy and nationalism. Our embarrassment is even more acute when the victim of present-mindedness is a great historian. We are unhappy when we watch Bishop Stubbs adding Victorian liberalism to the cargo that the Anglo-Saxons brought with them to England from their North German forests. And as the conviction of sin is brought home to us we are warned, "There but for the grace of history-mindedness go you."

Convinced by the dreadful examples arrayed before us we resolve to eschew the wickedness of modernism and thenceforth hew to our obligation to be history-minded. And then a clear and chilly voice says: "But my dear fellows, you can't be history-minded. It might be nice if you could, or it might not, but in any case it is impossible. So all this pother about the obligation to be history-minded is rather silly. Only a particularly repulsive sort of Deity would bind men to do what in the very nature of things they are unable to do." So an almost medieval emphasis on the duty to be history-minded is deflected by a rather Machiavellian observation as to the facts of life. Medieval assertions about what statesmen ought to do Machiavelli met with assertions about what statesmen—the human animal being what it is—are sure to do. History-minded assertions about what historians ought to do are met with present-minded assertions of what—the history-writing animal being what he is—the historian is certain to do. The harsh fact of life is that, willy-nilly, the present-day historian lives not in the past but in the present, and this fact cannot be altered by any pious resolve to be history-minded.

What we say about any historical epoch in some ways reflects our experience; and that experience was accumulated not in the fifteenth, in the sixteenth, or in any other century than the twentieth. When we look back on the past, we do so from the present. We are present-minded just as all earlier historians were present-minded in their day because for better or worse we happen to live in our own day. Indeed the very horrid examples cited by the proponents of history-mindedness afford irrefutable evidence that the best of former historians were in their day present-minded, and we can hardly hope to be different. So the best thing for us to do is to recognize that every generation reinterprets the past in terms of the exigencies of its own day. We can then cast aside our futile history-minded yearnings and qualms and deal with the past in terms of our day, only mildly regretting that, like all the words of man, our own words will be writ on water. By this intellectual stratagem the present-minded turn—or seek to turn—the flank of the history-minded.

We must admit that some points in the argument of the present-minded are true beyond dispute. It is certainly true, for example, that all that we think is related to our experience somehow, and that all our experience is of our own day. But though this be true, it is also trivial. It is a plea in avoidance dressed up as an argument. Granting that we can have no experience beyond what we have acquired in the course of our own lives, the question is, does anything in that experience enable us to understand the past in its own terms rather than in terms of the prepossessions of our day? Banal statements about the origin of our ideas in our own experience do not answer this question; they merely beg it.

In the second place, we must admit that in some respects all historians are present-minded, even the most determined proponents of history-mindedness. All historians are indeed engaged in rewriting past history in the light of at least one aspect of present experience, that aspect which has to do with the increments to our positive knowledge that are the fruit of scientific investigation. Consider a single example. Up to a few decades ago the Dark Ages before the twelfth century were considered an era of total regression, technological as well as political, social and cultural. Then Lefebvre de Noëttes described results of certain experiments he had made with animal power. He had reproduced antique harnesses for draft horses. In such harness the pulling power of the horse proved to be less than a quarter of what it is in modern harness. But "modern" harness, involving the use of a rigid horse collar, makes its appearance in Europe in the tenth century. So in the Dark Ages a horse could deliver about four times the tractive force that it could in antiquity. Now no historian would suggest that we disregard Lefebvre de Noëttes's experiments in our consideration of medieval agrarian history; a fourfold increase in the efficiency of a very important source of power is something that no economic historian can afford to overlook. Yet when we do apply the results of Lefebvre's experiments to medieval agriculture we are being present-minded in at least two ways. In the first and more simple way we are rewriting the history of the Middle Ages in the light of the present because until the present the particular bit of light that was the work of Lefebvre did not exist. But we must go further. It was not pure accident that such work had not been done in earlier ages. Historians in earlier ages would not have thought of going about the investigation of medieval agriculture as Lefebvre did. In making his historical investigations by the method of experiment and measurement, Lefebvre was distinctly reflecting the preoccupations of his own age and of no earlier one. In this particular area of study at any rate, scientific-mindedness is present-mindedness.

It seems to me that the proponents of history-mindedness must, and in most cases probably do, concede the validity of this kind of present-mindedness in the writing of history; and if this is all that present-mindedness means, then every historian worth his salt is present-minded. No sane contemporary scientist in his investigations of the physical world would disregard nineteenth-century advances in field theory, and no sane historian in his work would rule out of consideration insights achieved in the past century concerning the connection of class conflict with historical occurrences. But this is only to say that all men who are professionally committed to the quest of that elusive entity—the Truth—use all the tracking devices available to them at the time, and in the nature of things cannot use any device before it exists. And of course the adequacy of the historical search at any time is in some degree limited by the adequacy of the tracking devices. In this, too, the historian's situation is no different from that of the scientist. Adequate investigation of optical isomers in organic chemistry, for example, had to wait on the development of the techniques of spectroscopy. If this is what present-mindedness means, then present-mindedness is not just the condition of historical knowledge. For all knowledge at any time is obviously limited by the limits of the means of gaining knowledge at that time; and historians are simply in the same boat as all others whose business it is to know.

Now I do not believe that the proponents of present-mindedness mean anything as bland and innocuous as this. On the contrary I am fairly sure they mean that the historian's boat is different from, and a great deal more leaky than, let us say, the physicist's or the geologist's boat. What then is supposed to be the specific trouble with the historian's boat? The trouble, as the present-minded see it, can be described fairly simply. The present-minded contend that in writing history no historian can free himself of his total experience and that that experience is inextricably involved not only in the limits of knowledge but also in the passions, prejudices, assumptions and prepossessions, in the events, crises and tensions of his own day. Therefore those passions, prejudices, assumptions, prepossessions, events, crises and tensions of the historian's own day inevitably permeate what he writes about the past. This is the crucial allegation of the present-minded, and if it is wholly correct, the issue must be settled in their favor and the history-minded pack up their apodictic and categorical-imperative baggage and depart in silence. Frequently discussions of this crucial issue have got bogged down because the history-minded keep trying to prove that the historian can counteract the influence of his own day, while the present-minded keep saying that this is utterly impossible. And of course on this question the latter are quite right. A historian has no day but his own, so what is he going to counteract it with? He is in the situation of Archimedes who could find no fulcrum for the lever with which to move the Earth. Clearly if the historian is to be history-minded rather than present-minded he must find the means of being so in his own day, not outside it. And thus at last we come up against the crucial question—what *is* the historian's own day?

As soon as we put the question this way we realize that there is no ideal Historian's Day; there are many days, all different, and each with a particular historian attached to it. Now since in actuality there is no such thing as The Historian's Day, no one can be qualified to say what it actually consists of. Indeed, although I know a good number of individual historians on terms of greater or less intimacy, I would feel ill-qualified to describe with certainty what any of their days are. There is, however, one historian about whose day I can speak with assurance. For I myself am a historian at least in the technical sense of the word; I have possessed for a considerable time the parchment inscribed with the appropriate phrases to indicate that I have served my apprenticeship and am out of my indentures. So I will describe as briefly as I can my own day. I do so out of no appetite for self-revelation or self-expression, but simply because the subject is germane to our inquiry and because it is the one matter on which I happen to be the world's leading authority. Let us then hurry through this dreary journal.

I rise early and have breakfast. While eating, I glance through the morning paper and read the editorial page. I then go to the college that employes me and teach for two to four hours five days a week [1] Most of the time the subject matter I deal with in class is cobwebbed with age. Three fourths of it dates back from a century and a quarter to three millennia; all of it happened at least thirty years ago. Then comes lunch with a few of my colleagues. Conversation at lunch ranges widely through professional shoptalk, politics, high and ghostly matters like religion, the nature of art or the universe, and the problems of child rearing, and finally academic scuttlebutt. At present there is considerable discussion of the peculiar incongruence between the social importance of the academic and his economic reward. This topic has the merit of revealing the profound like-mindedness, transcending all occasional conflicts, of our little community. From lunch to bedtime my day is grimly uniform. There are of course occasional and casual variations—preparation of the ancient material above mentioned for the next day's classes, a ride in the country with the family, a committee meeting at college, a movie, a play, a novel, or a book by some self-anointed Deep Thinker. Still by and large from one in the afternoon to midnight, with time out for dinner and domestic matters, I read things written between 1450 and 1650 or books written by historians on the basis of things written between 1450 and 1650. I vary the routine on certain days by writing about what I have read on the other days. On Saturdays and in the summer I start my reading or writing at nine instead of noon. It is only fair to add that most days I turn on a news broadcast or two at dinnertime, and that I spend an hour or two with the Sunday paper.

Now I am sure that many people will consider so many days so

---

[1] A change in place of employment since the above sentence was written has resulted in a reduction in the number of hours I spend in teaching.

spent to be a frightful waste of precious time; and indeed, as most of the days of most men, it does seem a bit trivial. Be that as it may, it remains one historian's own day. It is his own day in the only sense in which that phrase can be used without its being pretentious, pompous and meaningless. For a man's own days are not everything that happens in the world while he lives and breathes. As I write, portentous and momentous things are no doubt being done in Peiping, Teheran, Bonn, and Jakarta. But these things are no part of my day; they are outside of my experience, and though one or two of them may faintly impinge on my consciousness tomorrow via the headlines in the morning paper, that is probably as far as they will get. At best they are likely to remain fluttering fragments on the fringe of my experience, not well-ordered parts of it. I must insist emphatically that the history I write is, as the present-minded say, intimately connected with my own day and inextricably linked with my own experience; but I must insist with even stronger emphasis that my day is not someone else's day, or the ideal Day of Contemporary Man; it is just the way I happen to dispose of twenty-four hours. By the same token the experience that is inextricably linked to any history I may happen to write is not the ideal Experience of Twentieth-Century Man in World Chaos, but just the way I happen to put in my time over the series of my days.

Now it may seem immodest or perhaps simply fantastic to take days spent as are mine—days so little attuned to the great harmonies, discords and issues of the present—and hold them up for contemplation. Yet I will dare to suggest that in this historian's own humdrum days there is one peculiarity that merits thought. The peculiarity lies in the curious relation that days so squandered seem to establish between the present and a rather remote sector of the past. I do not pretend that I am wholly unconcerned by the larger public issues and catastrophes of the present; nor am I without opinions on a large number of contemporary issues. On some of them I am vigorously dogmatic as, indeed, are most of the historians I know. Yet my knowledge about such issues, although occasionally fairly extensive, tends to be haphazard, vague, unsystematic and disorderly. And the brute fact of the matter is that even if I had the inclination, I do not have the time to straighten that knowledge out except at the cost of alterations in the ordering of my days that I am not in the least inclined to undertake.

So for a small part of my day I live under a comfortable rule of bland intellectual irresponsibility vis-à-vis the Great Issues of the

Contemporary World, a rule that permits me to go off half-cocked with only slight and occasional compunction. But during most of my day—that portion of it that I spend in dealing with the Great and Not-So-Great Issues of the World between 1450 and 1650—I live under an altogether different rule. The commandments of that rule are:

1. Do not go off half-cocked.
2. Get the story straight.
3. Keep prejudices about present-day issues out of this area.

The commandments are counsels of perfection, but they are not merely that; they are enforced by sanctions, both external and internal. The serried array of historical trade journals equipped with extensive book-review columns provides the most powerful external sanction. The columns are often at the disposal of cantankerous cranks ever ready to expose to obloquy "pamphleteers" who think that Clio is an "easy bought mistress bound to suit her ways to the intellectual appetites of the current customer."[2] On more than one occasion I have been a cantankerous crank. When I write about the period between 1450 and 1650 I am well aware of a desire to give unto others no occasion to do unto me as I have done unto some of them.

The reviewing host seems largely to have lined up with the history-minded. This seems to be a consequence of their training. Whatever the theoretical biases of their individual members, the better departments of graduate study in history do not encourage those undergoing their novitiate to resolve research problems by reference to current ideological conflicts. Consequently most of us have been conditioned to feel that it is not quite proper to characterize John Pym as a liberal, or Thomas More as a socialist, or Niccolò Machiavelli as a proto-Fascist, and we tend to regard this sort of characterization as at best a risky pedagogic device. Not only the characterization but the thought process that leads to it lie under a psychological ban; and thus to the external sanction of the review columns is added the internal sanction of the still small voice that keeps saying, "One really shouldn't do it that way."[3]

[2]*American Historical Review,* 51 (1946), 487.
[3]I do not for a moment intend to imply that current dilemmas have not suggested *problems* for historical investigation. It is obvious that such dilemmas are among the numerous and entirely legitimate points of origin of historical study. The actual issue, however, has nothing to do with the point of origin of historical studies, but with the mode of treatment of historical problems.

The austere rule we live under as historians has some curious consequences. In my case one of the consequences is that my knowledge of the period around the sixteenth century in Europe is of a rather different order than my knowledge about current happenings. Those preponderant segments of my own day spent in the discussion, investigation and contemplation of that remote era may not be profitably spent but at least they are spent in an orderly, systematic, purposeful way. The contrast can be pointed up by a few details. I have never read the Social Security Act, but I have read the Elizabethan Poor Law in all its successive versions and moreover I have made some study of its application. I have never read the work of a single existentialist but I have read Calvin's *Institutes of the Christian Religion* from cover to cover. I know practically nothing for sure about the relation of the institutions of higher education in America to the social structure, but I know a fair bit about the relation between the two in France, England and the Netherlands in the fifteenth and sixteenth centuries. I have never studied the Economic Reports to the President that would enable me to appraise the state of the American nation in the 1950's, but I have studied closely the *Discourse of the Commonwealth of England* and derived from it some reasonably coherent notions about the condition of England in the 1550's. Now the consequence of all this is inevitable. Instead of the passions, prejudices, assumptions and prepossessions, the events, crises and tensions of the present dominating my view of the past, *it is the other way about.* The passions, prejudices, assumptions and prepossessions, the events, crises and tensions of early modern Europe to a very considerable extent lend precision to my rather haphazard notions about the present. I make sense of my present-day welfare-state policy by thinking of it in connection with the "commonwealth" policies of Elizabeth. I do the like with respect to the contemporary struggle for power and conflict of ideologies by throwing on them such light as I find in the Catholic-Calvinist struggle of the sixteenth century.

Teaching makes me aware of the peculiarities of my perspective. The days of my students are very different from mine. They have spent little time indeed in contemplating the events of the sixteenth century. So when I tell them that the Christian Humanists, in their optimistic aspiration to reform the world by means of education, were rather like our own progressive educators, I help them understand the Christian Humanists. But my teaching strategy moves in the opposite direction from my own intellectual experience.

The comparison first suggested itself to me as a means for understanding not Christian Humanism but progressive education. There
is no need to labor this point. After all, ordinarily the process of
thought is from the better known to the worse known, and my
knowledge of the sixteenth century is a good bit more precise than
my knowledge of the twentieth. Perhaps there is nothing to be said
for this peculiar way of thinking; it may be altogether silly; but in the
immediate context I am not obliged to defend it. I present it simply
as one of those brute facts of life dear to the heart of the
present-minded. It is in fact one way that one historian's day affects
his judgment.

In the controversy that provided the starting point of this rambling
essay, the essential question is sometimes posed with respect to the
relation of the historian to his own *day.* In other instances it is posed
with respect to his relation to his own *time.* Having discovered how
idiosyncratic was the day of one historian we may inquire whether
his time is also peculiar. The answer is, "Yes, his time *is* a bit odd."
And here it is possible to take a welcome leave of the first person
singular. For, although my day is peculiar to me, my time, as a
historian, is like the time of other historians.

For our purposes the crucial fact about the ordinary time of all
men, even of historians in their personal as against their professional
capacity, is that in no man's time is he *really* sure what is going to
happen next. This is true, obviously, not only of men of the present
time but also of all men of all past times. Of course there are large
routine areas of existence in which we can make pretty good
guesses; and if this were not so, life would be unbearable. Thus, my
guess, five evenings a week in term time, that I will be getting up the
following morning to teach classes at my place of employment
provides me with a useful operating rule; yet it has been wrong
occasionally, and will be wrong again. With respect to many matters
more important, all is uncertain. Will there be war or peace next
year? Will my children turn out well or ill? Will I be alive or dead
thirty years hence? three years hence? tomorrow?

The saddest words of tongue or pen may be, "It might have been."
The most human are, "If I had only known." But it is precisely
characteristic of the historian that he does know. He is really sure
what is going to happen next, not in his time as a pilgrim here below,
but in his own time as a historian. The public servant Conyers Read,
for example, when he worked high in the councils of the Office of
Strategic Services did not know what the outcome of the maneuvers

he helped plan would be. But for all the years from 1568 during which he painstakingly investigated the public career of Francis Walsingham, the eminent Tudor historian Conyers Read knew that the Spanish Armada would come against England and that the diplomatic maneuvers of Mr. Secretary Walsingham would assist in its defeat. Somewhat inaccurately we might say that while man's time ordinarily is oriented to the future, the historian's time is oriented to the past. It might be better to say that while men are ordinarily trying to connect the present with a future that is to be, the historian connects his present with a future that has already been.

The professional historian does not have a monopoly of his peculiar time, or rather, as Carl Becker once put it, every man is on occasion his own historian. But the historian alone lives systematically in the historian's own time. And from what we have been saying it is clear that this time has a unique dimension. Each man in his own time tries to discover the motives and the causes of the actions of those people he has to deal with; and the historian does the like with varying degrees of success. But, as other men do not and cannot, the historian knows something of the results of the acts of those he deals with: this is the unique dimension of the historian's time. If, in saying that the historian cannot escape his own time, the present-minded meant this peculiarly historical time—which they do not—they would be on solid ground. For the circumstances are rare indeed in which the historian has no notion whatever of the outcome of the events with which he is dealing. The very fact that he is a historian and that he has interested himself in a particular set of events fairly assures that at the outset he will have some knowledge of what happened afterward.

This knowledge makes it impossible for the historian to do merely what the history-minded say he should do—consider the past in its own terms, and envisage events as the men who lived through them did. Surely he should try to do that; just as certainly he must do more than that simply because he knows about those events what none of the men contemporary with them knew; he knows what their consequences were. To see the events surrounding the obscure monk Luther as Leo X saw them—as another "monks' quarrel" and a possible danger to the perquisites of the Curia—may help us understand the peculiar inefficacy of Papal policy at the time; but that does not preclude the historian from seeing the same events as the decisive step towards the final breach of the religious unity of

Western Civilization. We may be quite sure however that nobody at the time, not even Luther himself, saw those events that way. The historian who resolutely refused to use the insight that his own peculiar time gave him would not be superior to his fellows; he would be merely foolish, betraying a singular failure to grasp what history is. For history is a becoming, an ongoing, and it is to be understood not only in terms of what comes before but also of what comes after.

What conclusions can we draw from our cursory examination of the historian's own time and his own day? What of the necessity, alleged by the present-minded, of rewriting history anew each generation? In some respects the estimate is over-generous, in one respect too niggardly. The necessity will in part be a function of the lapsed time between the events written about and the present. The history of the Treaty of Versailles of 1919 may indeed need to be written over a number of times in the next few generations as its consequences more completely unfold. But this is not true of the Treaty of Madrid of 1527. Its consequences for better or worse pretty well finished their unfolding a good while back. The need for rewriting history is also a function of the increase in actual data on the thing to be written about. Obviously any general estimate of the rate of increase of such data would be meaningless. History also must be rewritten as the relevant and usable knowledge about man, about his ways and his waywardness, increases. Here again there has been a tendency to exaggerate the speed with which that knowledge is increasing. The hosannahs that have greeted many master ideas about man during the past fifty years seem more often than not to be a reflection of an urge toward secular salvation in a shaky world rather than a precise estimate of the cognitive value of the ideas in question. Frequently such master ideas have turned out to be plain old notions in new fancy dress, or simply wrong. Perhaps the imperative, felt by the present-minded, to rewrite history every generation is less the fruit of a real necessity than of their own attempts to write it always in conformity with the latest intellectual mode. A little less haste might mean a little more speed. For the person engaged in the operation it is all too easy to mistake for progress a process that only involves skipping from recent to current errors.

If, instead of asking how often history *must* or ought to be rewritten we ask how often it *will* be rewritten, the answer is that it will be rewritten, as it always has been, from day to day. This is so because the rewriting of history is inescapably what each working historian in fact does in his own day. That is precisely how he puts in his time. We seek new data. We re-examine old data to discover in them relations and connections that our honored predecessors may have missed. On these data we seek to bring to bear whatever may seem enlightening and relevant out of our own day. And what may be relevant is as wide as the full range of our own daily experience, intellectual, aesthetic, political, social, personal. Some current event may, of course, afford a historian an understanding of what men meant five hundred years ago when they said that a prince must rule through *amour et cremeur,* love and fear. But then so might his perusal of a socio-psychological investigation into the ambivalence of authority in Papua. So might his reading of Shakespeare's *Richard II.* And so might his relations with his own children.

For each historian brings to the rewriting of history the full range of the remembered experience of his own days, that unique array that he alone possesses and is. For some historians that sector of their experience which impinges on the Great Crisis of the Contemporary World sets up the vibrations that attune them to the part of the past that is the object of their professional attention. Some of us, however, vibrate less readily to those crises. We feel our way toward the goals of our historic quest by lines of experience having precious little to do with the Great Crises of the Contemporary World. He would be bold indeed who would insist that all historians should follow one and the same line of experience in their quest, or who would venture to say what this single line is that all should follow. He would not only be bold; he would almost certainly be wrong. History thrives in measure as the experience of each historian differs from that of his fellows. It is indeed the wide and varied range of experience covered by all the days of all historians that makes the rewriting of history—not in each generation but for each historian—at once necessary and inevitable.

SIEGFRIED KRACAUER
Present Interest

"ON THE WIDE OCEAN on which we shall venture out," says Burckhardt in the opening passage of his *Renaissance,* "the possible routes and courses are many, and the identical studies made for this volume could, if dealt with by another man, . . . easily occasion essentially different conclusions."[1] Burckhardt's remark, made at so important a place, testifies to his intense awareness of the role which the historian's personal outlook and indeed temper play in the rendering and understanding of the past. (The reason why historical knowledge involves subjectivity to a larger extent than does strictly scientific knowledge lies primarily with the fact that different universes challenge the investigator's formative powers in different ways. While the establishment of the world of science, this web of relationships between elements abstracted from, or imposed upon, nature, requires mathematical imagination rather than, say, moral ingenuity, the penetration of the historian's world which resists easy breakdowns into repeatable units calls for the efforts of a self as rich in facets as the human affairs reviewed.[2] That these too may in a measure be subjected to scientific treatment proper is quite another matter.)

Because of the cognitive functions of the historian's self, a definition of its nature would seem to be all the more desirable. Should it not at least be possible to fasten, so to speak, this elusive entity to the peg of rationally controllable conditions? Here is where a theory comes in which—to express it in the terms of that theory—could not arise but in the wake of historicism. Since historical writings themselves are products of history, the argument runs, the views they convey depend on their authors' position in time and place. This proposition means two things—that the historian's mind is shaped by contemporary influences and that in turn his preoccupation with contemporary issues accounts for the why and how of his devotion to the past. The living present is thus identified as the fountainhead and goal of history. The foremost philosophical exponents of this "present-interest" theory are Croce and

---

[1]Burckhardt, *Die Kultur der Renaissance in Italien,* Wien (Phaidon Verlag), p. 1.
[2]Cf. Berlin, "History and Theory . . . ," *History and Theory* (The Hague, 1960), vol. I, no. 1:27.

Collingwood. Without neglecting the conditioning power of the historian's environment, they pay special attention to the need for his involvement, moral or otherwise, in the problems of his day. One knows Croce's dictum that history is contemporary history;[3] he supplements it by contending that "only an interest in the life of the present can move one to investigate past fact."[4] (As a person and historian, he himself was animated by a magnificent interest in the cause of liberty.) Similarly, Collingwood features the historian as a "son of his time"[5] who "re-enacts" the past out of his immersion in present-day concerns.[6] In addition, both thinkers are alert to the necessity for them to justify their emphasis on the present by endowing it with metaphysical significance. This gets them into deep waters, for both of them refute, or pretend to refute, any principle governing the whole of human history and yet cannot help re-introducing it in order to explain the uniqueness of the present moment. It will suffice to mention that Croce conceives of this moment as a phase—the temporarily ultimate phase—of a dialectical and, all in all, progressive movement. True, Collingwood, who radically reduces history to the (better manageable) history of thought, does not share Croce's belief in total progress,[7] but he too holds that the successive thoughts of the past form a comprehensible chain leading to, and climaxing in, the present. With the two of them, the ideal historian is the mouthpiece of History's last will, or, in Croce's words, of the "spirit" which *is* history and "bears with it all its history."[8] Whenever philosophers speculate on the "idea of history," Hegel's "world spirit" pops up behind the bushes. Finally, both thinkers insist that the historian cannot discover thàt which is essential in history unless he reconstructs the past in the light of what Collingwood calls his "a priori imagination"—an imagination which, according to premise, is geared to the requirements of the situation in which he finds himself. Indeed, if, as both Collingwood and Croce take for granted, the present moment virtually contains all the moments preceding it, only those who really live in and with the present will be able to get at the core of past life. In this view, historical truth is a variable of present interest. The time whose son

[3]See Croce, *History: Its Theory and Practice,* New York, 1960, p. 19.
[4]Ibid. p. 12.
[5]Collingwood, *The Idea of History,* New York, 1956. (A Galaxy Book) See, for instance, p. 305.
[6]Ibid. p. 282 ff.
[7]Cf. ibid. pp. 328-34.
[8]Croce, op. cit. p. 25.

the historian is not only transmits to him its preferences and prejudices but rewards his dedication to its peculiar tasks by offering him guidance as he ventures into the dark of times gone by.

No doubt there is something to be said in favor of this proposition. The first of the two assumptions it comprises—the assumption of the impact of the historian's "milieu" on his (unconscious) thought—is actually endorsed by many a practicing historian.[9] In fact, it sounds all but self-evident. On their way through time, nations, societies, and civilizations are usually confronted with problems which, delimiting their horizon, captivate the imagination of all contemporaries. Think of such present-day issues as the struggle for supremacy between the democratic and Communist power blocs, the revolutionary advance of Western technology, the transition from a national to a global frame of reference, the increase of leisure time and the ensuing demand for "mass culture" on a hitherto unheard-of scale, etc.: whatever we hope and fear relates to these issues, whether we know it or not. They literally hypnotize the mind; and arising from the crisscross patterns of divergent opinions, a confused din of them permanently fills the air. Their seeming inescapability lends weight to Carr's advice: "Before you study the historian, study his historical and social environment."[10] Given to studies in this vein, historians of historiography advance many observations to the effect that historical writings tend to reflect responses to the fixed topics of the periods from which they issue. Butterfield, for instance, shrewdly remarks that the stand which German 19th-century historians took in the then raging political dispute between pro-Austrians and pro-Prussians automatically colored their ideas about the beneficial or disastrous consequences of the German medieval monarchy. As a result, "problems of German medieval history were staged against the background of the nineteenth-century struggle between Prussia and Austria, even

---

[9]Cf., for example, Marrou, "Comment comprendre le métier d'historien," in Samaran, ed., *L'Histoire et ses méthodes,* Paris, 1961, p. 1505; Carl L. Becker, "What Are Historical Facts?" in Meyerhoff, ed., *The Philosophy of History in Our Time,* Garden City, N.Y., 1959, p. 133; etc.

[10]Carr, *What is History?,* New York, 1962, p. 54. Incidentally, Carr goes to the limit, or rather beyond it, in following his own advice; he sees fit to derive certain changes in outlook which the Meinecke of 1907 underwent in the 'twenties and 'thirties from the simultaneous short-term changes of his political environment (ibid. pp. 48-49). With Carr, the historian is not only the son of his time but the chameleon-like offspring of fractions of it.

though this involved a gigantic anachronism."[11] There is no end of such attempts to demonstrate the projective character of historiography. Here are, selected at random, some of the findings they yield: Kant's ethics flows from the moral convictions of German pietism;[12] Niebuhr's Demosthenes is a thinly disguised Stein or Fichte, his Chaeronea the counterpart of Jena;[13] Gibbon's work reveals him as a disciple of Voltaire, a "Européen de l'age des Lumières";[14] and of course, nobody can fail to notice that Mommsen's Roman History mirrors the views of the 1848 German liberals.[15] (Mommsen himself was quite conscious of the "modern tone" of his narrative in which he deliberately used contemporary political terms to "bring down the ancients from their fantastic pedestal into the real world.")[16]

Findings of this type immediately strike us as plausible because we are accustomed to credit environmental influences and the like with the power of swaying minds. So it is natural for us to think of the historian as a son of his time. I submit that this apparently self-evident assumption is the outcome of faulty reasoning. It cannot be upheld unless one accepts Croce's doctrine that the historical period is a unit informed by the "spirit" of that period, that any such period is a phase of the historical process, and that the historical process must be imagined as a dialectical movement whose successive phases are meaningfully connected with each other. (It goes without saying that Collingwood's thesis of the all-inclusiveness of "present thought" falls into line with Croce's.) Then it is possible indeed to define the historian's self in terms of its position in time; it fulfills its true nature if it conforms to the spirit of the period to which it belongs. However, the Croce-Collingwood doctrine suffers from two irremediable shortcomings: it rests on the untenable premise that the flow of chronological time is the carrier of all history; and it flagrantly conflicts with a large body of experiences regarding the structure of the period. . . . I shall confine myself here to a remark, somewhat provisional at that, on the doctrine's inadequacy to these experiences. Contrary to what Croce

---

[11]Butterfield, *Man on His Past* . . . , Boston, 1960, p. 25.
[12]Collingwood, op. cit. p. 229.
[13]Gooch, *History and Historians in the Nineteenth Century,* Boston, 1959, p. 21.
[14]Marrou, op. cit. p. 1506.
[15]Cf. Carr, op. cit. p. 44, and Gooch, op. cit. p. 461.
[16]Quoted by Gooch, ibid. p. 461.

postulates, the typical period is not so much a unified entity with a spirit of its own as a precarious conglomerate of tendencies, aspirations, and activities which more often than not manifest themselves independently of one another. This is not to deny the existence, at any given moment, of certain widespread and even prevailing beliefs, goals, attitudes, etc. I venture to guess that their presence, an empirical fact rather than a metaphysical "must," is in a measure accounted for by the "principle of mental economy";[17] . . . for the rest, would it not be surprising if there were no interaction of a short between the heterogeneous elements that make up a period? Simultaneity also favors cohesion. But if the period is a unit at all, it is a diffuse, fluid, and essentially intangible unit. Note the admirable caution with which Marc Bloch approaches an issue which Croce settles dogmatically. Bloch, truly a historian's historian, acknowledges the impact which, in the heyday of the feudal age, French culture as a whole exerted on Europe, and then tentatively adds a few reasons for its sweeping success. That he himself does not set great store by them follows from his concluding remark: "But this having been said, we may well ask ourselves if it is not futile to attempt to explain something which, in the present state of our knowledge of man, seems to be beyond our understanding—the ethos of a civilization and its power of attraction."[18]

And here is the point I wish to drive home. If the historian's "historical and social environment" is not a fairly self-contained whole but a fragile compound of frequently inconsistent endeavors in flux, the assumption that it moulds his mind makes little sense. It does make sense only in the contexts of a philosophy which, like Croce's, hypostatizes a period spirit, claims our dependence on it, and thus determines the mind's place in the historical process from above and without. Seen from within, the relations between the mind and its environment are indeterminate. Even supposing that contemporary influences were better definable than they actually are, their binding power would still be limited by the mind's freedom to initiate new situations, new systems of relationships. After having brilliantly deduced the effects of Periclean Athens on the formation of Thucydides' mind, Finley, the Harvard classicist, voices scruples about his own inferences; he declares that "the influence of the

---

[17]See chapter 1, Kracauer, *History: The Last Things Before the Last,* New York, 1969, pp. 17-44.

[18]Marc Bloch, *Feudal Society,* Chicago, 1964, vol. 2, p. 307.

contemporary world on any man is of a complexity which defies all but the crudest analysis."[19] His circumspection compares favorably with the kind of observations dear to students of historiography—observations which exhaust themselves in showing that this or that historian unintentionally projects influential contemporary ideas into his accounts of the past. To be sure, such projections do occur but they are by no means inevitable. Maitland, for example, knew how to avoid them, thereby improving on Bishop Stubbs, his contemporary, who unwittingly added Victorian liberalism "to the cargo that the Anglo-Saxons brought with them to England from their North German forests."[20] Nevertheless, at this point an objection suggests itself which seems to confirm the impact of time and place. Are we not usually able to trace documents, literary products, or works of art to the periods of their origin? We undoubtedly are. Upon closer inspection, however, this argument defeats its purpose, for as a rule achievements of the past can be dated only on the basis of characteristics which do not, or at least need not, involve their intrinsic intentions and meanings. Clues may be offered by stylistic peculiarities, references to otherwise familiar events, the recourse to knowledge unobtainable before a particular historical moment, etc. Moreover, as with all circumstantial evidence, the conclusions drawn from these secondary characteristics are anything but irrefutable truths. In sum, the whole assumption examined here stands and falls with the belief that people actually "belong" to their period. This must not be so. Vico is an outstanding instance of chronological exterritoriality; and it would be extremely difficult to derive Burckhardt's complex and ambivalent physiognomy as a historian from the conditions under which he lived and worked. Like great artists or thinkers, great historians are biological freaks: they father the time that has fathered them. Perhaps the same holds true of mass movements, revolutions.[21]

---

[19]Finley, *Thucydides,* University of Michigan Press, 1963, p. 74.

[20]Quoted from Hexter, *Reappraisals in History,* Evanston, Ill., 1961, p. 2. For the reference to Maitland and Stubbs, I am indebted to Prof. Sigmund Diamond.

[21]In his "Foreword" to Hexter's *Reappraisals* . . . , Prof. Laslett (Trinity College, Cambridge) raises a question which points in this direction. He asks "whether the whole enterprise of accounting for the dramatic events of the middle of the seventeenth century in England is not to some extent misconceived. Is it right to assume, as always seems to be assumed, that a long-term, overall explanation is necessarily called for? And he adds that "it may not be justifiable . . . to suppose that great events have great causes." (p. xiii)

According to the second assumption inherent in the present-interest theory, the historian is not only a son of his time but a son utterly devoted to it. He must be prompted by a deep concern with its problems, sorrows, and objectives, or else the past he wants to resuscitate will never come to life. Croce and Collingwood bring this line of thought to its logical conclusion by contending that present-mindedness is prerequisite to any significant reconstruction of historical reality.

Their radical proposition sheds light on the dangerous implications of the assumption underlying it. I intend to show that this assumption entails a shift of emphasis from the realistic to the formative tendency which threatens to upset the "right" balance between the two of them. Historians who proceed straight from present interest are apt to obscure, and indeed submerge, the evidence. A nice instance is the following: under the pressure of conventional preferences and, I presume, contemporary reader demands, Cortés' biographers have up to now featured only the more dramatic events of his life—the conquest of the Aztec, the expedition to Honduras, etc.—while leaving unused the rich source material in the archives of Mexico and Spain which would have enabled them to shed light on the Conqueror's later career.[22] The investigator's aggressiveness tends to frighten the past back into the past; instead of conversing with the dead, he himself does most of the talking. Remember Butterfield's remark on the "gigantic anachronism" to which 19th-century German medieval histories fell prey because of their authors' naïve indulgence in pro-Prussian or pro-Austrian sentiments.

It pays to take a good look at Collingwood's argument in support of his position. To be sure, exactly like Croce, he points to the necessity for the historian to secure the facts, or what we commonly believe to be facts, with scholarly accuracy; he even requests him to "re-enact" past experiences—a request which obviously calls for an effort on the historian's part temporarily to disregard present-day experiences. Yet at the same time Collingwood characterizes the ideal historian in terms which make it seem improbable that he should ever be able to live up to these obligations. A counterpart of the Baconian natural scientist, Collingwood's historian treats history as if it were nature. Instead of waiting for what the sources may wish to tell him, he questions his material in accordance with his

[22]Personal information by Prof. France V. Scholes, who kindly permitted me to make use of it.

own hunches and hypotheses and like a scientific experimenter forces it to answer his questions.[23] How the poor man will manage to get substantial answers from the past—a past which is not merely nature—without waiting for its possible communications, Collingwood does not care to reveal to us.

Or rather, he tries to clarify the issue by comparing the historian with the sleuth in detective novels.[24] As he sees it, both figures coincide in detecting hidden truths by way of active questioning. It is a particular detective Collingwood has in mind: Agatha Christie's incomparable Monsieur Hercule Poirot. This archetypal model of a Collingwoodian historian derides the police for collecting everything which might eventually turn out to be a clue and, strictly opposed to their pedestrian methods, emphatically asserts that the secret of detection consists in using one's "little grey cells." In Collingwood's words: "You can't collect your evidence before you begin thinking, he [Poirot] meant; because thinking means asking questions (logicians, please note), and nothing is evidence, except in relation to some definite question."[25] Now as much as I admire Hercule Poirot's miraculous "a priori imagination"—miraculous because it often hits the mark in the absence of any palpable clue—as an assiduous reader of detective stories I am bound to admit that he is not the only detective with a superior record and that some of his peers are little inclined to agree with him on this score. Superintendent Arnold Pike of Scotland Yard for one, the hero of Philip MacDonald's delightful yarn *Murder Gone Mad,* refuses to rely on his "little grey cells" at the beginning of an investigation: "I just try to collect facts whether they appear to have any bearing on the case or not. Then, suddenly, when I've been digging round long enough and hard enough, I maybe dig up something which seems to click in my mind and become a good starting-off place for a think."[26] I might as well add that his subsequent think is very ingenious indeed. There are, then, sleuths and sleuths. The moral is that Collingwood should have read more detective novels.

[23]Collingwood, op. cit. pp. 269-70.—Blumenberg, "Das Fernrohr und die Ohnmacht der Wahrheit," p. 21, emphasizes Galileo's aggressiveness as a scientist. He, the "founder of natural science" (p. 73), says Blumenberg, "is not the man who would simply look at things and patiently give himself up to his object; what he perceives always foreshadows the contexts of a theory, bears on the complex of theses comprising it." (My translation.)

[24]Collingwood, op. cit. pp. 243, 266-68.

[25]Ibid. p. 281.

[26]MacDonald, *Murder Gone Mad,* New York, 1965, p. 39 (An Avon Book).

Fortunately, the spell his theory casts over him wears thin at intervals—which, on some such occasion, permits Collingwood to realize that his historian is in a predicament; he is faced with the problem of resurrecting a past whose nature his involvement in present thought tends to conceal from him. The problem so posed admits only of one "solution": if the historian does not seriously reach out for the evidence and get close to it—if he insists on present-mindedness—the evidence must be made to move toward him. Collingwood, intent on demonstrating that pronounced aggressiveness and intimate contact with the given material may well go together, eagerly seizes on this seeming possibility. He claims that historians had better concentrate on events or developments for which they show genuine affinity.[27] The idea behind his advice is that the attraction which this or that aspect of historical reality exerts on the historian will be reciprocated in kind—i.e., cause all relevant facts to rush out of their hiding-places, as if drawn to him by a sort of magnetic power. They are his for the asking. Nor need he further look into them; thanks to his sympathy for his subject matter, he knows all that there is to be known about it from within. It is understood that Collingwood's advice—by the way, he is not alone to offer it[28]—fails to dispose of the problem it is meant to solve. Granted for the sake of argument that under certain circumstances the historian following this suggestion succeeds in bridging the gap between his "little grey cells" and the far-distant evidence, what will happen to those portions of the past which do not strike a sympathetic chord in him? Are they doomed to oblivion? More important, the device in which Collingwood takes refuge rests on the belief that love makes you see. Quite so. Yet the reverse holds true also, especially in the case where love is inseparably coupled with present interest. Then in all likelihood a historian's affinity for his topic will blind rather than sensitize him to its specific qualities. Arthur Schlesinger, Jr.'s *Age of Jackson*—certainly a product of sympathy for this age—is considered not so much a contribution to original historical scholarship as a "young humanitarian's politically inspired volume that succeeded in creating a popular image of Jackson as a forerunner of F.D.R."[29] Collingwood resorts to an

---

[27]Collingwood, op. cit. pp. 304-5.

[28]Cf. Lord Acton's remarks on this subject, as quoted by Butterfield, *Man on His Past . . .* , Boston, 1960, p. 220. See also Marrou, "Comment comprendre le métier d'historien," in Samaran, ed., *L'Histoire et Ses Méthodes,* Paris, 1961, p. 1521.

[29]Ratner, "History as Inquiry," in Hook, ed., *Philosophy and History,* New York, 1963, p. 329.

ineffective expedient; and he rejects precisely the kind of love which really serves as an eye-opener: love of the past for its own sake.

But his recourse to eligible affinities plays a marginal role after all. In the final analysis the Croce-Collingwood doctrine is founded on the two thinkers' conviction that history amounts to something like a comprehensible whole, an intelligible arrangement of things. Indeed, they *must* postulate the wholeness of the historical universe in order to justify their identification of history as contemporary history. This equation is meaningful only if the historian's material is thought of as making up a virtually consistent and surveyable "cosmos" of a sort. Only then is he in a position to indulge in present-mindedness and yet have access to the past; only then may he reconstruct past thoughts from present thought without running the risk of misconstruing them. As elements of a, so to speak, closed system all pieces of the evidence he gathers can be expected to fall by themselves alone into place. The present-interest theory hinges on the idea of such a system—on one of the pipe-dreams of unfettered reason, that is. Once this dream is abandoned, it is easy to see that present interest lacks the magic attributed to it by Croce and Collingwood; that the historical facts are stubborn enough not to yield their secret to a historian who just treats them after the manner of a scientific experimenter.

The ultimate consequences of this theory—consequences which Croce and Collingwood would hardly have sanctioned, though—are illustrated by a pseudo-historical genre which lies in the border region between history proper and prophecy. Born out of an existential concern with the present and the future in its womb, the genre I have in mind springs from the experience that the way in which we conceive of the past will help us achieve our goals (or interfere with their attainment). "History feeds on history."[30] I do not wish to suggest, of course, that all histories partial to a cause would fall into that border region. It all is a matter of degree. No doubt the various Catholic and Protestant accounts of the Reformation are to a larger or lesser extent "engaged," but even so numbers of them are true histories inasmuch as they originate in an often admirable effort to render their material with scholarly detachment. This property of theirs makes them differ from what I should like to call "existential" histories. No sooner does the historian's apologetic passion exceed his capacity for detachment than he crosses the

[30]Valéry, *History and Politics*, New York, 1962, p. 8. (Cf. also Valéry, *Oeuvres*, II, Pléiade, 1960, p. 917: *"L'histoire alimente l'histoire."*)

threshold which separates the past as a field of study from the past as a means of exhortation, as a whip, a fiery challenge. History, as envisioned by the Jewish Prophets, is a series of partly supernatural transactions, with God's wrath or forgiveness constantly intervening in the course of secular events. By the same token, peoples acquiring statehood or assuming a new existence are prone to invent a past which transforms them into the standard-bearers of significant destinies. A striking case in point is the young Nietzsche, who in his essay *Vom Nutzen und Nachteil der Historie fuer das Leben* champions such uses or abuses of the past. He condemns the historians of his day—this "generation of eunuchs"[31]—for indulging in aimless scholarly pursuits. Historicism, he has it, enlarges our horizon beyond our wants, destroys the instincts of the people, paralyzes vitality, etc.; it is altogether a vain human effort, a science got out of hand. Instead, he pleads for histories which serve "life," the life of the present. Croce's dictum: "History is contemporary history" still reverberates with Nietzsche's determination to make the past meet the needs of the living. But while Croce advocates present-mindedness as a prerequisite of knowledgeable interpretation, Nietzsche holds that the last thing we, the living, do need is knowledge: ". . . each people and in fact each man who is to become *mature,* wants . . . a delusion to be wrapped in, a . . . protective and veiling cloud . . . "[32] Plainly speaking, Nietzsche yearns for historians who surrender their preoccupation with what really happened to such representations of the past as foster the illusions that keep us going. The demands of "life," however deceptive, would thus take precedence over the, in his view, emasculated search for historical truth, much of which he deems unnecessary anyway. As for these demands, Nietzsche looks forward to a time when we will again disregard the masses and turn the spotlight on the individuals, "who form a kind of bridge over the arid stream of becoming."[33] Here you have the idea of the "superman" in a pupa state. (On the other hand, the phrase of the "arid stream of becoming" with its anti-evolutionary ring . . . is well worth remembering.) The rub in all of this is that Nietzsche, out of his inordinate and rather juvenile infatuation with "life," shuts his eyes to the enormous achievements

---

[31]Nietzsche, Friedrich, "Vom Nutzen und Nachteil der Historie fuer das Leben," *Unzeitgemaesse Betrachtungen, Zweites Stueck,* Leipzig, 1930, p. 137.
[32]Ibid. p. 156.
[33]Ibid. p. 177.

of historicism; that he just wants to liquidate it instead of uncovering its meanings and then telling us where we should go from there. His essay has traits of an adolescent's inconsequential rebellion. . . . It remains to be mentioned that the existential genre stands the best chance of materializing when the whole of history comes into view. The larger the units a historian is dealing with, the greater the temptation for him to lapse into purposeful constructions with prophetic overtones.

Yet I have no intention of throwing the child out with the bath water. It would be foolish indeed to deny that, like us other mortals, the historian is often moved by present interest. And this justly so; the fact that we live only once involves a moral obligation toward the living. The historian's concern with them—his desire better to understand the present—inspires many of his inquiries into the life of the dead. He may relate, somehow, the past to the present; and he may even wrest this or that secret from the past precisely by probing it in the light of contemporary needs.[34] Burckhardt, anxious to strengthen the awareness of historical continuity, considers it proper for historians to feature all those past facts whose consequences make themselves still felt in our time, our culture.[35] Is there a historian who would not see eye to eye with him? To find out how we have become what we are has ever since been one of the grand designs of history.[36]

However, none of these customary practices can be traced to the chimerical assumption that present interest is the master key which opens all the doors to the past, the axis around which everything revolves. Rather, whenever historians—I mean real historians—give the present its due, they do so, as Meinecke puts it, in the conviction that this is a "legitimate and necessary goal, but neither the only nor the highest one."[37] They would not dream of confusing present-

[34]Cf. Aron, *Dimensions de la conscience historique,* Paris, 1961, p. 13.

[35]Burckhardt, "Historische Fragmente aus dem Nachlass," in *Jacob Burckhardt Gesamtausgabe,* Bd. VII, Stuttgart, Berlin und Leipzig, 1929, p. 225.

[36]For instance, Droysen, *Historik,* Muenchen, 1960, p. 306, identifies the "didactic presentation" as a legitimate form of historical narrative and declares it to be its objective "to apprehend the essence and sum total of the past from the standpoint reached here and now, and . . . to explain and to deepen that which is, and is earned, in the present by its past becoming."

[37]Meinecke, "Historicism and Its Problems," in Stern, ed., *The Varieties of History . . . ,* New York, 1956 (A Meridian Book), pp. 267-88. For the quote, see ibid. p. 411, note 14.

mindedness with a methodological requirement. Take Marc Bloch: eager to transform history into a science, he insists, not unlike Collingwood, on the necessity for the historian to proceed with a scientist's aggressiveness from the very beginning; to cross-examine the past, that is, by means of constructs and models which flow from his "a priori imagination," or, by extension, his present-mindedness. Yet, historian that Bloch is, he hastens to add that the models are nothing but provisional scaffoldings: "Naturally, the method of cross-examination must be very elastic. . . . Even when he has settled his itinerary, the explorer is well aware that he will not follow it exactly."[38] (I wonder, though, whether the elastic method suggested by Bloch will always result in adjustments fitting the case. Elastic breaks if overextended.[39])

What counts, then, is the difference between present interest as a starting-point for, or terminus of, historical studies and present interest as defined by Croce *et al.*[40] Now present interest in the first sense so little precludes "antiquarian interest" that it is entirely consistent with an approach to the past which pays full tribute to the available evidence instead of neglecting, Collingwood fashion, its possible contributions over the allegedly superior constructions of "present thought." It is an approach patterned on Superintendent Arnold Pike's prudent devotion to the facts rather than Hercule Poirot's magisterial indifference to them. (But the contempt in which the little Belgian detective holds material clues makes him all the more an endearing incarnation of paternal omniscience.) The literature abounds with testimony in favor of this mode of treating the given data. Even historians who feel that present-mindedness is of the essence request the student of history to explore the past without regard for our well-being, our calamities. So Burckhardt.[41]

[38]Marc Bloch, *The Historian's Craft,* New York, 1959, pp. 65-66. The original reads: "Naturellement il le faut, ce choix raisonné des questions, extrémement souple . . . . L'itinéraire que l'explorateur établit, au départ, il sait bien d'avance qu'il ne le suivra pas de point en point." Bloch, *Apologie pour l'histoire ou métier d'historien,* 5th ed., Paris, 1964, p. 26.

[39]Max Weber's "ideal-types" give rise to exactly the same doubts.

[40]Turning against the followers of the Croce-Collingwood school of thought, Hexter, op. cit. p. 8 n., defines this difference with unsurpassable clarity: "I do not for a moment intend to imply that current dilemmas have not suggested *problems* for historical investigation. It is obvious that such dilemmas are among the numerous and entirely legitimate points of origin of historical study. The actual issue, however, has nothing to do with the point of origin of historical studies, but with the mode of treatment of historical problems."

[41]See Burckhardt, "Weltgeschichtliche Betrachtungen," in *Jacob Burckhardt Gesamtausgabe,* Band VII, Stuttgart, Berlin und Leipzig, 1929, p. 13.

His wavering in this respect marks an attitude fairly widespread among contemporary historians.[42] (He himself tried to escape the present, yielding to the "unfulfilled nostalgia for that which has perished."[43] Others promote, or indulge in, antiquarian pursuits pure and simple. Huizinga has it that true history probes the past also because it is significant in its own right.[44] And Namier never tired of looking for the seemingly irrelevant; "in fact, he spent all his life in byways."[45] Still other historians—e.g., Harnack[46]—make a point of combining their appreciation of disengaged research with critical comment on the tenets of the present-interest school of thought.

Thus Lovejoy explicitly attacks Dewey's proposition that "all history is necessarily written from the standpoint of the present. . . . "[47] (Dewey and Collingwood are strange bedfellows indeed; but *les extrêmes se touchent,* especially in the near-vacuum filled with sets of sharp-edged abstractions.) The attack is borne out by a statement palpably saturated with personal experience. Lovejoy not only wants the historian to get rid, as best he can, of the preoccupations of his time but argues that such an "effort of self-transcendence" will enrich his knowledge of the present.[48] He will find what he did not seek, precisely for turning his back on it.[49] At the very end of his *Social and Economic History of the Roman Empire,* a work of profound and completely detached scholarship, Rostovtzeff, as if emerging from a long dream, addresses himself to his contemporaries. The evolution of the ancient world, says he, has a lesson and a warning for us. Our civilization will not survive unless it be a civilization not of one class, but of the masses. But is not

---

[42]Cf., for instance, Geyl, *Debates with Historians,* New York, 1958 (A Meridian paperback), pp. 196 and 221; Bury, *The Ancient Greek Historians,* New York, 1958 (A Dover paperback), pp. 246-7; Marrou, "Comment comprendre le métier d'historien," in Samaran, ed., *L'Histoire et ses méthodes,* Paris, 1961, pp. 1505, 1506; Raymond Aron, *Dimensions de la conscience historique,* Paris, 1961, pp. 24 and 11, 13, 172.

[43]Burckhardt, op. cit. p. 206, values highly "unsere unerfuellte Sehnsucht nach dem Untergegangenen."

[44]Huizinga, *Im Bann der Geschichte . . . ,* Basel, 1943, p. 92.

[45]See John Brooke about Namier, as quoted by Mehta, "The Flight of Crook-Taloned Birds," *The New Yorker,* Dec. 15, 1962, p. 93.

[46]Harnack, *History of Dogma,* New York, 1961 (Dover books), vol. I, p. 39.

[47]Lovejoy, "Present Standpoint and Past History," in Meyerhoff, ed., *The Philosophy of History in Our Time,* Garden City, N.Y., 1959, p. 174.

[48]Ibid. p. 180.—Geyl, op. cit. p. 196, expresses himself in a similar vein.

[49]For an analogy to this phenomenon in the domain of film, see Kracauer, *Theory of Film . . . ,* New York, 1960, pp. 151-52 (under the title: "Music recaptured").

every civilization bound to decay as soon as it begins to penetrate the masses?[50] Unexpected, like a rare flower, this meditation grows out of the soil of the past.

One cannot discuss the relations between the past and the present without referring, sometime, to Proust. He is one of the highest authorities on these matters. Clearly, Proust sides with Lovejoy and the rest of the anti-Collingwood historians. In his view the past gives itself up only to those who lean over backward in an attempt to make it speak; and only an "effort of self-transcendence" in this vein will, perhaps, enable us to arrive at an understanding of our present condition. Proust's thought is thrown into relief by that episode in his novel where he tells us that he was suddenly overwhelmed with happiness when, during a carriage ride, he saw three trees which formed a pattern strangely familiar to him; he believed them to have surged out of the forgotten days of his infancy. The sensation of *déjà vu* he experienced went together with an awareness that the "phantoms of the past" were beckoning him. "Like ghosts they seemed to be appealing to me to take them with me, to bring them back to life." And why did they so anxiously try to capture his attention? Looking at them, he felt that they wanted to impart a message which concerned him personally. "I watched the trees gradually withdraw . . . seeming to say to me: '. . . If you allow us to drop back into the hollow of this road from which we sought to raise ourselves up to you, a whole part of yourself which we were bringing to you will fall forever into the abyss.'" Note that Proust leaves it in the open whether or not the message of the three trees bears on his infancy and through it on his present self. He asks himself: ". . . were they but an image freshly extracted from a dream of the night before . . . Or had I indeed never seen them before . . . ? . . . I could not tell."[51] Proust shares Burckhardt's nostalgia for lost causes.

It follows from what I have said so far that there is no peg onto which to fasten the subjective factor, operative in history writing, with any certainty. The historian is not just the son of his time in the sense that his outlook could be defined in terms of contemporary influences. Nor is his conception of the past necessarily an expression of present interest, present thought; or rather, if it is, his

[50]Rostovtzeff, *The Social and Economic History of the Roman Empire,* Oxford, 1926, p. 541.

[51]Proust, *Remembrance of Things Past,* New York, 1932 and 1934, vol. I, pp. 543-45.

aggressiveness may cause the past to withdraw from him. The historian's mind is in a measure capable of moving about at liberty. And to the extent that he makes use of this freedom he may indeed come face to face with things past.

Orpheus descended into Tartarus to fetch back the beloved who had died from the bite of a serpent. His plaintive music "so far soothed the savage heart of Hades that he won leave to restore Eurydice to the upper world. Hades made a single condition: that Orpheus might not look behind him until she was safely back under the light of the sun. Eurydice followed Orpheus up through the dark passage guided by the sounds of his lyre and it was only when he reached the sunlight again that he turned to see whether she were still behind him, and so lost her for ever."[52] Like Orpheus, the historian must descend into the nether world to bring the dead back to life. How far will they follow his allurements and evocations? They are lost to him when, re-emerging in the sunlight of the present, he turns for fear of losing them. But does he not for the first time take possession of them at this very moment—the moment when they forever depart, vanishing in a history of his own making? And what happens to the Pied-Piper himself on his way down and up? Consider that his journey is not simply a return trip.

MARTIN DUBERMAN
On Becoming an Historian

MANY HISTORIANS ARE TODAY discontented with their profession. The younger malcontents chiefly bemoan its "irrelevance"; historians, they argue, are not sufficiently engaged, either in their own lives or in their scholarship, with the pressing social problems of the day. The counter-model these malcontents suggest is an academic whose professional energies would be devoted to some such topic as the history of racist thought in America, and whose person, time and money would be actively committed to movements

---

[52]Graves, *The Greek Myths,* Baltimore, Maryland, 1955, vol. I, p. 112.

From *The Uncompleted Past* by Martin Duberman. (New York: Random House, 1969), pp. 336-356. "On Becoming an Historian" appeared in *Evergreen Review,* April 1969. Reprinted by permission.

championing egalitarianism. The historical investigations of such a man would provide contemporaries with perspective on current problems, and his personal engagement would contribute directly to the eradication of those problems.

A second, far smaller and older group of historians is dissatisfied with the profession for what I would call philosophical reasons—not primarily because of its unwillingness to help solve contemporary problems, but because of its inability to do so even where the will is present. These historians are unhappy because of what they take to be limitations inherent in the nature of their work. And especially two limitations: insufficient data, which makes it difficult, and in many cases impossible, to reconstruct the past with any fullness of detail or certainty of interpretation; and, secondly, the fallible abilities of any single historian commenting on the data. Because of the first limitation—the skimpiness of evidence—studies of the past are better at cataloguing particulars than extracting universals, and more adept at recounting actions than explaining the motives behind them. And because of the second limitation, human fallibility, any given historian is likely to project his subjective perspective onto the limited data before him, thereby further falsifying it.

In other words, discontent within the historical profession today can be roughly divided into two groupings. First, a large number of young historians who seem to have little doubt that the past can yield rich relevance for the present if only we decide that it should, and second, a small number of older historians who find the limitations that adhere to historical investigation so decisive that they do not believe the past can yield guidelines for the present even though the historian may be determined that it will (unless, that is, the historian turns propagandist, manipulating limited evidence in order to make resounding pronouncements about What the Past Tells the Present).

In trying to sort out my own discontents with history (I mean, of course, with history as a profession, not with history as the actual sum of man's past—we are all discontented with that, no matter how we read its partial remains), I find that they are drawn from both the activist and philosophical positions. This was probably predictable, given where I "fit" among the current generations of practicing historians. I am thirty-eight years old, a product of the campus ethos of the early 1950's, a member of the "silent generation." Preceding us was a generation fascinated by ideas, particularly those of Karl Marx; following us, there is a generation, typified by SDS, more interested in action. The generation preceding my own, true to its youthful devotion to ideas, makes up the small ranks of philosophical objectors to history as a discipline. The generation following mine, true to its disinterest in ideas, makes up the large ranks of young instructors who place chief emphasis on history as a tool for the active conversion of society.

My generation was the in-between one, never as attracted to a system of ideas as our predecessors had been, never as committed to active resistance to American society as our SDS successors currently are. Those of us in our mid- to late-thirties are the "floaters" of today's academic community. As undergraduates we equated a commitment to ideology with a religious turn of mind, one which required certainty and completeness at the expense of complexity (to us a synonym for "truth"). At the same time we regarded anyone with a commitment to "action politics" as probably more deranged still, for we felt, in the complacent fifties, that such injustices as existed in our country would be set right simply by continuing the ameliorative policies of the New Deal.

We matured, in other words, in an atmosphere distrustful of (or disinterested in) both ideas and action. Our obsessions instead were wholly traditional—grades, athletics, fraternities, sex—and perhaps the best that can be said of us, in retrospect, is that somewhere we seemed to have recognized our pettiness for what it was, for we adopted a cool, I-don't-give-a-damn-about-anything manner, as if to say that we knew our concerns didn't warrant the zeal we were investing in them.

In the last few years we have been educated somewhat by events. We now know the need for active opposition to some of the crippling policies and institutional arrangements in our country. We now know—if for no other reason than from watching the young activists, whom many of us admire, flounder in their search for philosophical underpinnings—that ideas, perhaps even those old-fashioned Marxist ones, are necessary for focusing action and sustaining commitment. Learning these lessons, we have, to some degree, changed. We are less scornful of systematic thought and less reluctant to commit ourselves to an active role in politics. Yet the scorn and the reluctance alike remain, residual testimony to the way my generation was programmed. It is still difficult for us to work up enthusiasm over ideas (for example, Herbert Marcuse's) or to feel in our gut that the United States is so rotten as to warrant an outright assault against the entire "system." (I am, of course, overgeneralizing; there are historians of roughly my own age—like Staughton Lynd or Eugene Genovese—who have less difficulty than most of us in committing themselves either to a philosophy or to organized action.)

Being a member of this particular generation, with its pervasive suspicion of advocacy, helped to condition the "mid-way" position that I discover I hold between the two centers of discontent—activist or philosophical—within the historical profession. But my conditioning as a member of the silent generation is only part of the explanation for my mid-way position—what might be called the sociological part. No one can understand himself simply by listing the cultural influences that worked upon him. Something more is needed: those unique relationships and events which make up his—and only his—experience. The way I have come to regard history as a profession is due at least as much (indeed, I think, more) to my personal history as to my shared membership in a particular generation. I would like to try to recall the relevant parts of that personal history. I apologize for the egotism involved, but discussing my own history is the best way I know of illustrating certain general propositions I would like to make about the historical profession itself.

When I set out to answer the question "How did I become an historian?" I soon discovered that my experience as a biographer failed to prepare me for the difficulties involved in autobiography. The biographer has before him only such tangible remains of his subject's life as have survived—letters, journals, published writings and the like. But the autobiographer has another kind of evidence to confront as well: all those hazy impressions of early events which are too vague even to be dignified by the word "memory." These recollections, the origins and outlines of which are so uncertain, keep the autobiographer perplexed about whether he is writing a true history of his own life or some fictionalized account in which events become merely the starting point, the pretext, for some invention whose necessity is itself not understood. The biographer can afford to pronounce on the "meaning" of this, the "motivation" for that, because his conclusions need only meet the evidence accumulated on his work desk. The autobiographer, haunted as well by all the unwritten, unendurable fragments, knows that what is piled on the work desk is not the whole story but some accidental, refracted trace of it. Biographers write about skeletons, autobiographers about remembered flesh.

As the biographer of Charles Francis Adams, for example, I had little difficulty describing why he decided to become a lawyer: the legal profession in his day carried promise of prestige and income; he came from a long line of lawyers; he wanted to demonstrate pecuniary and emotional stability to his future father-in-law; he doubted if he had the talent or interest to pursue any other work. These, at least, are the reasons I gave in my biography of Adams. Now, eight years after writing that book, I doubt the sufficiency, perhaps even the centrality of those reasons. It may well be that Adams' choice of career hinged on relationships or episodes about which we now have little or no evidence. Perhaps the real force behind his entering law school was the hope of duplicating the achievements of his father, John Quincy Adams, just as his ambivalence about the decision may have reflected his fear that he would not measure up to his father. Or it may be that some particular event, now entirely lost to us, proved to be the true catalyst—like a temporary fascination with a legal treatise or opinion; the subtle pressures of his fiancée to enter a prestigious calling; an unsuccessful attempt to write fiction.

As an autobiographer trying to discover why I became an historian, I find I can make up a neat little list for myself in much the way I once did as a biographer when trying to explain why Adams became a lawyer. The list would include a number of items special to my own circumstances, especially my friendship as an undergraduate with a young history instructor (my admiration for him led me to adopt his profession in the confused belief that thereby I would reproduce for myself his life style and personality as well). The list would also include a number of items standard for any academic: the influence of a few outstanding teachers, courses or books in high school and college, and a kind of generic fascination with what we like to call finding out "what makes this country tick," "what made it what it is."

It's this last factor that I have most trouble accounting for. *Why* was I fascinated with this country's past? Indeed, *was* I, or did the fascination represent some elaborate game of concealment I was playing with myself? In trying to answer these questions, I've hit on many possibilities, all of which seem to me true, though whether true to my current needs or to my actual feelings of fifteen years ago, I'm not sure. Nor do I know how to weigh their significance in relation to each other—which, in other words, were of minor and which of decisive importance.

I thought, for example, of the influence of my father's history on my own. He was already twenty years old when he emigrated to this country from Russia, a man without formal education and without any knowledge of English. He never talked to me about Russia; I knew of no antecedents, heard no tales of the Old Days. That is, with one exception: the story that my father, a peasant on a large estate, had stolen away to America in the dead of night—taking his own aged father with him—in order to avoid being drafted into the Russian army.

Thinking to check this story, I mentioned it recently at a family gathering. To my astonishment my mother's version turned out to be markedly different from the one I had long believed to be true. As she told it, my father had been an overseer on a beet plantation (the only Jew, she added, who worked there). He did suddenly leave Russia to avoid the army but didn't bring his own father over to this country until several years later. At this point in her narrative my mother was interrupted by a cousin also present at the family gathering. "You've got it all wrong," he said; "just before Joe (my father) died, he gave me a complete account of what happened. He didn't run away to avoid the draft, he ran away *from* the army after he had already been inducted." After much discussion (and considerable shell-shock) all around, my mother finally decided that my cousin's version was the correct one; she was persuaded by recalling that a "laundry chute" had been involved in my father's escape and the chute only seemed to make sense in connection with an army barracks.

One thing was clear: *my* recollection had been almost wholly inaccurate; my father did not escape in the dead of night and did not bring his own father with him. How I came by that tale remains a mystery. Perhaps I invented it to supply some version of a father-son cooperative venture which in fantasy held enormous appeal for me because of the lack of communion with my own father. Or perhaps my father himself told me the story, producing it out of some obscure wish to save us both from what he took to be a less digestible truth. In any case I believe I have made the point that I know almost nothing of my father's past (and perhaps secondarily have also provided an apologue of how both "first-hand" accounts and the historian himself can create obstacles to "reconstructing the past").

It was not only my father, but my mother, too, who seemed devoid of antecedents. Her family had come to the United States two generations earlier from Austria, but I was given no sense of what that background had meant. My mother always seemed to me (as did her parents) one of those present-minded Americans whose very insistence on living exclusively from day to day suggests, as a correlative, a suffusing dislike of what has gone before. It may well be that I became an historian in order to compensate for this lack of family roots. It may be that I became an historian of the United States out of some unconscious drive to end our displaced status within it. To have this country depend upon me for its official interpretation was in some way to possess it, to achieve over it the kind of mastery for which my father seemed unequipped, and my mother uninterested.

But that is not the whole story either. A "life in history" held out attractions for me for reasons still more personal. I had, in fact, grown up the family "presentist" *par excellence.* My life lacked continuum, connections with what preceded. Every day seemed new, unrelated to others; events, feelings, relationships, did not so much build on each other as cancel each other out. I seemed as little able to retain the satisfactions of yesterday as its pain. It was as if an enormous blackboard eraser were suspended down my back to the floor and as I walked it instantly erased all trace of my footsteps.

Why this was so, I hardly begin to understand. In part I had simply internalized an attitude common to my family: the past was something to forget as rapidly as possible; it was an encumbrance, the source of useless anguish rather than useful experience. For a long time I liked to think of this attitude as an emblem of emancipation. The moment was what counted, I said, and the moment could be most fully experienced when the fewest preconceptions were brought to it.

But as I belatedly came to understand, when I talked of "living in the moment" I was theorizing about my life rather than describing it. In fact I was as little committed to the present as to the past. I disliked depth experience of any kind, today's as well as yesterday's, and if, by some chance, I found myself undergoing such an experience, my impulse was to terminate it as rapidly as I could and obliterate its traces as fully as I was able. I preferred, in other words, to pass quickly from one mild encounter to another, avoiding as much as possible binding associations, for those I tended to link with the threat of pain.

It seems bizarre that someone so eager to dissociate himself from his own past should decide to devote his life to collecting and explaining other people's pasts. But that paradox itself contains the heart of the explanation. It is one that eluded me until a few years ago when I found myself trying to express the contrast between my professional devotion to history and my personal distrust of it, in a short poem I called "Historian":

> I am a guardian of memories,
> collective ones, the race—
> to give it all the best light.
> My own I do not care for,
> fear the shadow line they throw,
> suppress their bite.
> Neat balance for a life,
> If one believes a blank brings peace—
> and fright.

Apparently my personal amnesia—the "blank"—frightened me more than I could consciously admit. Skating on a thin layer of ice (and on a new pond) every day carried special thrills; but at the same time, I recognized the dangers involved and longed for some thickness beneath the surface—especially if it could be artificially manufactured from someone else's refrigerator.

In short, though I had little sense of it at the time, I now think I became an historian largely out of the need to find some balance for a life tipped heavily toward the immediate, the momentary, the present occasion. There was little in my motivation which had to do with what might be called a "passion to know" about the American past—certainly not one which I can separate from my subjective need for "ballast." My guess is that such subjective needs are the chief ingredients of any historian's pursuit of the past. Doubtless those needs vary widely with individuals; some historians may be drawn to the seeming stability of a world of "hard" facts, some to the isolation (and safety) of dealing with the dead, some to the authoritarian pleasures of being able to pass judgment on others without fear of retaliation.

But if my main motive for joining the historical profession was one of personal compensation, my actual experience within the profession has modified that motive. From the first I found myself asking questions of the past which carried me a good distance from my starting point. This broadening of my concerns was a matter of fits and starts, a development that took place almost behind my own back. Only when its accumulated force became pronounced did I become conscious of what had been going on in my professional life for some time.

My first book—that biography of Charles Francis Adams—was inspired by accident and finished by will power. When I entered graduate school at Harvard in 1952, I was put in a dormitory room with a student whose mother had at one time been social secretary to Brooks Adams and who was currently curator of The Adams Mansion in Quincy, Massachusetts. She invited me out to Sunday dinner, gave me a tour of Adams memorabilia and further caught my interest with her private storehouse of anecdotes and recollections. At about the same time, The Adams Trust announced that the family's enormous collection of private papers, so long withheld from scholars, would henceforth be open for research.

This conjunction of personal exposure to the Adams milieu and the public availability of the family's papers seemed to me, when the time came to choose a topic for my doctoral dissertation, something like a mandate. Like most graduate students, I had no one burning interest I was eager to pursue, but rather a desultory half dozen or so. Such burning as I felt was knowing that a thesis topic had to be chosen and had to be chosen expeditiously lest I lose my hard-won status as a graduate student Seriously Devoted to the Study of Our Past. And so I chose—not, as it turned out, wisely or well.

In truth, most of the five years I ended up devoting to the Adams biography was drudgery. This is not hindsight but in fact the way I felt at the time. For a brief period in graduate school I kept a diary (I think because I needed an outlet for my feelings which my academic work was not providing), and in rereading that diary recently, I find my discontent with working on Adams' biography pervasive. In one entry I wrote that my research into state politics of the 1850's was proving so "exasperatingly dull and inconsequential" that all the familiar doubts about being a professional historian had begun to return. "*Why* the academic life," I wrote. "*What* the significance of scholarship either as a vehicle for my self-expression or as a tool for others?" On another day I wrote:

> I don't really give a healthy damn for "the past," nor for scholar-ship and its laborious recollections . . . I *use* the past, I do not purposely elucidate it. I write about Charles Francis Adams because I wish to write *a good book* . . . I don't give a damn for his personality, nor do I wish to immortalize his achievements. He is a vehicle, nothing more. Does anyone feel differently? I doubt it . . . How *can* one feel interest in the past "for its own sake"? One can only feel *from* oneself. True, if personality has become meaningless, if one wishes to submerge oneself in someone else's life, or times, then

selflessness can be approached. But then it is the devotion of a
nonentity . . .

Yet I persisted with the Adams biography. At first because I
wanted to get my doctorate; then, the doctorate completed, because
I wanted to publish a book, and with two years of my life already
invested in studying Adams' career, it seemed uneconomical to start
all over on a new topic. I also persisted for what some might call
"better" reasons (though these were never uppermost), primarily
the interest I had begun to develop in Adams' leadership of the
moderate "free-soil" wing of the antislavery movement. I found the
issue of slavery in politics increasingly absorbing and the position
Adams took on it increasingly persuasive. "Spent most of the day,"
I wrote at one point in my diary,

> reading the *Boston Whig* in New England Deposit library—not bad
> work—the slavery issue is absorbing—I lean more and more to
> outright sympathy with the overtly aggressive position of the anti-
> slavery leaders—though some abolitionist tactics were deplorable.
> Many parallels with today & the desegregation issue: what to do?—to
> insist forcefully on equal rights or to leave improvement to "time" &
> Southern evolution? Reaction knows no progress; stability or worse is
> its operational level. Yet force must be tempered with a reasonable
> understanding of the complexity of the problem—a thin line to define
> & tread—but Charles Francis (and *not* the abolitionists) once man-
> aged to do so. He presents an admirable ideal (if disagreeable
> personality)—the "right," moderately insisted upon.

I should add, immediately, that in the dozen years since writing
those lines I have felt ever diminishing sympathy for the Adams'
moderates and ever increasing admiration for those who, like
William Lloyd Garrison, called for outright abolition of slavery. This
radicalization of my views might have come about simply as a
response to public events of the last dozen years, events which have
demonstrated clearly that the white majority in this country does not
wish to give the American Negro equal access to the benefits of our
society, and that a large and determined minority still believes in the
Negro's biological inferiority. These events, as I say, might alone
have moved me "leftwards," have made me realize the necessity for
firm resistance to racism. But aside from the education of public
events, I was also moved to a more radical stance as a result of my
historical studies themselves (though because my scholarship itself
probably took the particular turns it did under the influence of public

events, I would say my historical researches reinforced rather than initiated my changing opinions).

What happened was that when I finished the Adams biography in 1961, I decided to pursue further the one strand in it that had consistently sustained my interest—the antislavery movement. For a while I thought of writing a full-scale history of the movement, or perhaps of its radical wing, abolitionism. But my temperament worked against that idea. I've always been more inclined toward the particular than the general and more interested in the workings of human personality than in the panorama of public affairs. How individuals differ from each other concerns me more than how they are alike; biography and intellectual history—the study of what made a few men, and their works, special—holds far more fascination for me than sociology, the study of group behavior, of what a disparate collection of individuals have in common. To study the abolitionists as a *group* would have meant concentrating on impersonal factors and shared traits, whereas I preferred to investigate idiosyncratic ones.

I finally satisfied such interest as I had in the abolitionist movement as a movement by writing two speculative articles and by putting together a volume of new essays by young historians entitled *The Antislavery Vanguard,* a volume aimed at providing enough new evidence and perspective to touch off the full-scale reevaluation I thought needed. I turned the bulk of my energies toward writing a new biography, this time of James Russell Lowell.

I had been attracted to Lowell on several levels. Though his aristocratic New England background was similar to that of Adams, Lowell had taken up a more radical position in the antislavery struggle by becoming an active abolitionist. I wanted to know why he had (and why Adams had not), chiefly, I think, in order to find out more about where I stood (and why I stood there) in the current spectrum of opinion on the Civil Rights struggle.

I was also interested in Lowell as a literary man. By 1962, when I began work on his biography, I was feeling the constrictions of my role as an "objective" historian. I wanted to get more of myself into my writing, and it was this need (among others) which led me in 1963 to write the documentary play *In White America,* and which has led me since then to spend increasing amounts of my time writing plays. In other words, more and more attracted to "literature" as an outlet and career for myself, I was drawn to the prospect of finding out more about what made a literary man "tick." Writing a biography of Lowell seemed the ideal way to focus and go further with two matters of concern to me—the Civil Rights movement and literature.

I again spent close to five years on the Lowell book. The years were much more pleasant than those given over to Adams, largely because Lowell was a far more genial companion. I came to like him enormously as a man, and to feel—as I had not with Adams—involvement in his life. There was also drudgery and discouragement, as with any book, but on the whole I felt the time with Lowell well spent.

The trouble is, I'm not sure why. When I finished the biography, I wrote another poem, entitled "A Biographer to His Subject":

> Upon your grave
> a wreath of words,
> circling about your life.
>
> Joint commemoration:
> Your image molded now in time;
> My own, unsettled by the mime.

What I was trying to express in that poem was my general sense of uneasiness at what had happened—to Lowell and to me. I felt glad to have gotten to know Lowell and somewhat changed by the contact. But I wasn't sure how much I had been in touch with the actual Lowell, as opposed to my reconstruction of him, and therefore, whether I had been changed by contact with another person or with my own fantasies; nor in any case, could I have said *how* I had been changed. Finally, though I knew in some vague way that I had profited from writing the book, I wasn't at all convinced anyone else would profit from reading it.

For the fact was I had found out very little about those matters that had originally led me to undertake Lowell's biography. The kind of introspective evidence I needed to help me understand why Lowell became a radical in the antislavery movement, and what inspired or drove him to seek a life in literature, was available only in fragments. Nor do I think its paucity is peculiar to a study of Lowell. In fact a comparatively large number of his private papers have survived and his formal writings were voluminous. It is true he did not keep a continuous diary and that he was not a particularly introspective man. But although Charles Francis Adams did keep a journal almost every day of his life and did tend to brood (although in a rather stereotypic way) about the motives behind his actions, I am equally unable to tell you why Adams became a "free-soiler" rather than an abolitionist or why he did not devote his life to literature.

I can, of course, tell you something of what went into the decisions of both men; I don't mean to overstate the case. I can (and did), for example, describe the atmosphere in Lowell's home when he was growing up—his father's strong antislavery views and his mother's deep interest in literature; I discussed the Christian radicalism of his first wife, Maria White; I tried to delineate the literary ferment operative in ante-bellum Cambridge—and so forth. But these hardly satisfy me as *sufficient* explanations for Lowell's major decisions in life. Many boys grew up in New England under influences seemingly comparable in every way to those surrounding Lowell, but they did not become abolitionists or writers. Moreover, when I look at the actual turning points in Lowell's life—the points at which he decided to abandon the law for poetry and decided to take out membership in the Massachusetts Anti-Slavery Society—I am as unclear about what immediate events precipitated those decisions as I am about the preconditioning that disposed Lowell to regard those events as critical.

What I am saying, in other words, is that I cannot tell you what made Lowell tick, and to that very large extent, therefore, I cannot tell you much about what ever makes for literature or for political radicalism. I can describe the dominant outlines of Lowell's personality—its buoyancy, its grace, its wit—and I can describe most of his activities in behalf of literature and abolition—his writings, his attendance at meetings, his positions on public questions, etc.—but I cannot *explain* why his personality or his activities took on the particular shape they did. I find the source of his motivation pretty much cut off from my view—as indeed, it may have been from his own, for few of us can master (even when we have the will) that maze of impulse, determination and sheer circumstance that leads us to do or say certain things and not others.

Did I—to focus on one of the two questions which were of central concern to me—learn *anything* from studying Lowell's life about the impulses that lie behind political radicalism? Not much. I think I learned that radicals are made, not born, that childhood experiences produce certain predispositions which public events then activate. In Lowell's case, for example, I found that his upbringing predisposed him to be compassionate toward the suffering of others and particularly toward the black slave; and that this predisposition was activated by his marriage to Maria White, who was already deeply committed to the abolitionist cause, and also by certain public developments, especially the growing threat in the early 1840's that slavery's boundaries would be extended through the annexation of land belonging to Mexico.

But that is all I can tell you, and it doesn't seem to me much. I can't tell you *precisely* what influences in Lowell's home or what attitudes in the surrounding community may have predisposed him to public protest, and therefore I can't come close to generalizing about what kinds of upbringing produce which predispositions in the young. Many New Englanders grew up in homes much like Lowell's; the subtle areas in which they differed are crucial for understanding what does or does not produce "radicals," but it is exactly these fine points of difference which are least available for historical scrutiny. We can say only that although many New Englanders were aware of the growing threat of slavery's expansion, few joined Lowell in advocating abolition—just as today many are aware of the inequities in our society but few become active members of SDS or the Peace and Freedom Party.

It seems to me that *if* we are interested in finding out what produces radicals, we would learn far more by studying radicals today than by investigating the life histories of radicals in our past. The studies done on contemporary radicals by social scientists like Kenneth Keniston, Nevitt Sanford and Richard Flacks provide that very abundance of detail and analysis so absent in historical efforts. Because men like Keniston deal with live subjects who can be interviewed directly and repeatedly, and who can be subjected to a sophisticated variety of testing devices and laboratory controls, they have been able to tell us much about the kinds of environmental stimuli that produce disaffection and protest in the young. Their techniques, of course, are subject to challenge, but not, it seems to me, much challenge, given the fact that the dozen or so studies thus far completed were made independently of each other and yet closely agree in their major findings (for example, that young radicals tend to come from liberal, middle-class homes, to have been brought up permissively, and to be more mature and more intelligent than their non-activist counterparts).

In other words, if an historian is interested in the past primarily because of the light he hopes it will throw on present-day problems (his own or his society's), he would do better, it seems to me, to study the present itself. If, for example, he is interested in the phenomenon of youthful radicalism today, he will learn a great deal more about it from reading the psychological and sociological work done by Keniston and others than he will from studying previous groups of radicals in our history—for the latter operated in a widely different context and, in any case, have left only fragmentary evidence on the roots and shape of their activism.

One can, of course, be interested in history for any number of reasons other than "problem-solving" and could thereby justify its study by any number of other rationales. One could claim, for example, that the chief reason for studying past experience is not to help us *solve* the problems that confront us, but only to make us aware of how those problems developed through time, how, in other words, we got into the predicament in which we currently find ourselves. Thus it could be said that we must know the history of slavery in this country before we can understand the current crisis in race relations. (A plausible rationale, though also a debatable one, for the fact is that historians differ so widely among themselves about the nature and effect of the slave experience that it is difficult to say *precisely* what contribution it made to our current dilemma.)

Or one could eschew the "problem" approach entirely as extrinsic to the study of history—and yet still defend that study for its relevance (of a more generalized kind) to our life today. One could, for example, insist that investigating past experience makes us aware that people have at times behaved according to different norms from those we know and sanction—and that discovering this puts us in touch with our own potential range. Or one could claim that by learning how difficult it is to "account" for past events, we become more aware of the complexity of contemporary ones, become more able to recognize and sustain uncertainty, more humble in the face of it.

My point in this essay is not to argue these or other possible justifications for the study of history. It is only to say that *my* dissatisfactions with history (as a source of insight, as a way of life) reflect my initial expectation (shared, I feel sure, by many other historians) that it *could* help us "problem-solve," could help us to understand not only how we got where we are, but also where we want to go and how to get there. Like many of the younger historians, I am increasingly disturbed that we spend so much of our time investigating materials (in my case, ten years in writing the lives of two men) of so little immediate import either to ourselves or to the society at large. Like them, I wish we could find a way of making the past yield information of vital concern to contemporary needs. But unlike them, I have little hope that we can. Here I join the older group of philosophical skeptics who feel that the limited evidence available from the past, the very different context in which past experience took place, and the clouded perspective of any historian trying to evaluate that limited evidence and that changed context, all combine to keep historical study of marginal utility for those concerned with acting in the present.

There cannot be a New History, in the sense our younger malcontents are calling for it—that is, a History researched, written and taught in such a way as to aid directly in the eradication of social ills—because we can neither manufacture the needed data for "problem-solving" nor decontaminate the scholars who will deal with it. For those among the young, historians and otherwise, who are chiefly interested in changing the present, I can only say, speaking from my own experience, that they doom themselves to bitter disappointment if they seek their guides to action in a study of the past. Though I have tried to make it otherwise, I have found that a "life in history" has given me very limited information or perspective with which to understand the central concerns of my own life and my own times.

V History and Analogy

The study of historical analogies has been neglected by both historians and philosophers. Statesmen use analogies in justifying and perhaps in formulating foreign policies, and everyone uses analogic reasoning to some extent. Indeed, as Arthur Koestler has noted in *The Act of Creation,* analogic reasoning may be at the heart of creative thinking. Yet historians seem to feel that their main function in this area is that of analogic debunker. When statesmen or journalists come up with an analogy, the historian crosses swords with them in the name of historical particularism.

While agreeing that there is some value in exploding bad analogies, Arno Mayer asks that the historian contribute to present concerns by suggesting alternative analogies as well. Mayer argues that although no analogies are perfect, some throw more light on the problems of the day than others. In his critique, David Hackett Fischer accuses Mayer of ignoring his own advice. For although Mayer recognizes that there can be no exact correspondence between historical events, he treats "Greece" an an analogic refer-ent without discussing the differences between it and Vietnam. According to Fischer, Mayer has substituted one bad analogy for another. Fischer goes on to claim that the war in Vietnam is historically unique and that analogies only blind us to the peculiari-ties of this event.

It might be helpful, however, if historians used their talents to point out similarities and dissimilarities in *all* attempts to set up historical analogies. During the debate over the relevance of "Munich" to Vietnam, for example, no historian took the time to examine this analogy carefully in order to see how it did and did not relate to the possibilities of negotiations in Vietnam. This was understandable given the passions that were aroused in this case, but it might have been useful if historians had embarked on this task. For, if the historian is unwilling to apply his talents to a careful analysis of analogies, he is destined to a very negative role in policy formation. Statesmen will continue to use analogies and the historian will continue to serve merely as an analogic watchdog. At best, he will be little more than a vigilante, guarding a sacred and unique past from abuse by the present.

ARNO J. MAYER

Vietnam Analogy:
Greece, Not Munich

EVEN, OR PERHAPS ESPECIALLY, in this secular age the citizen craves reassurance that history follows a patterned and discernible course. In his quest for direction he is predisposed to welcome, and any government is inclined to provide, reminders of past events or situations which make those of the present and future recognizable. That being the case, he is likely to look askance at critics who question the legitimacy of a prevalent analogy without proposing a better one to take its place. Particularly in the United States, where any critic of government is suspect if he refuses to propose concrete remedies, this failure reduces his effectiveness.

Further, many critics leave the impression that anything short of a perfect analogy should be proscribed. But in the absence of perfect analogies, which exist only in the world of formal abstractions, this is equivalent to ruling out analogic arguments altogether. What, then, is an analogy? According to Webster it is "a relation of likeness between two things or one thing to or with another, consisting in the resemblance not of the things themselves but of two or more attributes, circumstances, or effects." In short, analogy is not identity. Reasoning by historical analogy consists of isolating two or more circumstances or processes which have structural, relational and/or causal resemblances in a context of differences and indeterminacies, the resemblances being emphasized for the purpose of proceeding to the clarification of a situation, a process, or an effect which appears not to be characterized by unalloyed uniqueness.

If E. H. Carr is right in saying that the current era is exceptionally history-conscious and if today's citizen has that pronounced need for and is peculiarly susceptible to analogies—and these two points await empirical verification—then any administration may be expected to harness only such analogies as will bolster up and justify its policies. Moreover, government spokesmen and supporters, as well as dissident action intellectuals, will tend to violate the canons

"Vietnam Analogy: Greece, Not Munich" by Arno J. Mayer. From *The Nation* (March 25, 1968), pp. 407-410. Reprinted by permission.

of sound analogic explanation: rather than give due weight to degrees of similarity or difference, they will tend to speak in terms of immaculate identity or contrast.

Accordingly, present government spokesmen and supporters seek to press into service the analogy of Munich, hoping thus to rally public and Congressional support for a resolute, forward policy in Vietnam. The opposition on the Left tends to reject this analogy— without, however, providing the citizen with alternate historical sign posts.

By its proponents, the Munich analogy is designed to stress the identity, not the similarity, of Hitler and Mao; of the Nazi German and the Communist Chinese political systems and foreign policy objectives as well as methods; and of the externally incited subversion as well as the strategic significance of Czechoslovakia and South Vietnam. The ensuing lesson is presented as self-evident: no self-respecting American should want in the White House a Chamberlain or Daladier, who by surrendering South Vietnam to the Chinese-controlled North Vietnamese and Vietcong would encourage Peking to activate its timetable for aggressive expansion into Southeast Asia and beyond.

Needless to say, government critics, including professional historians, have excelled in exposing the flaws in this Munich-Vietnam analogy. They have sought to demonstrate that the South Vietnamese insurgency, *unlike* the Sudeten insurgency, is essentially and authentically indigenous and popular and is directed against a corrupt regime; that South Vietnam, *unlike* Czechoslovakia, is at best of marginal strategic importance; that Communist China, *unlike* Hitler Germany, does not appear to be intent on military aggression; and that the United States of the 1960's, *unlike* the Anglo-French allies in 1938, has overwhelming military capabilities in readiness if Peking should, after all, embark on a course of outright military aggression.

But these corrections, though well-grounded, do not come to grips with the pivotal assumption underlying the Munich parable. Today's anti-appeasers imply that if the Anglo-French statesmen had stood their ground firmly on Czechoslovakia, Hitler would have climbed down and the Second World War would have been averted. Quite apart from the fact that such counter-factual events are difficult to prove, this particular proposition is left intentionally vague. Specifically, it begs the question of whether, in order to persuade Hitler to desist or delay, it would not have been necessary to confront him with the unequivocal prospect of a two-front war arising from a timely and binding military alliance between the two Western allies and Soviet Russia, including arrangements for the transit of Soviet military power through Poland and Romania.

It is worth noting that many critics, who rightly question the accuracy of the Administration's interpretation of the nature and purpose of the struggle in South Vietnam, tacitly accept its representation of Munich, thereby ignoring or concealing the anti-Communist mainsprings and objectives of Western diplomacy since 1917. Concern and priority for the containment of Russian Bolshevism and for the maintenance of the domestic *status quo* significantly influenced many of the provisions in the post-1918 peace treaties which during the thirties quickened Europe's diplomatic and political crisis. This twin concern and priority also inhibited England and France from entering into an operative mutual security pact with Moscow, either before or immediately following Munich. The allies thereby denied themselves substantial and credible military support for their diplomacy. If the Western powers, by then including the United States, eventually combined with the Soviet Union to defeat the Axis, the alliance was in the nature of a momentous but short-lived and precarious political truce in an international civil war that began in 1917 and resumed before the Second World War was over. In this larger perspective, not only Munich but also the Nazi-Soviet pact—both of which have the outward earmarks of classic moves of power politics in a stable international environment—are diplomatic maneuvers in an international civil war, with World War II and the extermination camps the diabolic wages of revolution and counter-revolution in a pre-atomic age.

Today, most spokesmen for the Left opposition as well as the self-styled anti-appeasers prefer not to go into those aspects of Munich and appeasement which stem from the anti-Soviet and anti-Communist texture of inter-war politics and diplomacy. They have good reasons. After all, the one-dimensional lesson of Munich—stand fast, refuse to negotiate, rearm, and prevent war—figured prominently in Washington's justificatory and explanatory rhetoric from 1945 to 1956. Specifically, successive administrations proclaimed that since the nature, dynamics and objectives of Stalin and the Soviet system were analogous to, if not identical with, Hitler and the Nazi system, the only way to contain expansionist Russia and surging Bolshevism in third countries was to stand up to Stalin as the allies should have stood up to Hitler. As of 1948-49 even the ADA, not to speak of allegedly scholarly historians and political scientists, accepted, legitimized, and propagated the cold-war eschatology according to which Nazism and Bolshevism were essentially identical totalitarian systems bent on unlimited expansion by a crude blend of outright military force and externally engineered subversion. It thus became the American consensus that, even though the Marshall Plan contributed substantially to the removal of those economic and social grievances which fed the Communist conspiracy in so many European countries, in the last analysis superweapons and NATO were what kept Stalin's Red hordes from sweeping across the Elbe.

It is thus understandable, if paradoxical, that most of the Establishment critics of President Johnson's Vietnamese policy cling to this time-bound interpretation of the nature and purpose of the Soviet Russian threat, the Communist insurgency and American containment. They seem to be saying that, though Stalinist Russia was blatantly expansionist, militarist and interventionist, Maoist China is launched on an altogether more prudential course; that though European communism was monolithic and Moscow-controlled, Asian communism is polycentric and independent of Peking; that though communism in Greece, France and Italy was an externally fostered conspiracy, communism in Vietnam is an authentically indigenous rebellion: and that though American containment in Europe was defensive, in Asia this containment policy is aggressive. Behind this polyphonic position lurks the questionable assurance that, provided a Communist revolution is indigenous rather than externally instigated and controlled, the United States has not and should not intervene militarily to either thwart or overthrow it.

In actual fact, the confrontation of the so-called Free World and the so-called Communist World in Europe is so similar in origins, dynamics and purposes to that confrontation in Asia that it is somewhat puzzling that neither the Administration nor its critics have drawn the parallel. For it would seem that, with due allowance for specific dissimilarities, the intervention in Greece is the most striking and meaningful positive analogue to the intervention in Vietnam. Historians are beginning to note that in Greece Stalin played a reticent role, not unlike Mao Tse-tung in Vietnam today; that the Greek guerrillas were thoroughly indigenous, not unlike the

Vietcong today; and that Tito, rather than Stalin, most eagerly supported the insurgency from across the border, not unlike Ho Chi Minh rather than Mao today. As for U.S. policy, both then and now Washington at first intervened primarily with sea and sea-borne air power coupled with a military mission, in one case in the wake of British retrenchment, in the other of French retrenchment. After 1945, President Truman and his advisers took advantage of Russia's momentary military and economic incapacity to risk supporting the Greek revolutionaries, just as since the mid-1950's Washington has taken advantage of China's glaring but impermanent weakness. And last, whereas for the benefit of Congress and the public President Truman invoked the so-called domino theory to warn of the disastrous consequences of a Communist breakthrough in Greece for the nearby Middle East, as well as for France and Italy, so today President Johnson invokes the domino theory to warn of the consequences of a Communist breakthrough in Vietnam for nearby Southeast Asia and the developing nations beyond.

Vital official and private archives for the study of the origins of the cold war continue to be inaccessible. Even so, there is sufficient evidence to postulate that, because of Stalin's caution and Tito's backdown, America was spared in Greece a test of the length to which it was prepared to go to defeat revolutionary insurgency. Once the Marshall Plan and NATO were erected on the foundations of the Truman Doctrine, the Greek operation was hailed with the same enthusiasm and rationale with which the American-supported restoration in Western and Central Europe had been celebrated. After the defeat of Henry Wallace, the shift to strident anti-communism by the non-Communist Left and the ravages of McCarthyism, few critics remained to question the assumptions, methods, costs and results of this containment crusade in Europe.

Greece was the only country in which guerrilla forces had to be defeated. Even there, quite apart from the rapid victory, others did the fighting, America's contribution being confined to the offshore fleet, the Van Fleet military mission and money. In the rest of Europe—including "pacified" Greece—American intervention took the form of deliberate and massive economic, technical and military assistance. American divisions were stationed on the Continent, but they never went into action and the Berlin airlift further encouraged the assumption that air power would be decisive in limited as well as in general war.

As for Korea, there the international civil war was fought across rather than within fixed boundaries, so that even that bloody war failed to show Americans, including liberal Americans, the realities of guerrilla warfare. For quite some time Americans could tell themselves that only the English, the French, the Dutch and the Belgians fought guerrillas in their last-ditch struggle for the preservation of empire. Many Americans, including John F. Kennedy, were outraged by the barbarous methods of counterinsurgency and pacification in overseas territories. Before long, however, these transgressions were legitimized as part of the wages of ordered decolonization from above.

Throughout NATO Europe, except in Greece, the restorative containment of communism, pump primed by American economic aid, paved the way for significant and rapid improvements in per capita income and welfare, with the result that the sources for revolutionary agitation were quickly and effectively undercut. But now that the battlefield of the cold war has shifted away from Europe the question arises whether this containment strategy, so appealing to the anti-Communist Left, will work in pre-modern societies, including Greece, where development is held back or blocked by rapid population growth, adverse terms of trade and, above all, ossified political and social elites. Or will the containment of communism, which has been and continues to be central to America's world project, require interventionist means and methods that will be increasingly difficult to square with the reformist persuasion? The Bay of Pigs, the Cuban missile crisis and the war in Vietnam (as well as the coup in Indonesia?) suggest that the iron fist of counterrevolution is beginning to show through the velvet glove of Point Four and the Alliance for Progress.

Why this crescendo of violence, notably in Vietnam? Notwithstanding an occasional call for a turn to isolationism, America does not seem to be on the verge of resigning its role as the chief architect, carrier and coordinator of anti-communism, a role it has played with consummate skill and unprecedented success ever since 1945. At present, the crisis managers in Washington, who rigidly adhere to the anti-revolutionary assumptions underlying America's world mission and project, are searching for a containment formula that will work in the developing countries, many of which hover on the brink of grave internal disturbances. In this sense, Vietnam is not only an execrable and taxing civil war but also a testing ground for political and military strategies of revolution and counterrevolution.

Particularly when placed in the context of this century's international civil war, whose primary battlefield has shifted to nonmodernized, semi-colonial and ex-colonial countries, the similarities of the Greek and Vietnamese situations are striking. The question arises, therefore, as to why the Greek-Vietnamese analogy has not been enlisted either by the Administration or by its Establishment opposition on the Left.

For the Administration to use it *publicly* would be to give too much away. The analogy would only lend credence to Mao Tsetung's interpretation of the instrumental and experimental nature of the Vietnamese conflict in America's—as also in China's—project; it would exacerbate Moscow's embarrassment vis-à-vis Peking; and it would serve notice to a restless black-ghetto population at home that counterrevolutionary forays and wars on poverty in the Third World are likely to enjoy continued precedence over the war on poverty in America.

At the same time, the Greek-Vietnamese analogy presents grave difficulties for liberal-action intellectuals like Schlesinger and Galbraith. From the very start they, too, portrayed the cold war as a battle between light and darkness, insisting that the underlying thrust and ultimate purpose of containment were not only politically libertarian but also economically and socially reformist. With the anti-Communist Left in Europe, they canonized the Marshall Plan. For a while they balked at the galloping military build-up, criticized the rearmament of Germany, and protested the inclusion of Spain in the military system of the Atlantic world. Before long, however, they rationalized such restorative and conservative costs and consequences of containment, whether intended or unintended, by simply moving their vital center farther to the right. In Western and Central Europe, as also in America, Schlesinger and Galbraith increasingly trusted corporate and welfare capitalism to provide the sinews for consensus politics.

Yet not only Greece—as the recent coup demonstrates—but also many of the developing countries lack the political integration, the social cohesion, and the economic sinews to sustain gradual and ordered modernization and reform, even with considerable foreign aid. In particular, throughout the developing world, whenever the Left—whether reformist or revolutionary—threatens or seems to threaten the *status quo,* significant components of the ruling political classes switch from tolerating or cooperating with the Center-Left to praetorian guards which, at a minimum, undertake to uphold order. Not only the local grandees but also important segments of the entrepreneurial and professional middle classes have good reason to assume that Washington wishes them and the military to err on the side of caution. In fact, the most retrograde elements are so confident that Washington considers them essential backstops to order that they impudently block those ameliorative structural reforms which Washington normally would like to see fostered in exchange for aid.

When historical analogies are used for political purposes, professional and professorial historians have an obligation to correct and qualify them, as they have done with the Munich-Vietnam analogy. But historians who at the same time are critics of power have the additional obligation to raise analogic controversies to a level where they stimulate and enhance meaningful political discourse and debate. The opaque censure of the Johnson Administration's one-dimensional Munich-Vietnam analogy has at best made a marginal contribution to the critical examination and assessment of America's course in Vietnam. The Greek-Vietnamese analogy could conceivably throw a more intense searchlight on the context and implications of the Vietnamese crisis. Though it has not been invoked publicly, perhaps for fear of quickening Congressional and public distrust of the direction and design of America's postwar foreign policy, the Greek-Vietnamese analogy may well have guided the inner circle of the Johnson Administration in setting and maintaining its course in Vietnam.

It is by correcting and criticizing the uses and abuses of history that historians mount that "true vigil at arms" to which Croce summoned them and in which he wisely insisted there was "no use for either narcotics or intoxicants."

DAVID HACKETT FISCHER

Analogies

THE FALLACY OF THE PERFECT ANALOGY consists in reasoning from a partial resemblance between two entities to an entire and exact correspondence. It is an erroneous inference from the fact that *A* and *B* are similar in some respects to the false conclusion that they are the same in all respects. One must always remember that an analogy, by its very nature, is a similarity between two or more things which are in other respects unlike. A "perfect analogy" is a contradiction in terms, if perfection is understood, as it commonly is in this context, to imply identity.

This sort of error often appears in attempts at evaluation by analogy, in arguments such as the following.

> *A* and *B* are analogous in some respects.
> *A* is generally a good thing.
> Therefore, *B* is generally a good thing.

This set of propositions is structurally fallacious, for it shifts the analogy from a partial resemblance to an identity, which is implied by the holistic value judgment. If *B* were existentially analogous to *A* in respect to *X* and *Y*, then it might be fairly though not conclusively inferred that it is evaluatively analogous in the same limited sense. But it can never be inferred that *B* is equivalent to *A* in either an existential or an evaluative way.

Two examples of invalid historical analogies of this sort have appeared in debates over American intervention in Vietnam. Spokesmen for the United States government have tended to find an analogue in Munich. A critic of the administration and its Vietnam policy, Arno J. Mayer, has accurately criticized this unfortunate comparison, which is, I think, not merely a rhetorical device, invoked by Washington policy makers to justify their acts, but rather an operating assumption, upon which their acts are based. Mayer protests that

> By its proponents, the Munich analogy is designed to stress the identity, not the similarity, of Hitler and Mao; of the Nazi German and the Communist Chinese political systems and foreign policy objectives as well as methods; and of [the] externally incited subversion as well as the strategic significance of Czechoslovakia and South Vietnam. The ensuing lesson is presented as self-evident: no self-respecting American should want in the White House a Chamberlain or Daladier, who by surrendering South Vietnam to the Chinese-controlled North Vietnamese and Vietcong would encourage Peking to activate its timetable for aggressive expansion into Southeast Asia and beyond.[1]

---

[1]Arno J. Mayer, "Vietnam Analogy: Greece, Not Munich," *The Nation,* March 25, 1968, pp. 407-10.

Mayer proceeds to summarize the differences between Munich and Vietnam: the disparity between the Vietcong and the Sudeten Germans; the difference between the Czech government and the Saigon regime; the difference between the strategic significance of Czechoslovakia and Vietnam; the difference between the intentions of Nazi Germany and Communist China; the difference between the military capability of Anglo-French forces in 1938 and American power in the late 1960's. Mayer also challenges the assumption that Hitler would have changed his aggressive plans in any significant degree had the allies stood their ground at Munich, and suggests that the only effective deterrent would have been an effective alliance between Soviet Russia and the Western nations, with rights of transit for Soviet troops through Rumania and Poland. Such an alliance, he believes, was inconceivable, given the intense and obsessive anti-Bolshevism of the Western powers. Finally, Mayer denounces all "allegedly scholarly" historians and political scientists who have "accepted, legitimized, and propagated the cold war eschatology according to which Nazism and Bolshevism were essentially identical totalitarian systems bent on unlimited expansion by a crude blend of outright force and externally engineered subversion."

Many details of Mayer's thesis are doubtful, as to his understanding of both the Czechoslovakia crisis and the war in Vietnam. But his protest is surely sound. There probably cannot be any sustained analogy which will stretch from Munich to Saigon without breaking down. But more important, there can never be an identical analogy, such as Cold Warriors customarily draw between the 1930's and their own predicament.

But Mayer is not done. He believes with E. H. Carr that the "current era is exceptionally history-conscious" and that "today's citizen has that pronounced need for and is peculiarly susceptible to analogies." On this assumption, he concludes that a historian's duty consists not merely in knocking over bad analogies but in setting up good ones, in order to provide "the citizen with alternate historical sign posts." His alternative to the Munich-Vietnam analogy is a Greece-Vietnam analogy, in which parallels are drawn between the "reticent role" of Stalin and Mao; between indigenous Greek guerrillas and the Vietcong; between Tito and Ho Chi Minh; between English retrenchment in Greece and the French retreat from Vietnam; between the temporary military and political weakness of Russia vis-à-vis the United States in the late 1940's and the temporary weakness of China twenty years later; between the domino theory of the Truman Doctrine and similar assumptions in what might be called the Johnson Doctrine for Southeast Asia. Mayer suggests that American policy—which includes containment of Communism, ordered modernization, and gradualist reform—is similar in Greece and Vietnam. He implies that it has failed in Greece and that it will fail in Southeast Asia as well. Moreover, "Not only Greece—as the recent coup demonstrates—but also many of the developing countries lack the political integration, the social cohesion, and the economic sinews to sustain gradual and ordered modernization and reform, even with considerable foreign aid."

But Mayer has refuted one bad argument only to replace it with a worse one. In his Greek analogy to Vietnam he commits the same fallacy that others have done by analogizing from Munich to Southeast Asia. Mayer concedes that there are "specific dissimilarities" between Greece and Vietnam, but nowhere in his article does he specify them. Instead, he tends to leap from analogy to identity, in the manner of his opponents.

There are, of course, many major differences which he does not take into account. Ho Chi Minh's concern with South Vietnam is of a very different order from Tito's interest in Greece. The political culture of Vietnam is far removed from that of Greece. The British presence in Greece was of a different nature from the French regime in Indo-China. American assistance to Greece was unlike our intervention in Vietnam, both in quantity and in quality. Most important, international political, military, and economic conditions have changed radically from the late 1940's to the late 1960's. Vietnam is a painful and difficult dilemma for the United States precisely because there is nothing in our recent or distant past (or anybody else's) which is more than incidentally and superficially similar.

Many analogues to Vietnam have been suggested—not merely Munich and Greece, but the Mexican War, the Philippine Insurrection, the Korean War, the insurgency in British Malaya, guerrilla warfare in German-occupied Europe, the American Revolution, the Spanish rising against Napoleon. In each of these instances, the analogy is very limited, if indeed it exists at all. And there is surely no identity between any of these happenings and the situation which American policy makers face in Vietnam. That problem must be studied and solved in its own terms, if it is to be solved at all. There are many particular historical lessons which might be applied, in many limited and special ways, with due allowance for intervening changes. There are restricted and controlled analogies which might suggest hypothetical policy commitments for possible use. But there are no comprehensive analogies which serve as a short cut to a solution. A satisfactory historical approach to the problem will not be oriented toward a search for an analogue but rather toward a sense of environing continuities and changes within which the present problem in Vietnam exists; combined with a keen and lively sense of treacherous anachronisms and false analogies such as have deluded so many well-meaning architects of American policy—and their critics, too.

There are many other examples of the identical analogy, a few of which might be briefly noted. Ranke supported his government in the Franco-Prussian war with the flat assertion that "We are fighting against Louis XIV." This is a classic case of the abuse of historical knowledge. A sophisticated sense of history consists not in the location of analogues such as this but rather in an ability to discriminate between sound analogies and unsound ones.

Another quaint example, by an able historian who ought to have known better, is the following assertion by Richard Pares: "It does help us if we can realize that Charlemagne was just like an enlightened American millionaire, for this recognition brings him into a class about which we may know something."[2] This curious comparison may tell us more about the extraordinary ideas which one British historian entertained on the subject of enlightened American millionaires. And as it stands, it is a false inference from resemblance to identity. Charlemagne may or may not have been like an enlightened American millionaire in some respect—though I cannot think of one, and Pares mentioned none in particular. But he was surely not "just like" an American millionaire. Therein lies a fallacy.

[2]Richard Pares, *The Historian's Business and Other Essays* (Oxford, 1961), p. 8.

VI History and Tragedy

To view history as tragedy seems at first a counsel of despair. If history is no more than sound and fury signifying nothing, then why study it? But tragedy has always meant more than despair. We do not go to a Shakespearian tragedy only because we want to drown ourselves in hopelessness. We go because great tragedy shows men acting nobly as well as basely and because it helps us to make contact with certain truths about the human condition that should not be forgotten. In tragic drama we enter into a world where good grows out of evil and evil out of good. We come face to face with the harsh fact that in human affairs the punishment seldom fits the crime, that the innocent suffer beyond our understanding, and that good and seemingly rational decisions can lead to disaster. Understanding tragedy means facing up to the fact that there are conflicts in human affairs that cannot be resolved peacefully and that in many of these conflicts, each opponent has some right on his side. It means becoming aware that in some confrontations, in Herbert Butterfield's words, "there was a terrible knot beyond the ingenuity of men to untie." Understanding tragedy also means understanding the dilemma of choice in an imperfect world. Pericles could not know the consequences of the decisions that led Athens into the debilitating war with Sparta any more than Brutus could know that in murdering Caesar he would bring about the destruction of the Roman Republic that he was trying to save. Tragedy puts one in contact with the irony of action. Furthermore, it makes us recognize that in some cases all choices are equally bad. In the words of Walter Kaufmann:

> That the hero is confronted with a choice that leads him into guilt, whatever he does, is not a feature of all great tragedies, but of many of the greatest. If Oedipus stops his inquiries as he is advised to do, he

fails in his duty as king and is responsible for the continuation of the plague; if he presses his questions as he does, he incurs responsibility for his mother's death and wrecks the lives of his children. It was the genius of Sophocles that found *this* situation tragic instead of trying to construct the play around the hero's murder of his father.[1]

Seeing history as tragedy may not make us happy or even hopeful, but it may play some small part in enlarging our perspective. Perhaps that is all we can expect from studying the past.

[1]Walter Kaufmann, *The Faith of a Heretic* (Garden City, N.Y.: Doubleday, 1963), p. 345.

HERBERT BUTTERFIELD

The Tragic Element in Modern International Conflict

I

In the nineteenth century, when many people were optimistic in their views of human nature, and confident that the course of progress was going to be continued into an indefinite future, there were one or two prophets who feared and foretold that the twentieth century would see great wars of peoples, popular military dictatorships and the harnessing of the machines of industry to the science of warfare. It is interesting to note that, without knowing whether one country or another was going to emerge as the chief offender, and without basing his prediction upon any view that Germany was likely to present a special problem to the European continent, a writer could still feel assured, a generation beforehand, that this age of terrible warfare was coming. He could see, in other words, that, apart from the emergence of a special criminal, the developments in the situation itself were driving mankind into an era of conflict. In the midst of battle, while we are all of us in fighting mood, we see only the sins of the enemy and fail to reflect on those predicaments and dilemmas which so often develop and which underlie the great conflicts between masses of human beings. While there is battle and hatred men have eyes for nothing save the fact that the enemy is the cause of all the troubles; but long, long afterwards, when all passion has been spent, the historian often sees that it was a conflict between one half-right that was perhaps too wilful, and another half-right that was perhaps too proud; and behind even this he discerns that it was a terrible predicament, which had the effect of putting men so at cross-purposes with one another. This predicament is the thing which it is the purpose of this paper to examine; and first of all I propose to try to show how the historian comes to discover its existence.

If we consider the history of the historical writing that has been issued, generation after generation, on a given body of events, we shall generally find that in the early stages of this process of reconstruction the narrative which is produced has a primitive and simple shape. As one generation of students succeeds another, however, each developing the historiography of this particular subject, the narrative passes through certain typical stages until it is brought to a high and subtle form of organisation. It would be difficult to give names to these successive stages in the development of the historiography of a given theme, but there is an early period in the writing-up of a subject, particularly when the subject itself is one form or another of human conflict, which seems to me to belong to the class of literature sometimes described as "Heroic." It does not matter whether the topic which the historian is writing about is the victory of Christianity in the Roman Empire, or the struggles of the modern scientists in the seventeenth century, or the case of either the French or the Russian Revolutions. There is a recognisable phase in the historical reconstruction or the chronicle writing which has distinctive features and shows a certain characteristic form of organisation; and on more than one occasion in my life I have found myself saying that this kind of historiography bears the marks of the Heroic age. It represents the early period when the victors write their own chronicles, gloat over the defeated, count their trophies, commemorate their achievements, and show how righteousness has triumphed. And it may be true that the narrative has a primitive sort of structure that we can recognise, but it is a structure that requires little thought on the part of the writers of the history; for it was ready-made for them all the time—it is nothing more than the sort of organisation that a narrative acquires from the mere fact that the author is taking sides in the conflict. We who come long afterwards generally find that this kind of history has over-dramatised the struggle in its aspect as a battle of right versus wrong; and to us it seems that these writers refused to exercise imaginative sympathy over the defeated enemy, so that they lack the perspective which might have been achieved if they had allowed themselves to be driven to a deeper analysis of the whole affair. In England our own Whig interpretation of history is only a development from the "Heroic" way of formulating the issues of human conflict—as though the parliamentarians of the seventeenth century were pro-voked to war by mere personal wickednesses and deliberate aggres-sions on the part of Charles I and his supporters.

Though I have no doubt that the progress of historiography to a higher level than this is really to be regarded as a collaborative achievement, I have always understood that the name of S. R. Gardiner is particularly associated with the developments which led to a drastic refocusing of these English constitutional conflicts of the seventeenth century. It seems to have been the case furthermore that with him as with other people the refocusing resulted from what in the last resort might be described as the method of taking compassion on the defeated. Gardiner's mode of procedure led him to be careful with the defeated party, and he tried by internal sympathetic infiltration really to find out what was in their minds. And this is a process to which there ought to be no limits, for historical imagination comes to its sublimest achievements when it can succeed in comprehending the people not likeminded with oneself. Once such a process is embarked upon, the truth soon emerges that it is an easy thing to produce a Whig history of a constitutional conflict or alternatively a Royalist version of the affair; but it is no easy matter to comprise the two in a single survey, since clearly they cannot be just joined or added to one another. In reality you find that at every inch in your attempt to collate the outlooks of the two belligerent parties you are driven to a higher altitude—you have to find a kind of historical truth that lies on a higher plane before you can make the evidence square with itself, or secure a story that comprehends all the factors and embraces the purely partial visions of the two opposing sides. Then, after much labour, you may achieve something more like a stereoscopic vision of the whole drama. Similarly, if an English foreign secretary and an Austrian ambassador give curiously divergent reports of a conversation that they have had with one another, the historian would not be content merely to add the two reports together. Collating them inch by inch, he would use one document to enable him to see new folds of implication in the other. So he would be carried to a higher version of the whole affair—one which embraces the contradictions in the original accounts and even enables us to understand how the discrepancies should have occurred. In the long run the historian will not limit himself to seeing things with the eyes of the Royalist or with the eyes of the Roundhead; but, taking a loftier perspective which puts him in a position to embrace both, he will reach new truths to which both sides were blind—truths which will even enable him to see how they came to differ so much from one another.

When the historiography of the English seventeenth-century constitutional struggles has developed through the work of Gardiner and his successors, and has been brought to a higher state of organisation by virtue of processes somewhat on the pattern that I have described, what emerges is a new and drastically different formulation of the whole conflict. And this new way of presenting the entire issue has a peculiar characteristic which I wish to examine, because it shows us what the revised perspective really amounts to—it provides us with almost a definition of what is implied in the progress of historiography as it moves further away from the events that are being narrated, further away from the state of being contemporary history. The progress of historiography takes us away from that first simple picture of good men fighting bad; and not merely in the case of seventeenth-century England, but in one field of history after another we find that it contributes a new and most uncomfortable revelation—it gradually disengages the structural features of a conflict which was inherent in the dialectic of events. It shows us situations hardening, events tying themselves into knots, human beings faced by terrible dilemmas, and one party and another being driven into a corner. In other words, as the historiography of a given episode develops and comes to be further removed from the passions of those who were active in the drama, it uncovers at the basis of the story a fundamental human predicament—one which we can see would have led to a serious conflict of wills even if all men had been fairly intelligent and reasonably well-intentioned. Perhaps it was this reformulation of the conflict which Lord Acton had in mind when he suggested that it needs the historian to come on the scene at a later time to say what it was that these poor seventeenth-century Royalists and Roundheads were really fighting about.

In the new organisation of the narrative the personal goodness or badness of Charles I may still appear to be operative but it ceases to be the central issue, ceases to be the basis for the mounting of the whole story. We see the English monarchy coming into a serious predicament in this period in any case; and something of a parallel kind is seen to take place as we study the conflicts of the reign of George III. The central fact—the one that gives the new structure to the whole narrative—is a certain predicament, a certain situation that contains the elements of conflict irrespective of any special wickedness in any of the parties concerned; and the personal goodness or badness of Charles I or George III operates only, so to speak, on the margin of this, and becomes rather a fringing issue. So, while contemporary ways of formulating the human conflict have the structure of melodrama, the white hero fighting the black villain of the piece in a straight war of right versus wrong, historiography in the course of time leads us to transpose the lines of the picture and redraft the whole issue, especially as we come to comprehend more deeply the men who were not like-minded with ourselves. The higher historiography moves away from melodrama and brings out the tragic element in human conflict.

If all this is true, then we who are so deeply engaged in an age of conflict are under an obligation not to be too blindly secure, too wilfully confident, in the contemporary ways of formulating that conflict; and it is incumbent upon us not quite to forget how future historiography may expose the limitations of our vision. If all this is true, then an issue is drawn between the view which the contemporary historian so often tends to possess and the view associated with a higher and riper stage of historiography—the view of what I hope I may be allowed to call "academic history." The issue is drawn because the two kinds of history differ in the actual structure of the narrative and formulation of the theme, unless the contemporary history has been written after great prayer and fasting, which seldom happens to be the case. If what I have said is true, then the examination of the actual structure of a piece of historical narrative can be at any rate one of the tests of the intellectual quality of the work and the genuineness of its historical perspective. Furthermore, if any people should desire to envisage the events of their own day with a certain historical-mindedness, then we have at least a clue to the kind of direction in which they should move in their attempt to achieve the object. For if we realise the way in which historical science develops in the course of time—if we know even only one of the laws which govern its development as it proceeds further away from the merely contemporary point of view—then we have at any rate a hint of the kind of thing which historical perspective requires of us; and we can be to that degree more hopeful in our attempt to hasten or anticipate the future verdict of historical science. Behind the great conflicts of mankind is a terrible human predicament which lies at the heart of the story; and sooner or later the historian will base the very structure of his narrative upon it. Contemporaries fail to see the predicament or refuse to recognise its genuineness, so that our knowledge of it comes from later analysis—it is only with the progress of historical science on a particular subject that men come really to recognise that there was a terrible knot almost beyond the ingenuity of man to untie. It represents therefore a contribution that historical science itself has added to our interpretation of life—one which leads us to place a different construction on the whole human drama, since it uncovers the tragic element in human conflict. In historical perspective we learn to be a little more sorry for both parties than they knew how to be for one another.

II

The international situation of the present day is so difficult, and we are so greatly in need of a deeper vision that we ought to be ready to clutch at anything which might have a chance of leading us to fresh thoughts or new truths. We might ask, therefore, whether in the modern world there is any hint of the kind of human predicament that we have been considering and whether the idea can be of any use to us when we are seeking light on our contemporary problem. For the purpose of illustrating an argument I should like to describe and examine an imaginary specimen case in diplomacy—one which will enable me to isolate and to put under the microscope that very factor in human conflict which so often emerges at a later time, when historians have long been reflecting on the issue, but which is so often concealed from contemporaries in the heat of action and in all the bustle of life. For the purpose of assuring that the issue shall confront us more vividly I should like to present this imaginary instance in the guise of something real, something which will come to us as an actual problem of the present day.

Let us suppose, then, that the Western Powers on the one hand and Russia on the other hand have just defeated Germany and have reduced that country to total surrender. And let it be granted that the Western Powers, confronted by the Russian colossus, feel that they cannot afford to allow the defeated Germany to be drawn into the orbit of the Communist system; while Russia, for her part, faced by what to her is the no less formidable West, is ridden by the mathematically equal and opposite fear that the balance will be turned against her for all the future if Germany is enlisted in the non-Communist group. Here then is a case in which the objects of the two parties are mutually exclusive, since if the one side is satisfied the other feels the situation to be utterly desperate; and it is a case not difficult to imagine, since it might be argued (though we need not commit ourselves to the fact) that it has actually existed in our world since 1945. If we can take this situation for granted for the purpose of argument, and then persuade our minds to perform a piece of abstraction, we may arrive at a result upon which we can do some mathematics. What is required is that we should stretch our imagination to the point of envisaging this particular international predicament in a purer form than either it or anything else ever exists in history. Let us assume that the Soviet group of States on the one hand and the Western group on the other are absolutely level in point of virtue and in the moral qualities of the statesmen who conduct their affairs. Further, we will postulate that the level shall be a reasonably high one, that the statesmen on both sides are not saints, of course, competing with one another only in self-renunciation—a situation which would defeat our mathematics—but are moderately virtuous men, as men go in politics, anxious that their countries shall come to no harm, and moved by national self-interest to a degree that we must regard as comparatively reasonable. We will postulate that they have just those faults which men can have who feel themselves to be righteous and well-disposed—both sides anxious to avoid a war, but each desperately unsure about the intentions of the other party; each beset by the devils of fear and suspicion, therefore; and each side locked in its own system of self-righteousness.

Allowing for all this—which means that the problem before us is presented in what I should call its optimum setting—then I should assert that here is a grand dialectical jam of a kind that exasperates men—a terrible deadlock that makes ordinary human beings even a little more wilful than they ordinarily are. Here is the absolute predicament and the irreducible dilemma—for I shall have something to say later to those who assert that it is no genuine predicament at all, and that every schoolboy knows the solution to the problem. Even granting throughout the whole of human nature no more than the ordinary amount of human wilfulness such as we ourselves may be said to possess, here are the ingredients for a grand catastrophe. The greatest war in history could be produced without the intervention of any great criminals who might be out to do deliberate harm in the world. It could be produced between two Powers, both of which were desperately anxious to avoid a conflict of any sort.

Though the example that I have given is a purely hypothetical one, as I have said—for in the complicated realm of history so clear a pattern will never be found in its absolute purity—still there is a sense in which it typifies an essential human predicament; it illustrates a certain recalcitrancy that may lie in events as such, an intractability that can exist in the human situation itself. Here, in other words, is the mathematical formula—or perhaps one of the formulas—for a state of things which produces what I should call the tragic element in human conflict. As regards the real world of international relations I should put forward the thesis (which, if it is true, would seem to me to be not an unimportant one) that this condition of absolute predicament or irreducible dilemma lies in the very geometry of human conflict. It is at the basis of the structure of any given episode in that conflict. It is at the basis of all the tensions of the present day, representing even now the residual problem that the world has not solved, the hard nut that we still have to crack. So far as the historian is concerned, here is the basic pattern for all narratives of human conflict, whatever other patterns may be superimposed upon it later. Indeed, as I have said, when the historical reconstruction of a given episode has been carried on for generation upon generation, this is the structure the story tends to acquire as it becomes revised and corrected and reshaped with the passage of time. This tragedy of the absolute human predicament enters into the very fabric of historical narrative in proportion as we move further away from being mere contemporary historians.

Turning again to the hypothetical case which we have been using as our pattern, we may note that not only could the greatest war in history be produced between two Powers both of which were moderately virtuous and desperately anxious to prevent a conflict, but such a struggle, far from being a nice, quiet and reasonable affair, would be embittered by the heat of moral indignation on both sides, just because each was so conscious of its own rectitude, so enraged with the other for leaving it without any alternative to war. It is the peculiar characteristic of the situation I am describing—the situation of what I should call Hobbesian fear—that you yourself may vividly feel the terrible fear that you have of the other party, but you cannot enter into the other man's counter-fear, or even understand why he should be particularly nervous. For you know that you yourself mean him no harm, and that you want nothing from him save guarantees for your own safety; and it is never possible for you to realise or remember properly that since he cannot see the inside of your mind, he can never have the same assurance of your intentions that you have. As this operates on both sides the Chinese puzzle is complete in all its interlockings—and neither party sees the nature of the predicament he is in, for each only imagines that the other party is being hostile and unreasonable. It is even possible for each to feel that the other is wilfully withholding the guarantees that would have enabled him to have a sense of security. The resulting conflict is more likely to be hot with moral indignation—one self-righteousness encountering another— that it would have been if the contest had lain between two hard-headed eighteenth-century masters of *realpolitik*. In such cir- cumstances the contemporary historians on each side will tend to follow suit, each locked in the combative views of his own nation, and shrieking morality of that particular kind which springs from self-righteousness. That is one of the reasons why contemporary history differs so greatly from what I have called academic history. In all that I am saying I am really asserting, moreover, that the self-righteous are not the true moralists either in history or in life. Those who are less self-righteous may face the world's problems more squarely, even when they are less clever, than other people.

Pandit Nehru, when he was speaking at Columbia University, made a somewhat moving criticism of both East and West, because in his view they were intent upon what he called a race in armaments. Some people even say that a race in armaments is a cause of war—but nobody actually wills a "race"; and I personally would rather pity both sides than blame them, for I think that the race in armaments, and even the war that seems to result from it, are caused rather by that tragic human predicament, that situation of Hobbesian fear. All that we can say is that the predicament would not exist, of course, if all the world were like St. Francis of Assisi, and if human nature in general were not streaked with cupidities. The predicament, the race in armaments and the war itself are explained in the last resort, therefore, as the result of man's universal sin. Similarly, suppose two great groups of alliances have been at virtual deadlock for some years, so that even neutral States have begun to assert that war is inevitable—meaning that war is inevitable, human nature being what it is. Suppose you have such a situation, and then one party to the predicament becomes overexasperated and makes too wilful a decision; suppose in particular that he does it because he thinks that somebody must take a strong line at last; and we will say that he even intends to bluff, but the bluff does not come off and so a great war is brought about. Then, though this man has done wrong I could not personally agree that he should be charged as the sole author of the war and loaded with all the misery of it as though he were the only villain in a melodrama. I could not agree that he should be regarded as guilty in just the way he would have been if he had fallen unprovoked on a flock of innocent lambs. When war arises in such circumstances, its true origin must be traced rather to the whole predicament; and on this basis the melodrama re-shapes itself, assuming more of the character of tragedy—the kind of tragedy in which it is so to speak the situation that gives one a heartache, and sometimes, as in the case of *King Lear,* what seem to be little sins may have colossally disproportionate consequences.

The truth is that when faced by this human predicament—this final unsolved problem of human relations—the mind winces and turns to look elsewhere, and statesmen, for their ease, pile all the blame on the handiest scapegoat. Men fix their attention upon what in reality are fringing issues, and they remove these from their proper place on the fringe to the centre of the picture—you can evade all problems by saying that everything is due to the wickedness of King Charles I. The point can be illustrated best perhaps by the process of looking for a moment at its converse. Let us make it clear to ourselves: if in our present-day crises Stalin and his colleagues could be imagined to be as virtuous and well-intentioned as the statesmen of the Western world, still our predicament would exist, and there would be the same dilemma concerning the future of Germany—especially as we, because we look at him from the outside, could never be sure that Stalin's intentions were as good as ours. In any case we could never be sure that if we put our trust in him we should not really be placing weapons into the hands of some villain who might succeed to his power next year, supposing he passed off the stage. Of course, if we are in this same international predicament and the Russians happen to be thieves or adventurers or aggressors or drunkards or sexual perverts to boot, then that is an extra boon which Providence throws into the lap, so to speak, of the Western Powers—the kind of boon which, to judge from our assertions over a number of centuries, Providence has generally vouchsafed to the British in their wars. Even in such circumstances, however, we are evading an essential problem if we lose sight of the basic predicament—a predicament so exasperating sometimes that it can be responsible for making people more wicked and desperate than they otherwise would have been. It is like the case of the person who owed his neighbour £5 and refused to pay it on the ground that the neighbour was an immoral man and would make a bad use of the money. The moralising might not be without its justice, but in this case it would be introduced as a screen to cover a delinquency of one's own. Or it is like the case of those people who so often, as in 1792, would judge a revolution entirely by its atrocities—evading the structural problem and pouncing upon an incidental issue. I have no doubt it would be a boon to me, supposing I were challenged in debate on a point of history, if I could say: "Take no notice of this man; he has just come out of prison after serving sentence for forging a cheque." I should be picking up a fringing issue and turning it into the central issue; and in this way I might use the other person's immorality most unfairly for the purpose of evading a challenge that happened to be inconvenient to myself.

Not only may the problem of war present itself in the acutest possible form, irrespective of any difference in morality between the contending parties, but the whole problem and the whole predicament that we are discussing exists absolutely, irrespective of any differences in ideology. All the evidence that we have—and it seems to me that we have had very much in the last one hundred years for this particular case—shows that the basic problem would not be fundamentally altered, and would certainly not be avoided, supposing what we were confronted with at the moment were all the power of modern Russia in the hands of the Tsars, instead of the regime of the Soviet. The predicament would not be removed even if there were no Communism in the world at all, or supposing that every State involved in the problem were a Christian State in the sense that so many countries were Christian throughout most of the centuries of modern times. Even supposing Russia were liberal and democratic—supposing the Great Powers on either side were so situated that their populations could put pressure on the government in the very matter of foreign policy—still the populations would be just as fearful or suspicious or exasperated or angry as the foreign offices themselves. Indeed it seems to be generally the case that they are more so, unless the knowledge of the predicament is withheld from them. In any case we did not have our present fears and panics on the subject of Communism till Communism had come to be identified with the formidable European position of Russia as it has existed since 1945.

In so far as international conflicts are concerned, therefore, I am suggesting that after many of the more incidental features of the case have been peeled away, we shall find at the heart of everything a kernel of difficulty which is essentially a problem of diplomacy as such. In fact I personally think that in the international crises of our time, we are muddying the waters and darkening our own minds and playing the very game the Russians want us to play, when we mix our drinks and indulge in a so-called "ideological" foreign policy, forgetting that the fundamental problems exist, as I have said, independent of the differences in ideology. The truth is that we could very well say to the Russians: "We would not have allowed you to steal this particular march on us, or to encroach in this particular direction or to dominate defeated Germany even if you had been a Christian empire as in the time of the Tsars." And, given the distribution of power which existed in Europe in 1945, the old Tsardom would have dominated Poland, Czechoslovakia, Hungary and the Balkans, just as the Soviets do now, though it would have used something different from the Marxian ideology to facilitate the execution of its purpose. All this carries with it the further corollary that we ought to attach very great importance to a study which in England at least has gravely declined and is woefully out of fashion, namely, pure diplomatic history regarded as a technique in itself; for it was just the characteristic of this technical diplomatic history to lay bare the essential geometry of the problem and isolate for examination the fundamental predicament that required a solution. Indeed what I am doing in this paper is to elicit the moral implications of that whole system of thought which is invoked in diplomatic history—and I am asserting that the new diplomacy of our time, as well as its dependent forms of historiography, though they are more self-righteous than the old, are in reality less moral, at any rate in certain respects.

We have already noted, however, that in the complicated realm of historical events, no pattern ever appears in a pure and unadulterated form—and certainly, when a diplomatic issue is presented to us for resolution, we can never say that both sides are exactly balanced in point of morality, exactly equal in the virtues of their leading statesmen. The original issue may be aggravated and greatly intensified by the aggressiveness of a politician in one country or the barbarism of a regime in another country; and our fear of the expansion of Russia is considerably increased if Russia implies either a Tsarist despotism or the Communist system. All the same, it is wrong to overlook that original diplomatic predicament which forms the kernel of the problem requiring to be solved; and it is a mistake to allow the incidental matters or the attendant circumstances to drive that essential issue out of our minds. I could express the point, for example—or I could illustrate its implications—by noting that we should not like to be conquered by Russia even if Russia were not a Communist State. Alternatively I might say that supposing it could be made out that there were general reasons for conceding that Spain had a right to Gibraltar, it is not clear that the British would be justified in withholding that possession merely because they disliked the present regime in Spain and disapproved of General Franco. It was perhaps one of the virtues of the older type of diplomacy that in time of war it did not allow itself to be entirely obsessed by the question of the responsibility for the resort to violence—did not merely hark back continually to the actual occasion of the outbreak—but recognised that the war itself was partly tragedy, that is to say, partly due to a predicament. Attention was concentrated rather on the kind of world which would be produced once the victory had been achieved, and the aim was not so much to punish the culprits, but rather to make sure that there was a tolerable balance of forces at the finish. In times past it would have been realised that the most essential thing of all is to guard against the kind of war which, if you win it absolutely, will produce another "predicament" worse than the one you started with.

III

The great diplomatic issue that emerged—or rather reemerged—in Europe in the early years of this present century concerned the question whether Russia on the one hand or Germany on the other hand should dominate those countries of Central and Eastern Europe which run from Poland, through Czechoslovakia and Hungary to what we now call Yugoslavia and the Balkans. This is how it came about that the occasion for the war of 1914 was an episode involving Bosnia and Serbia, while the occasion for the war of 1939 occurred in regions concerning which Lloyd George had long before expressed his apprehensions—namely in Czechoslovakia and in Poland. Those two wars were embarrassing in certain respects for Great Britain, for though we claimed that we were fighting for democracy we were allied in the former case with Tsarist Russia, where the Jews had been oppressed, and the Poles were held in subjection, and the Baltic nations were prevented from achieving statehood; while in the case of the Second World War we were the allies of the Soviet system. So far as I can interpret European history in general, the line of central European States which were in question—Poland, Czechoslovakia, Yugoslavia, etc.—can flourish beautifully when both Germany and Russia are reduced to impotence, as they were in the fifteenth century, and as they came to be again for a period after 1919. The same States may preserve their independence provided both Germany and Russia are strong, so that when the giant on the one side seeks to oppress them they can look for help to the giant on the other side. It is bound to be sad, however, for Poland, Czechoslovakia, etc., if only one of these giants is left standing and there is no other great Power in the vicinity to challenge or check this monster. Indeed, we have seen how even in the last few years America, England and the nations of Western Europe have been unable to prevent this whole line of States from coming almost entirely into the power of the Russian bear. Even in our moment of victory we had to let these States fall under what we regarded as the oppressor—a fact even more remarkable (when the whole situation is considered) than the case of Munich itself. Supposing wars to be necessary and unavoidable—as indeed they seem to be sometimes—it might still be a question whether we have conducted ours with a right mentality or with a proper grasp of the essential issues. In respect of the great diplomatic problem of the twentieth century, we may wonder sometimes whether Russia was so much more virtuous than Germany as to make it worth the lives of tens of millions of people in two wars to ensure that she (as a Communist system—or even as a Tsarist empire) should gain such an unchallenged and exclusive hold over that line of Central European States as Germany never had in all her history, and never could have had unless Russia had first been wiped out as a great State. For it is just that kind of question—the question of the redistribution of territorial power—which war decides. We cannot actually spread democracy by war, which barbarizes peoples and tends rather to make democracy more impracticable over a greater area of the European continent.

The supporters of the new diplomacy, which has emerged since the opening of the epoch of world-wars, like to tell us that the whole problem we have been discussing does not exist, because it ought not to exist. In any case, there is no Chinese puzzle at all, they say, for, whatever the issue might be, we could easily dispose of it by referring it to a conference or sending it to the United Nations. Against these specialists in wishful thinking it must be asserted that the kind of human predicament which we have been discussing is not merely so far without a solution, but the whole condition is a standing feature of mankind in world-history. If the whole of Russia and the entire body of its satellites were to be buried under the deepest oceans from this very night, the predicament would still be with us tomorrow, though the terms of it would be transposed by a regrouping of the remaining Powers. Supposing there were no Russian Power in existence, supposing Germany herself were lying prostrate as a beaten and ineffective nation, and supposing the help of America were not essential to everybody concerned—all that fine show of unanimity between the countries of Western Europe, all that co-operation induced by the threat of an immediate danger, would break down into bitterness and anarchy. And if the issue which divides the world at a given moment were referred to a conference table, then, though many good things might be achieved, we should not have eliminated the predicament which was most crucial—we should merely find it transplanted into the bosom of the conference itself. That is why those people were wrong who despaired of the League of Nations because it failed in the greatest of tests. Wise men had always given the warning that it could not cope with the last extremes of crisis; and it was wrong to forget how many good things it had in fact achieved. Even the organisation of the United Nations has not proved essentially different in this respect from the case of the League; and though the problem is transposed somewhat, so that different nations and different issues now produce the stumbling-block, the new international order has not in fact prevented Powers from remaining armed as never before, and racing one another in the development of the atomic bomb.

It was once my feeling that if, in a European crisis, Great Britain pressed for the assembly of a conference, while Germany rejected that procedure, then Germany was clearly in the wrong and my own country was plainly on the side of the angels. Unfortunately it comes to be borne in upon one's mind as one studies these matters that conferences themselves are only too liable to be the arena for a kind of power politics; and the greater States, in the very nature of things, hold a predominance in them which bears some proportion to their might. It even became evident to me that sometimes it was calculable in advance how the votes would be distributed if a conference met, since these would be affected by the alliances and affilations of the various governments concerned, and might even be decided by sympathies in ideology. Let us suppose it to have become clear that if a conference were assembled the result was a foregone conclusion and Germany was so to speak outvoted in advance. I began to wonder whether in such a case she was necessarily more selfish than anybody else when she refused to put her head in the noose—I began to wonder also whether the virtues of Britain were quite so much to boast about when they coincided so nicely with her interests. This argument might be projected on to a wider canvas altogether; for without doubting the good intentions of the men who have ruled England in the last few decades, one must note that if a Machiavellian imperialist statesman had happened to be governing us with purely egotistical purposes in view, he would have found the conference method the best way of promoting our national interests, indeed the only way in view of the decline of actual British power and in view of the general distribution of forces in the world. In other words Great Britain in our time has been in a position which we must regard as fortunate in a certain respect, in that the policy which altruism would have dictated to her happened to be the same as the one which self-interest would demand—so that, though the conference method has been promoted so often by Englishmen who were only conscious of it as a noble aspiration, it has also been described as the only method of *realpolitik* left to us. The conference method is more advantageous to us than any decision to measure forces with a rival, even if the voting should go against us on occasion in a matter of some moment to us.

But when I take this crucial case and imagine a real predicament—when I think of the kind of issue which decides whether a State or an empire goes up or down in the world—then I find myself in a position of some doubt even in regard to Great Britain. Supposing it to be the case that the loss of our overseas possessions would bring about a serious reduction in the standard of living of the British people, and supposing a motion were to be proposed that all forms of colony or of subjection or of dependency were to be abolished through the wide world—I, in a situation of this kind, should like to know what the attitude of the government of my country would be. In particular I should like to know what its attitude would be towards the idea of submitting such an issue to a conference or assembly in which the Communists were known in advance to have the majority of votes. I should like to know what my country would do on the assumption that we still had enough power to make a valid and independent choice. Where the conflict is really a cut-throat one it seems to me that the conference method does not put an end to the predicament but merely changes the locality and the setting of it. The whole method is liable to break down if either the Communists or the non-Communists can be fairly sure in advance that on critical issues the other party is going to have the majority. And in any case I am not clear that anybody has ever devised a form of political machinery that could not somehow or other be manipulated by ill-intentioned people in the possession of power.

Like the Germans, we sometimes allow the academic and professorial mind to have too much sway among us; and with us this has helped to give currency to the heresy that everything can be settled if men will only sit together at a table—a view which may be justified on many occasions but which does not prove to be correct when the conflicting parties are in the extreme kind of predicament we have been discussing. Where the predicament really exists and the question is one of those which decide whether States are to go up or down in the world, those who do have the power will not allow themselves to be talked or voted out of their strategic positions, any more than empires will go under without putting up a fight, supposing a fight to be possible at all. Europeans have had hundreds of years in which to discuss theological problems, but mere discussion round a table has not brought them into agreement on the disputed points. This was the kind of issue upon which men can at worst agree to disagree, though I note that ecclesiastical systems were slow to come to this arrangement and they went on fighting one another, using weapons that kill, as long as it was feasible to fight at all. But if two different countries are claiming Gibraltar it is not so easy to settle the matter by saying that the parties can agree to disagree. The conference method does not get rid of the difficulty—it merely transplants the whole predicament into another place.

While we are at war, and the conflict is a matter of life or death for us, we may hardly have any part of our minds free for devoting to a genral survey of the whole predicament in which the human race is standing. When the war is over, however, a time of healing ought to come, and it is our duty to carry all our problems to further analysis. Politicians, in the hurry of affairs and in the stress of conflict, may hardly have an opportunity to cover the problem in an all-embracing survey, for we must regard them as generally acting under great pressures. We in universities, however—and especially those of us who study history—have a duty to think in longer terms and seize upon the problem precisely where the difficulties are most challenging. We ought to be straining our minds to think of new things and to enlarge the bounds of understanding; for though our enlarged understanding of the problem will not necessarily prevent war, it may remove some of the unwisdom which has made victory itself so much more disappointing in its results than it otherwise might have been.